Knowledge, Pedagogy and

Over the course of the late-twentieth century Basil Bernstein pioneered an original approach to educational phenomena, taking seriously questions regarding the transmission, distribution and transformation of knowledge as no other before had done. Arguing tirelessly for change, more than any other British sociologist it is Bernstein who presents to us education as a social right and not as a privilege. It is this objective today that makes his work so important.

Knowledge, Pedagogy and Society seeks to clarify the broad brushstrokes of his theories, developed over the span of more than forty years, by collecting together scholars from every corner of the globe; specialists in education, sociology and epistemology to test and examine Bernstein's work against the backdrop of their own research. From teaching content and the social, cognitive and linguistic aspects of education, to changes in the political climate in the early-twenty-first century, this collection represents an open dialogue with Bernstein's work using a forward-looking and dynamic approach.

Originally published in French with the explicit aim of locating Basil Bernstein's theories alongside those of Pierre Bourdieu, one of the most important European sociologists, the French editors draw together a collection that offers a diverse background and perspective on Bernstein's work and thought. This will be a relevant resource for anyone interested in Bernstein, his reception and importance, as well as individuals working in the sociology of education, theory of education and education policy.

Daniel Frandji is Senior Lecturer in Sociology at the National Institute of Pedagogical Research (INRP) in Lyon, France.

Philippe Vitale is Senior Lecturer in Sociology at the University of Provence (Aix en Provence), France.

Knowledge, Pedagogy and Society

International perspectives on Basil Bernstein's sociology of education

Edited by Daniel Frandji and Philippe Vitale

Routledge
Taylor & Francis Group

LONDON AND NEW YORK

First edition published 2011
by Routledge
2 Park Square, Milton Park, Abingdon, Oxon OX14 4RN

Simultaneously published in the USA and Canada
by Routledge
711 Third Avenue, New York NY 10017

Routledge is an imprint of the Taylor & Francis Group, an informa business

First issued in paperback 2012

Typeset in Garamond by Wearset Ltd, Boldon, Tyne and Wear

British Library Cataloguing in Publication Data
A catalogue record for this book is available from the British Library

Library of Congress Cataloging-in-Publication Data
Knowledge, pedagogy, and society : international perspectives on
Basil Bernstein's sociology of education / edited by Daniel Frandji
and Philippe Vitale. – 1st ed.
p. cm.
Includes bibliographical references.
1. Bernstein, Basil B. 2. Educational sociology. 3. Education–
Philosophy. I. Frandji, Daniel. II. Vitale, Philippe.
LB880.B462K67 2010
306.43–dc22   2010011186

ISBN13: 978-0-415-56536-3 (hbk)
ISBN13: 978-0-415-50057-9 (pbk)
ISBN13: 978-0-203-84393-2 (ebk)

Contents

Illustrations

Figures

Tables

Contributors

Elisabeth Bautier, Professor, University of Paris VIII, ESSI–Escol, France.

Harry Daniels, Professor, Centre for Sociocultural and Activity Theory Research, University of Bath, England.

Brian Davies, Professor, Cardiff University, School of Social Science, Wales

Jean-Manuel De Queiroz, Professor, University of Rennes 2, France.

Roger Establet, Professor, University of Provence, LAMES–MMSH, Aix-en-Provence, France.

Daniel Frandji, Senior Lecturer, INRP, Lyon, LAMES–CNRS–MMSH, Aix-en-Provence, France.

Claude Grignon, Professor, Maison des sciences de l'Homme, Paris.

Catherine Mangez, PhD student, researcher, Catholic University of Louvain–UCL, Belgium.

Éric Mangez, Researcher, Catholic University of Louvain–UCL, Belgium.

Karl Maton, Senior Lecturer, Department of Sociology and Social Policy, Faculty of Arts, University of Sydney, Australia.

Rob Moore, Senior Lecturer, Faculty of Education, University of Cambridge, England.

Ana M. Morais, Professor, Centre for Educational Research, University of Lisbon, Portugal.

Johan Muller, Professor, School of Education, University of Cape Town, South Africa.

Isabel P. Neves, Professor, Centre for Educational Research, University of Lisbon, Portugal.

Nadège Pandraud, PhD Student, University of Provence, LAMES–CNRS–MMSH, Aix-en-Provence, France.

Nicole Ramognino, Professor, University of Provence, LAMES–MMSH, Aix-en-Provence, France.

Jean-Yves Rochex, Professor, University of Paris VIII, ESSI–Escol, France.

Sophia Stavrou, PhD Student, University of Provence, LAMES–CNRS–MMSH, Aix-en-Provence, France.

Philippe Vitale, Senior Lecturer, University of Provence, LAMES–CNRS–MMSH, Aix-en-Provence, France.

Acknowledgements

This volume includes extended versions of papers delivered at the international conference on "Social issues, knowledge, language and pedagogy: the current relevance and usefulness of Basil Bernstein's sociological work", held at the Ecole normale supérieure in Lyon, France from 31 May to 2 June 2007. The event was organized by the Centre Alain Savary at the Institut national de recherche pédagogique (CAS–INRP, Lyon; National Institute of Pedagogic Research), in partnership with the research group Education et Scolarisation (ESCOL, Université de Paris VIII Saint-Denis, France; Centre for Research in Education and Schooling), the Institut universitaire de formation des maîtres in Lyon (IUFM, Université Lyon 2, France; the teacher training college), the Laboratoire méditerranéen de sociologie (LAMES–CNRS–MMSH, Aix-en-Provence, France; the Mediterranean Centre for Sociological Research), and the Réseau national de recherche sur l'enseignement, les inégalités et les différenciations dans les apprentissages (RESEIDA, France; National Network of Research on Teaching, Inequalities and Differentiation in Learning).

Organizational support was provided by Professor Elisabeth Bautier (ESCOL–CIRCEFT, University of Paris VIII Saint-Denis), Professor Jean-Manuel De Queiroz (University of Rennes 2), Professor Nicole Ramognino (LAMES, University of Provence) and Professor Jean-Yves Rochex (ESCOL–CIRCEFT, University of Paris VIII Saint-Denis).

We are also particularly grateful to:

Brian Barrett (Assistant Professor, Department of Foundations and Social Advocacy at the State University of New York College at Cortland, USA) for his close readings of all the texts collected in this volume and for his invaluable suggestions.

Brian Davies (Professor, Cardiff School of Social Sciences) for his readings, helpful comments and encouragement.

Dr Beryl Exley and Dr Catherine Doherty (Faculty of Education, Queensland University of Technology, Australia) for their final reading of the manuscript.

Sylvie Chiousse (Engineer, LAMES–CNRS–MMSH, Aix-en-Provence, France) for her help in the preparation of the manuscript.

We are also grateful for the support provided by Sally Power (Professor, Cardiff School of Social Sciences) and Ginette Ramognino-Le Déroff (Agrégée d'anglais, School Inspector, France).

This volume is a revisited version of *Actualité de Basil Bernstein. Savoirs, pédagogie et société* (Frandji, Vitale 2008) published in France by the Presses Université de Rennes.

Foreword

Rob Moore

This collection is an especially welcome contribution to the growing body of work that is both about Basil Bernstein and taking place within, while also developing, his problematique. It is *especially* welcome because the chapters collected here were originally presented at a conference in France. The French connection is important because, as Bernstein never ceased to proclaim, his intellectual roots were with Durkheim and, indeed, he could well be considered as one of the greatest inheritors of the Durkheimian legacy. But this fact has consistently been a problem in the understanding of Bernstein and the interpretation of his thought and his intellectual project. The basis of this problem is that in the Anglo-Saxon sphere of sociology and social theory, the conventional understanding of Durkheim has been very different from Bernstein's own understanding of him. To understand Bernstein it is necessary to understand how *he* understood Durkheim. French social theorists will come to Bernstein from a different direction because they come to him with an understanding of Durkheim that is in significant respects different from that into which their Anglo-Saxon colleagues have been socialized. Hence, their perspective can illuminate Bernstein's thought in a way that can provide new insights and extends the growing global, international engagement with Bernstein's corpus.

The chapters illustrate a number of features of the enduring impact of Bernstein's work and also of its special character. In the first place, they represent the "open-endedness" of his project – it constantly evades closure. Bernstein had a *problematique*, not *a* theory. He always wanted to open things up by identifying new problems, not close them down by announcing solutions. He begins with a problem: the fundamental Durkheimian one of the nature of "the social". This problem is understood in terms of a crucial relationship: that between the inner and the outer. Human beings become *social* beings or (as Durkheim proclaims in the "Introduction" to the *Elementary Forms of Religious Life*) fully *human* beings by virtue of how the "outer", society, becomes "inner" as the structuring of consciousness. This is the process that Bernstein follows Durkheim in calling "pedagogy" and which is, in this deep sense, the most fundamental of social processes – the process of "humanization". In order to address this issue, Bernstein, throughout his life, searched for resources to bring to bear upon it and upon the increasingly complex refinements in his understanding of its forms, levels and sites, and their interactions and transformations. Much of what Bernstein did was concerned with the mapping of the terrain of this problematique, a conceptual cartography that traced its contours and the pathways between the key locations within it.

The chapters in this collection reflect the complexity of the structure that Bernstein erected upon the foundations of that problematic. Contributions range from the epistemological, through relations between the state and the education system to the investigation of the teaching/learning process in the classroom. What makes this possible is not just that there was an ad hoc interest in a large number of different issues, but the deeper theoretical and methodological concern with how to conceptualize transformations between levels and across sites. The process of conceptualization in Bernstein's work was primarily concerned with "recovery" – that is, how can a form in one place be recovered as the same form in another place? For instance, how can a certain structural location in the economic division of labour be so defined that it can be conceptually recovered within family structure and this, in turn, be identified in speech patterns? For Bernstein, this was primarily a *research* question. His concern was more with *systematic conceptualization* rather than with theoretical or paradigmatic purity.

There are three aspects to systematic conceptualization in Bernstein's work. The first is to reduce the ambiguity between a concept and that to which it points in the world – how would we *know* it if we *see* it? In his later work, he began to theorize this in terms of "grammaticality" and "the languages of description". The second is the translation between levels and sites and the transformation of forms (what above I termed "recovery"). The third is, sociologically, the most important: how to theorize *systematically* the relationships between social structures, symbolic systems and the structuring of consciousness and how these things are *differentially* distributed in complex modern societies in ways that have implications for social inequality and justice. This returns us to Durkheim. It is also the case that, at the substantive level, Bernstein's problematique provides so many places *within which* to work, but, also, so many tools *with which* to work. Bernstein's theory "works" because it can be *put to work* by so many others.

Bernstein has left a legacy that is exceptional in its fecundity – in its power to generate so much energy in thinking and research across the world. In contrast to many other major social theorists, those working within his problematique do not merely *invoke* his concepts, they *work* with them and develop and extend them. This is exactly what he would have wanted. To a significant degree this reflects the *rigour* of his methodological approach to conceptualization. But it is also the case that Bernstein remains in certain respects enigmatic and even "mysterious". He is "enigmatic" in that he says very little about the complex matrix of influences that inform his approach. He is "mysterious" in that he appears to have quite independently formed an understanding of Durkheim that was radically different from that which came to the fore in Anglo-Saxon sociology in the 1960s and early 1970s. In part, this might be because of historical and biographical aspects of the intersection between the development of the intellectual field of the sociology of education in Britain and Bernstein's personal career.

In the 1960s, with the emergence of so-called "critical", interpretative sociologies, Durkheim came to be positioned in Anglo-Saxon social theory as a conservative "positivist" and conventionally contrasted as the "social order" theorist against Marx as the revolutionary theorist of "social change". In fact, of course, Durkheim was a great, reforming secular republican, a socialist and, with Marx, a major theorist of historical materialism. This conventional interpretation of Durkheim was mediated by a Parsonian structural-functionalist reading of his work. Bernstein, however, came to Durkheim slightly earlier as a student at the London School of Economics and did so through *anthropology*. Whereas the "critical" sociologies that fed into the New Sociology of Education of the early 1970s took as their touch stone a positivistic interpretation of *Suicide*, for Bernstein the key Durkheimian text was, *The Elementary Forms of Religious Life*. In the formative period of Bernstein's beginning as a sociologist, a number of key figures in the expanding field of sociology in the UK were in fact *anthropologists* for the very simple reason that there were not enough sociologists to meet the demand for professorial places. Bernstein came to Durkheim *through* anthropology. This connection is powerfully underwritten by the seminal intellectual collaboration between Bernstein and the Durkheimian anthropologist, Mary Douglas, in the second half of the 1960s which resulted in Bernstein's papers on classification and framing and visible and invisible pedagogies (Bernstein 1977) and Douglas' book *Natural Symbols* (1970).

Bernstein sits enigmatically outside the mainstream of Anglo-Saxon sociology. To work with and beyond Bernstein across the terrain of his problematique is also to *discover* Bernstein and the starting point is with Durkheim and the French connection.

Introduction

Daniel Frandji and Philippe Vitale

A theory of practice for opening of the "possible"

The publication in French of Basil Bernstein's last book, *Pédagogie, contrôle symbolique et identité* (2007; originally titled *Pedagogy, Symbolic Control and Identity*), the final magnum opus of a life devoted to sociological research, provided the initial impetus for an international colloquium held in Lyon, France, from 31 May to 2 June 2007 titled "Social issues, knowledge, language and pedagogy: The current relevance and usefulness of Basil Bernstein's sociological work". This conference would not have been possible without the support of several institutions and researchers to whom we wish once again to reiterate our gratitude.

The purpose of the event was to provide a forum for a range of theoretical views and debates surrounding and extending Bernstein's work rather than merely an occasion for an exegetic memorial. Contributions by researchers from different parts of the globe, including South Africa, Britain, Australia, Belgium, France and Portugal, illuminated the current nature of issues of pedagogical transmission of skills and knowledge not merely in schools but in a wide range of human institutions and relations. In reading Bernstein it is clear that transmission of knowledge and skills is not only of relevance to democracy in general but to the rights of individuals to gain critical understanding, active participation and new opportunities. The challenge he raised was how humans can "live together" in our so-called "knowledge" societies, in which symbolic control and social production and reproduction are synonymous with power and control.

This volume, bringing together papers delivered at the Lyon conference, is designed to consider the gaps and paradoxes that hinder the circulation and sharing of knowledge at an international level, especially between researchers in French- and English-speaking worlds. The gaps are not merely ones of translation and availability. While the circulation and globalized sharing of knowledge appear to be valued and promoted, important areas of sociological research have been insufficiently shared and discussed. Like all social science, sociology has been built on the basis of interwoven, interdependent, international dialogue. However, sociological inquiry into what is (or is not) translated or, though published or translated, remains insufficiently read, discussed, used or integrated into legitimate bodies of sociological knowledge and research, remains nonetheless deeply instructive. We are driven by the recognition of a number of academic dead-ends and scholarly oddities that have often prevented more widespread circulation and sharing prerequisite to its understanding and appreciation.

For various reasons (see the chapters in this volume by Brian Davies and Roger Establet), Bernstein's work has not been given the same reception in every country and period. Leaving aside various ideological and political misunderstandings, as well as numerous over-simplifications and misuses of his theory of linguistic codes, it is hard to avoid the conclusion that the English-speaking academic world has yet failed to take stock of the significance of Bernstein's work. Likewise it appears that it remains relatively unfamiliar in the French sociological field, which continues to shun Bernstein's considerable contributions or, at best, to refer to works[1] from the 1960s and early 1970s which Bernstein significantly revised. Meanwhile, publication in English of contemporary French research has proved to be highly pertinent. The golden era of "French theory", established largely as a result of the work by Pierre Bourdieu and Michel Foucault, contributed to the critical culture of the 1960s and 1970s. Bernstein's encounter added to this productivity; his life-long debate with the work of Pierre Bourdieu is discussed in this volume, as is the line of descent of his inquiries from Durkheim. Engagement with international and particularly French sociology was to be a permanent feature of Bernstein's research outlook. Reading French texts in the original was never an easy task for him, though it did prove to be both possible and productive: consider his concern to remain closely aware of the products of what he sometimes referred to – somewhat testily – as "the Parisian versions of the sociology of reproduction" (Bernstein 2000, p. 5). It is not merely that Bernstein read all of Bourdieu's work, as well as that of Foucault, Althusser and others, he also developed an intense interest in the work of his collaborators, followers and dissidents and fed selectively from them. Yet in France Bernstein's work paradoxically remained for many years an object of derision and caricature largely as a result of misunderstanding of *Class, Codes and Control*, volume 1 (1971). Sociological research and its relevance to education, conducted in both French and English, continued to develop, in Maton's terms, somewhat segmentally.

For such reasons we are particularly grateful to Routledge and our anglophone colleagues who initiated and contributed to this volume and reopened the debate. This volume, hopefully, partially remedies some of the gaps noted above. Comprehensively collecting and presenting French research initiated by the "theories of reproduction" to an English-speaking readership is a task that still remains. Here we present exchanges between researchers who do not necessarily share the same language and often have only very limited knowledge of each other's work but who appear increasingly to be addressing common concerns in Bernstein's language, using his wide range of theoretical tools. These exchanges have been made possible because of the vitality and relevance of the set of questions and problems articulated in *Pedagogy, Symbolic Control and Identity*.

Three issues for the circulation of knowledge

The chapters in this volume are intended, within the context of the epistemological debate and the findings derived from empirical inquiries conducted in widely differing contexts, to help establish better understanding of the specificities and implications of Bernstein's complex theories. Some chapters serve to increase the coherence and singularity of this difficult body of work and invite rereading of it, as well as consideration of the development of empirical work challenging his models. Three major issues have been raised through critical readings of his work and provide the *raison d'être* of this volume.

1   The first issue concerns Bernstein's ambition to develop a theory of education and pedagogy in the broad and somewhat unusual sense[2] construed as symbolic control of "the production, reproduction and transformation of culture" (Bernstein 2000, pp. 37–8). His sociological theory aims to describe, understand and articulate the dynamic relations between education, families, language, curriculum, pedagogy, class relations, the state and work. As early as the 1970s it was acknowledged to have shifted the conventional limits of sociology, psychology and linguistics, integrating and revising their disciplinary contributions.[3] It was always concerned with articulating "micro" and "macro" levels of analysis across a surprising range of associated epistemological and methodological arguments, among other things analysing linguistic forms, data drawn from experimental inquiries, elements of the history of curricular and educational practices, relations between social classes and forms of the division of labour in modern societies. The articulations initiated have since been promoted and extended by research centres, some of which communicate their findings in this volume.

Yet the rarity of this type of global theorization and its intrinsic difficulty is itself worthy of detailed analysis in relation to what Bernstein calls the "regionalization of knowledge", the current, predominant response to pressures exerted by the development of research and debate surrounding issues of interdisciplinarity. Thought on education in every country is subject to regionalization, i.e. the development of new academic boundaries "recontextualizing singulars into larger units which operate ... in the intellectual field of external practice" (Bernstein 2000, p. 52). This tends to weaken the autonomous, discursive and political basis of disciplinary knowledge. It also tends to limit the scope of analyses to relevant social issues of the time, the categorical boundaries of local markets and administrative or professional categories in the name of instrumental knowledge, a logic of administrative control and regulation of organizational structures.

Tensions over identity, if not the "narcissistic" closing-in of disciplines upon themselves (take sociology as a prime example) are equally apparent. They are illustrated in France by a relative decline of sociological interest in education, in particular in schools, a delegitimated, concealed or shunned disciplinary field, zealous control of academic boundaries, reinforcement of critical postures, relativistic and even anti-realist tendencies (see the critique by Jean Molino (1989) on this point) and, above all, a renewed disdain for "normative action".[4] At the level of episteme the type of research for which public funding may be justifiably allocated becomes dictated by demands of efficiency and productivity. Evaluative research dominates the field, appearing to be immediately operational for states that have become evaluators and regulators, seeking "facts" and "evidence". Academic debates often appear to be limited to methods, indices and data. Educational processes are construed in terms of inputs and outputs in economistic operation of statistical models highlighting efficiency of institutional configurations (Mons 2008) which are often reduced to "institutional effects". Cognitive psychology, and even neuroscience, is well integrated within this outlook, thereby marginalizing research in the psychology of development. The "macro" level is confined to nation states and comparisons are made in terms of performance based on standardized tests or studies carried out on the basis of criteria and items defined at national or international level that are remote from the contextualized processes surrounding implementation of policies and practices. The "micro" level is reducible to detailed analyses focusing almost obsessively on a handful of elements of teacher practice and, at best, on a small number of pedagogical situations, straining to distance itself from immediate lived and professional experience. To paraphrase Claude Lessard (2007), the current issue precisely follows this trend implying that "numbers" are increasingly replacing "theory" which is accorded "the status of modes from which the field of education needs to be liberated" (translated from Lessard 2007, p. 71).

Though this distinctly biased and partial view of research in education requires much qualification, if we were to retain just one major interest from Bernstein's work, it is its capacity to provide an alternative view of the subject rooted in the vast network of critical theories dictated by an interest in emancipatory knowledge.[5] This is a theory that is keen to integrate earlier theories and to enable them to render it obsolete in describing and understanding connections linking social and educational relations.

2   Currently sociology appears to have become the target of attack and criticism, charged with a fatalistic outlook and "demobilizing determinism", accusations that serve to turn the ammunition of critique against it. These are highly paradoxical views in so far as they themselves tend to foster new forms of essentialism in public debate. At the same time, this rejection of sociology is not solely related to factors that are external to the field and to its analytical models, as Pierre Bourdieu himself appeared to bemoan.[6] Even if the emancipating ambition of sociology is "taken seriously", as when it claims to want to "deploy defence weapons against symbolic domination"

(translated from Bourdieu 2001), there still needs to be the possibility of some change in the social world. Yet, for us, the second and indeed main interest of Bernstein's analytical framework and theory is precisely its capacity to render operational the fundamental social and epistemological challenge of sociological research, its capacity to enable emergence and construal of "the possible" prospects for political action and choice (as Johan Muller and Jean-Yves Rochex emphasize in this volume). This capacity arises out of a relational epistemology and, ultimately, from a revision and complexification of the theories of reproduction through the intermediary of a theory of pedagogical activity and practice.

Bernstein's never-ending debate with the work of Bourdieu and his many claims of wanting to distance himself from sociological developments, commonly initiated in the name of the sociology of education, were highly symptomatic. The latter, not unlike his Parisian counterparts, strongly critical of attempts to maintain social inequalities and the continued prevalence of specific power relations, lacked any attempt at understanding the factors that enable power to be thus maintained and any attempt at reconstructing what these phenomena tend to alter or impede. This outlook was deeply problematic both for the social world and for these "dominocentric" theories, conferring an aporetic character to their theoretical and social project.[7] Basil Bernstein's views are in this respect quite explicit: at best, he argues, the sociologies of reproduction merely offer a "diagnosis" of the pathology of school (Bernstein 2000, p. 4), supplemented by a conceptual architecture that has an explanatory intent which merely serves to erect into law-like, nomological statement that which is precisely social construction collectively maintained and, therefore, in principle alterable, as with the theories of habitus and fields, pedagogical practice as "symbolic violence", cultural distance and cultural relativism.[8] Bernstein argues that they require a "theory of description".

Pedagogy, Symbolic Control and Identity (2000) opens with the formalization of a set of pedagogical rights designed to raise "fundamental questions about the limitations on democracy" (Bernstein 2000, p. xix) and to provide principles of analysis for studying schools and educational institutions. The inscription of this sociology in critical theory is assumed to be a given, since it is required to analyse the social biases of education. These biases "can reach down to drain the very springs of affirmation, motivation and imagination" (p. xix), thereby constituting "an economic and cultural threat to democracy" (p. xix). They are realized in the very structure of the processes of transmission and acquisition within the educational system and related hypothesis. His formalization of a model of "pedagogical rights" directs sociological analysis towards an epistemology designed to avoid the pitfalls of "dominocentrism" that may undermine critical analysis and may, of course, be viewed as normative. But it derives primarily from a relational mode of reasoning that seeks to avoid an essentialist view of past statistical regularities or other observable data. For Bernstein, as indeed for many others, educational institutions including schools are shaped by the social and power relations that underpin our societies, contributing to the reproduction of social and cultural inequalities, functioning as processes of social and cultural normalization and even as privileged instruments of bourgeois sociodicy. Yet, and herein lies the uniqueness of Bernstein's sociology, they may not (or need not) operate in this way: sociologically there is no such thing as inevitability at the level of individual development of socialized "man" (hence the debate with Vygotsky) and at social, institutional and political levels. Demonstrating this required elaborating a descriptive language capable of founding a theory of activity and pedagogical practice. Bernstein devoted most of his work to a language of description enabling understanding of pedagogical "social action" and its integration within social relations that are external to education and its potential alternatives. This theoretical and highly complex language needs to be abstract and generalized to provide the means of describing the "social action" that constitutes the facts announced by sociologists as well as the possibility of unrealized facts:

> In summary, how does power and control translate into principles of communication, and how do these principles of communication differentially regulate forms of consciousness with respect to their reproduction and the possibilities of change? ... I shall be concentrating very much on being able to provide and create models, which can generate specific descriptions.
>
> (Bernstein 2000, pp. 3–4)

Bernstein's contribution has been to the initial stages of the ambitious research programme flowing from his magisterial arguments which he dug deep and fought hard to defend in the midst of the international corpus of modern and contemporary research in the social sciences. The concepts of classification and framing, visible and invisible pedagogies, pedagogic text, privileging discourses, recontextualizing, recognition and realization rules, horizontal and vertical discourses, instructional and regulative discourse and a whole host of others have already articulated a language of description. This provides operationalizations that help to translate between social relations and pedagogical practice, the relations of continuity and discontinuity between the world inside the school and the world beyond, relations of power and pedagogic discourse, knowledge and social classes, established or emerging identities and global social forms. As we shall see with many of the analyses collected in this volume, the validity of the language may also be measured by its capacity to describe pedagogic and educational situations in very different contexts.

   3   It is time to draw some initial conclusions concerning the scope and progress state of advancement of this research programme, what we know about pedagogic discourse and activity, the state of descriptive theory and,

therefore, the elements of a solution for the overly simple diagnoses of reproduction, social control, inequalities, educational differentiation and exclusion. If we were to justify interest in Bernstein's work we would emphasize
its capacity to provide understanding and analysis of significant transformations that are currently tending to alter social and educational relations in
developed countries. As Professor Solomon reminds us (see Bernstein 2000,
ch. 11), it is not altogether inconceivable that these transformations may
serve to challenge or question the generalizability of the theory and to generate new developments. Many of the contributors to this volume have tended
to adopt this perspective, challenging the theory to confront the issues and
new contexts that characterize their specific areas and objects of inquiry. The
theories' suppleness is reinforced by multiple revisions in the course of a
40-year period of substantial political and social upheaval. As early as the
1960s, for Bernstein and many others, the central issue was the question of
social inequalities. He somewhat ironically put it in one of his earliest papers
as the issue of "the wastage of the educational potential of the working-
class". The political project initiated in Britain and later elsewhere, articulated around the notion of the welfare state, focused in part on the
development of a comprehensive educational system established in the name
of equality. The issue for Bernstein was to identify relationships between
intentions to democratize education and new educational policies, for
example, of "compensation" and class pressures for, and professional willingness to provide, "invisible pedagogies". In his last book his focus shifted to
the "infringement of pedagogical rights", transformations affecting pedagogic discourse manifested in the objectives of educational policies connected with transitional capitalism, marked predominantly by short-term
vision. Close observation of British educational reforms initiated by Thatcher
and extended by New Labour governments, prompted significant revision of
his last book shortly before his death in 2000, serving to increase the intelligibility of the principle of new public management and the subsumption of
curriculum under "an entrepreneurial competitive culture" (Bernstein 2000).
New conceptions of pupil learning, knowledge and education shaped the referents of international educational policies, ordinary school practices and
their expert analysis. Bernstein was concerned both with the prevalence of an
idealistic model of competence marked by an "emancipating tendency" fed
by the social sciences of the 1970s ("there is no such thing as a deficiency;
there are only differences") and with the emergence of unlikely new models
of generic performance in the name of principles of trainability and life-long
learning. This analysis illuminates curricular shifts that currently prevail in
primary, secondary and higher education in most developed countries entail-
ing the need for a new definition of "pedagogic identities". We are witnessing the replacement of pedagogical models aimed at developing "introjected"
identities by those aimed at producing "projected" ones centred on the
instrumental value of economic production. Whereas introjected modes
could be characterized as narcissistic, hierarchic and elitist, the new forms

"erode a collective base and replace inner commitments and dedications by short-term instrumentalities" (Bernstein 2000, p. 62). While these shifts may have been initiated in the name of a "knowledge society" and may not impede the possibility of change, they reveal a divorce between knowledge and knower, and render opaque a major new social rupture unfolding before our very eyes:

> Knowledge is divorced from persons, their commitments, their personal dedications. These become impediments, restrictions on the flow of knowledge, and introduce deformations in the working of the symbolic market. Moving knowledge about, or even creating it, should not be more difficult than moving and regulating money. Knowledge, after nearly a thousand years, is divorced from inwardness and literally dehumanized. Once knowledge is separated from inwardness, from commitments, from personal dedication, from the deep structure of the self, the people may be moved about, substituted for each other and excluded from the market.
>
> (Bernstein 2000, p. 86)

Beyond the matter of the reasons that account for affiliation, the logic of citation, professional competition or networking, social reality and educational challenges require the pursuit of an analysis and research into the accumulation of sociological knowledge. What tends to circulate in the realm of educational policy-making are "evidence-based" facts, "quality indicators" and "best practices" appropriate for benchmarking. Contemporary societies claim to be simply knowledge economies. Educational systems now ensure mass education; yet pedagogical rights do not appear to be any more guaranteed today than they were in the past for considerable numbers of children and teenagers attending school. New, large-scale instruments of statistical analysis purport to enable a far better description at a quasi-global level, indicating how some countries are better able to address these issues, legitimating the temptation to seek out and import "best practices" wherever they may be discerned, careless of the risks of transplant.

These views are open to naturalist construal (Crahay 2006) based, for the most part, on an implicit postulate that the processes of teaching and learning are inscribed in an universe of actually identifiable situations, such that mere observation of practices to identify those associated with the highest educational achievements is all that is required to establish what needs to be done. As Crahay eloquently states, this comes down to assimilating the situations observed in schools and classrooms to:

> A natural environment that has its own laws from which no one may escape ... the reasoning perfectly illustrates what Popper (1982) called the common sense problem of induction, i.e. deeming it legitimate to make predictions based on regular patterns observed in the past and

firmly believing in their validity, and even their inevitability, in so far as these are founded on a large number of observations.

(Crahai 2006, p. 141)

We prefer the view from Basil Bernstein keen on both solid theorization and confrontation with reality:

> If I now look at vulnerabilities within the theory I think these have been and will be revealed by empirical research. And as a consequence lead to the development, modifications and replacement of the theory. Thus the theory, for its own sake, is crucially dependent on research. There is therefore an obligation to construct a conceptual language and provide models which facilitate empirical research. And this I have tried very hard to do.
>
> (Bernstein 2000, pp. 211–12)

Meeting the challenge

The chapters collected in this volume have been grouped into five parts, each developing something from the major questions, though sharing many common threads. Some contributors adopt theoretical or epistemological approaches to Bernstein's work, focusing both on discussion of its global significance and more particular issues; others extend the same questions by focusing more particularly on empirical investigations.

"Legacies, encounters, continuities, misunderstandings" includes contributions by two major observers of, and actors within, the sociology of education, Roger Establet (University of Provence, France) and Brian Davies (Cardiff School of Social Sciences, Wales). The former focuses on the reception of Bernstein's work in France, while the latter examines its reception in the English-speaking world, both deeply paradoxical for a number of reasons. Establet emphasizes, for instance, the capacity of Bernstein's concepts to account for the results of certain analyses that have yet to be referred to, while Davies focuses on significant developments of the theory that have occurred, for the most part, outside Bernstein's country of origin.

Part II, "The social and the psychic: the interdisciplinary debate", focuses on the development of Bernstein's theory of pedagogic activity in comparison with theories of socialization. Jean-Manuel De Queiroz (University of Rennes 2, France), unravels the significance of Durkheimian influences on Bernstein's work, observing that Durkheim's *Rules* (1982 [1895]) and its claim to explain the social merely by the social provides one of the essential foundations for Bernstein's theory, allowing a distancing from Parsonian structural-functionalism and all forms of sociologism that tend to downplay the complexity of the subject. The originality of Jean-Manuel De Queiroz's chapter lies in its detailed knowledge of Durkheim's work and articulation around the notion of "mode of subjectivation". For many who depend on modern recontextualizations of Durkheim's texts, the portrayal of Bernstein as one of the holistic authors par excellence may appear somewhat paradoxical. Bernstein's work appears to be in direct descent from Durkheim's analyses of interiority in *Evolution of Educational Thought: Lectures on the Formation and Development of Secondary Education in France* (Durkheim, 1977 [1938]).[9]

Jean-Yves Rochex (University of Paris VIII, France) and Harry Daniels (University of Bath, England) return to the central issue of the social formation of mind emerging from the fruitful encounter between Bernstein's work and the theory of activity developed by the Russian psychologists Vygotsky and Leontiev. Both integrate a pragmatic dimension of learning within their theories, giving central importance to language in individual and social development. Daniels, an activity theory expert, uses Bernstein's work to show how analysis of the production of cultural artefacts still needs to be widened and extended. His argument is designed to demonstrate how Bernstein provides a descriptive language that helps to widen and extend Vygotsky's account of the social formation of the mind based on an understanding of the social processes that shape the specific modalities of pedagogic practice. He argues that Vygotsky and Leontiev fail to take sufficient account in their analyses of the capacity of macro-constraints to direct interactions and institutional structure. Jean-Yves Rochex, who has been working for many years at the interface of sociology and psychology, provides a counter-point to this critique, calling for strong acceptance of psychism for the acceptance of a strong definition of the social. Such developments called for by Vygotsky and Leontiev, among others, would help to put the finishing touches to Bernstein's work which remains inadequate in this regard, in spite of its significance within the field of sociological research. The challenge for Rochex is ultimately to construe the cultural, linguistic and subjective changes which the experience of schooling represents. In this respect, the most significant contribution of Bernstein's non-sociological work remains its elaboration of a non-deterministic theory providing useful critiques of ongoing debates on the theory of habitus and other "dispositional" models.

The following two sections extend these arguments through empirical analyses. Part III includes three chapters that focus more specifically on language and the transformations of pedagogic discourse. Claude Grignon (Maison des Sciences de l'Homme, Paris, France) returns to debates surrounding the notions of restricted and elaborated linguistic codes and to the constitution of social hierarchies of cultures. Referring to one of Bernstein's earliest articles, he reminds us how restricted code and the social relations to which it refers do not merely refer to socialization and are not a distinctive attribute of the working classes but pertain, as Bernstein insisted, to certain contexts and specific situations and activities. Using the criterion of the predictability of discourse, Grignon provides many useful illustrations of restricted code observed in a wide range of situations at every level of the social hierarchy, from situations involving "technical routines" to "superior forms of social comedy". The very nature of elaborated code and its connection with dominant culture is re-examined and specified. These clarifications lead to a reconsideration of linguistic, social and intellectual handicap theses and the "deficit perspective" unjustly attributed to Bernstein, demonstrating not only the possibility but necessity of a rupture with populist and miserabilistic (see note 6) views, which still tend to affect analyses of inequalities in school learning.

The object of the chapter by Elisabeth Bautier (University of Paris VIII, France) is to pursue and extend discussion of cognitive and linguistic socialization in relation to the position taken by Bernstein in *Pedagogy, Symbolic Control and Identity*. Her reading suggests that the work is of major significance in an era of the "desociologization" of the issue of educational inequalities while providing a synthesis of the results of a wide range of empirical analyses of classroom learning. Using Bernstein's work, Bautier describes and conceptualizes the impact of a school discursive genre with socially differentiating effects that currently appears to prevail in French educational practices, especially those concerning children from working-class backgrounds. She provides a detailed account of "horizontal discourse" which chiefly governs their pedagogical relations. Horizontal discourse is a local discourse rooted in practical procedures; it is oral and wholly contextualized, and treats knowledge segmentally. It is invariably contextualized and connected with a specific task. It stands in contradiction to official school expectations which pertain to "vertical discourse", the "specialized symbolic structures of explicit knowledge" (Bernstein 2000, p. 160). The existence of horizontal discourse is problematic in so far as it does not help to elaborate the resources required for appropriation of knowledge. Its discursive genre thus appears to contribute to misleading pupils as to the nature of the expectations of the institution which paradoxically proceed from a set of values with an overriding sense of democratic overtones concerning participation, respect of individual identities, valorization of ordinary and spontaneous experience, and so forth. In Bernstein's (2000, p. 43) terms, an idealistic model of competence is achieved at the price of "abstracting the individual from the analysis of distributions of power and principles of control which selectively specialize modes of acquisition and realizations".

The convergence between Bautier's article and the analysis provided by Karl Maton (University of Sydney, Australia) is particularly fruitful. The juxtaposition of these studies demonstrates the capacity of Bernstein's models to account for processes at work in very different national contexts in the realization of pedagogic discourse. Maton's argument is based on observations made in Australia and his twofold contribution. First he seeks to enrich the conceptual architecture of Bernstein's model using the concept of "semantic gravity" to avoid dichotomous use of Bernstein's categories and the notion of the legitimation codes that helps to integrate a range of analyses drawn from fields theorized by Pierre Bourdieu. The concept of semantic gravity aims to establish the degree to which signification depends on its context. Maton demonstrates how segmentalism (strong semantic gravity) haunts current educational practices: knowledge is strongly connected to its context and has no value beyond its context. The strong semantic gravity he observes in different pedagogic situations in professional university teaching in the humanities derives from the dominance of a knower code, in the absence of a knowledge code, legitimating pedagogic practices; what appears to matter is not "what we know" so much as "who we are". Maton's second major contribution extends Bernstein's analysis in signifying how segmentalism is not just an educational issue. Learners, especially from working-class backgrounds, encouraged to acquire knowledge that can be used "throughout one's life" through situations of "authentic learning", find it increasingly difficult to transfer into new contexts. Contradictory current educational policies require cumulative learning, yet foster segmented learning. But this contradiction tends to disappear as segmented learning fulfils the expectations of a new economic and social order that projects identities directed towards the short term and newly emerging markets for symbolic goods.

Part IV, "Classification and framing: the revision and permanence of curricula", includes four chapters that use Bernstein's models and extend arguments on current pedagogic and curricular transformations. Sophia Stavrou (University of Provence, France) focuses on the current state of affairs in curricular recontextualizations at the university level in relation to policy aimed at developing a "European space for higher education". Her argument focuses on the development of professional pluridisciplinary training and, in particular, on the emergence of what Bernstein calls "regions of knowledge". We are currently witnessing a weakening of singular disciplinary discourses and the emergence and elaboration of broader pedagogic discourses (for example, urbanism, communication and management in most universities, especially at master's level), and indications of global change rather than simple institutional prescription. The notion of recontextualizing fields helps conceptualize the dynamics of these processes of construction of training and curricular structures which involve appropriation struggles between many different actors, including agents promoting official discourse, ministerial experts on higher education in charge of certifying and allocating funds to particular educational programmes, professional societies and "resisters" within the pedagogic field. Tensions may give rise to compromises between those with intrinsic disciplinary and instrumental knowledge interests. The originality of the analysis provided resides in its ambition to question/challenge such structuring of knowledge and the social and power relations within. The master's in urbanism in France is in this respect highly illuminating. Disciplinary knowledge in sociology, geography and law undergoes recontextualization within a new framework independent of the theoretical models in which it was originally elaborated. Within the sociology component there is displacement of any explanation of social action and relations by focusing on the issues which they tend to generate. Training is subject to control external to the pedagogic field; the questions and tools produced by professionals within the field of urbanism tend to guide and direct what is conceivable and inconceivable within the training framework. Teaching cannot be accused of being "overly abstract" but at the cost of elaboration of the articulation of theory and practice in the knowledge transmission.

Eric and Catherine Mangez (Catholic University of Louvain, Belgium) focus on transformations affecting pedagogic discourse in the two schooling networks in French-speaking Belgium: the private, free Catholic and the public network of the French educational community. Both have had to retranslate new legislative injunctions formulated in the late 1990s, aiming to foster convergence (official texts speak of "reducing liberties") within their curricula. Mangez and Mangez base their analysis on earlier Bernsteinian concepts of visible and invisible pedagogy, using lexical and factorial analysis of texts and programmes within the two networks. Their analysis indicate a distinct polarization between the public network's visible pedagogies, and the private's invisible pedagogies, and how these pedagogies are related to the various structures of positions occupied by intermediary agents in charge of reform implementation, particularly institutional configurations of professional development.

The chapter by Nadège Pandraud (University of Provence, France) is more concerned with observing pragmatic learning dimensions while integrating different levels of observation. Her argument is articulated around observation of the activity of writing a tale in a sixième (first year secondary) class in a French school. The purpose of this case study is to understand how curriculum shapes learning activities and to define the conditions of, and possibilities for, the productivity of pedagogic actions in terms of learning. In the last ten years or so, significant shifts have occurred in the French curriculum which now focuses on the use of discourses rather than language. Starting from observation of the narrative activity of the pupils, Pandraud emphasizes the effects of framing on the learning activity. Official curriculum formulation and framing do not necessarily determine what happens *in situ*, where different possibilities can be observed. Classroom pedagogy may either reiterate or transform existing classifications and the social and power relations which they (re)produce. Currently, at the curricular level, instructional discourse appears to have become more opaque, the status of written work in French teaching more blurred, and the ends for which it is undertaken more uncertain. This tends to generate insecurity both in teachers and pupils and exacerbates social inequalities in knowledge acquisition. Yet change, and also the productivity of pedagogic action for all, entail *in situ* framings, as Pandraud argues, thereby following Bernstein, who had already underlined the possibilities of change at the level of framing.[10] Pandraud illustrates how the teacher produces revisions of framing "for every individual case" in his/her interactions with pupils who allow themselves, or are allowed, to speak and articulate reasons for what they do. She also shows that cognitive acquisition depends on the visibility given to scholarly and ordinary knowledge, showing a degree of convergence with Bautier's analysis of the status of speech in class and the relation between horizontal and vertical discourse.

Finally, Ana M. Morais and Isabel P. Neves (University of Lisbon, Portugal) offer a synthesis of a 20-year research programme designed to optimize a model of pedagogic practice in school science. They adopt a praxeological research stance somewhat different from that of previous chapters, aiming to conceptualize a school pedagogic practice capable of leading children to school success which narrows the gap between the results of children from different social milieux. Yet their argument is not so very far removed from the studies outlined above, seeking, as it does, through critical analysis, to identify conditions for more egalitarian knowledge acquisition. Such argument is, indeed, called for by Bernstein's own aim to produce "models which can generate specific descriptions" (Bernstein 2000, p. 3), while accounting for the unplanned and unexpected. The approach is resolutely experimental in pursuit of a form of "mixed pedagogic practice" based on Bernstein's conceptual language. Conditions for its optimization are articulated, as are conditions for its extension to teacher training contexts and curriculum development. Though the relational perspective of the theory entails that the model employed cannot be expected to work in all contexts, a number of ideal-type characteristics of pedagogic practice that appear to be indispensable for successful learning are outlined.

As noted above, Basil Bernstein never sought to circumvent the epistemological issues raised either in sociology generally or his own research.

Part V, "Epistemological perspectives", brings together two chapters by Johan Muller (University of Cape Town, South Africa) and Nicole Ramognino (University of Provence, France) which invite a reflection on the questions raised by Bernstein's work for the discipline as a whole. Rooted in the disciplinary debate between science and literature initiated by C.P. Snow in *The Two Cultures* (1993 [1959]), Muller's chapter aims to provide an irenic discussion of Bernstein and Bourdieu's epistemological theses. Muller views these as more similar in terms of their sociological interests and preoccupations than they are opposed and conflicting. Following a curricular and epistemological exploration of "hard" and "soft" disciplines, Muller challenges both the normative and the relativistic approaches adopted by sociologists of science, with regard to the call for "realist rationalism" as the distressed conclusion to the last book by Bourdieu (2001), depicting sociology as torn between constructivism and positivism. Bourdieu's analytical angle is articulated around discussion of the "truth" in science, appropriating epistemological and philosophical questions that have been objects of intense exploration in scientific and disciplinary fields throughout the twentieth century. While an underlying interest in rehabilitating sociology can also be found in Bernstein's work, the way in which he sets out to question epistemology is markedly different. Adopting a Durkheimian perspective, Bernstein sees an ideal-type schema of knowledge where, for example, disciplines (preferred to the term "field") such as sociology and physics inhere respectively in horizontal and vertical structures whose difference pertains both to their internal epistemology (accumulation, increasing generality, etc.) and legitimacy within the scientific "arena". In Muller's view, Bernstein and Bourdieu offer, in their own ways, alternatives to the "essential tension" between the hard and soft sciences, the former offering an answer to the tension between normativity, value judgement and reasoned choice.

Adopting a "practical epistemology" perspective initiated by Jean-Claude Gardin *et al.* (1987) among others, Ramognino contends that Bernstein's work has made two fundamental epistemological contributions: inquiring into connections between the social and action that characterizes reality, and searching for a specific language of description designed to account for their qualities. Her highly original approach aims to integrate observed social practice activity within a theory of cultural reproduction. It originates from an idealist principle, the right to democracy for all, a normative premise which enables her to question relations between scientific work and action, developing different levels of observation devised by Bernstein such as classification and framing and language of description. Yet, of heuristic value, Bernstein's model is seen to suffer from "a political orientation towards history and by an epistemic framing that hierarchizes statistics over the future", thus requiring revision of his conception of activity, time and space.

The chapters collected in this volume present several logics, readings and uses of Bernstein's work. While the common threads are numerous, there is no consensus or unanimity surrounding the sociology of the "master". This should by no means be taken as a cause for complaint! Perhaps "Give, receive and repay", the Maussian principle of economic, social and symbolic exchange, is an apt description of the way in which Bernstein envisaged research. Paraphrasing him loosely, we might say that while the circulation of theories and empirical research is required from a scientific, pedagogic, intellectual and social point of view, fidelity to these same theories and to these empirical findings is undoubtedly the sign of their heuristic exhaustion. As such, these discussions, questionings, borrowings and revisions of Bernstein's work are the very condition of their vivacity, fertility and respect. This volume presents itself as an opening. It is an invitation to (re)read Bernstein and to engage in research with and beyond his sociological oeuvre.

Notes

1 As noted above, it was not until 2007 that a French version of *Pedagogy, Symbolic Control and Identity*, a major contemporary work by Bernstein, finally became available. Although three articles by Bernstein were published in French between 1975 and 2007 they attracted very little attention and French sociologists tended to refer merely to *Langage et classes sociales* (1975), the translated version of *Class, Codes and Control* (1971).
2 "I also want to make it very clear that my concept of pedagogic practices would include the relationships between doctor and patient, the relationships between

psychiatrist and the so-called mentally ill, the relationships between architects and planners. In other words, the notion of pedagogic practice which I shall be using will regard pedagogic practice as the fundamental social context through which cultural reproduction-production takes place. Operating with this rather wide definition of pedagogic practice, the models of description that I shall try to create necessarily have a certain generality in order that they can cope with the differentiation of the agencies of cultural reproduction" (Bernstein 2000, p. 3).

3 As argued for instance by J.-C. Chamboredon in the preface to the French edition of *Class, Codes and Control*, vol. 1 (translated as *Langage et classes sociales. Codes socio-linguistiques et contrôle social* in 1975).

4 Normativity means here "spheres of activity". This notion refers to Canguilhem's distinction (1966) between normativity and normalization. There are internal conditions in spheres of activity which are not the only concern of arbitrary social norms. In any case, we think that sociology has to ask the question of this distinction. Otherwise it leads to a homogenization and a depreciation of all the constraints and all the conditions of practices which nevertheless allow people to think, to work, etc.

5 Although they would gain much from a comparison with Bernsteinian concepts, we refer here to the analytical categories developed by Habermas (1968), who defined three types of interest of scientific knowledge: a technical interest connected with the technosciences; a practical interest for those sciences with an interest in the regulation of social processes; and an emancipatory interest that may be the product of the so-called praxeological sciences geared towards critical ends.

6 See for instance the interview entitled "Une science qui dérange" (Bourdieu 1980).

7 The aporetic nature of Bourdieu's theory of the social is usefully highlighted by Alain Girard (1996): it is the aporia of a sociology that is keen to "liberate" agents from what it tends ultimately to construe as being constitutive of social relations, i.e. "symbolic violence". In French sociological research at least two significant theoretical trends have sought to elaborate this critique. Both were initiated by former collaborators of Bourdieu, the first by C. Grignon and J.-C. Passeron, whose book *Le Savant et le populaire* (1989) develops a fruitful reflection on Bourdieu's theory of cultural legitimacy and the applicability of the concept of "symbolic domination". Rejecting the cultural and scientific relativism that entered the realm of the social sciences in the 1980s, Grignon and Passeron identified the two poles of an alternative in research into the culture of dominated groups: (1) construing a dominated culture autonomously and as popular culture (i.e. as self-sufficient culture) or (2) construing it on the basis of the social domination that constitutes it as a dominated culture and reduces it to the status of an "absence" or a "lesser being". Sociological research ran the danger of falling into the trap of what the authors refer to as "populism" or "miserabilistic thought" (or "legitimism", precisely the tendency of the theory of cultural legitimacy elaborated by Bourdieu). A second was initiated by Luc Boltanski, who, along with Laurent Thévenot, had initially set out to demonstrate the need to shift from a sociology of critique ("the paradigm of dis-covery") to a "sociology of critical society" (Boltanski and Thévenot 1991; Boltanski 1990). This sociological paradigm has since developed significantly, generating a large number of empirical studies in a range of fields. The object of their critique is also to mark

a departure away from the kind of dominocentrism that is apparent, for instance, in Bourdieu's theory, played out in the process of invisibilization of different types of relations that results from the theory (e.g. cooperation, love, friendship, sense of justice, etc.), which cannot be reduced to relations of domination. In one recent publication, Luc Boltanski has attempted to re-articulate the two approaches, the sociologies of critique and domination and the pragmatic sociology of critique (Boltanski 2009). Such research might usefully be assessed in relation to Bernsteinian theory.

8 Indeed, one may wonder if this critique still applies to current "sociologies" of education while claiming simultaneously to stand as a revision of the theory of habitus. On this point, see the chapter in this volume by Jean-Yves Rochex.

9 This is yet another paradox, in view of the relative lack of interest in French sociology of education in this book.

10 The forms of control at work in the interaction: see in this respect the comments on "The message and the voice" in the chapters by De Queiroz and Ramognino's discussion of the issue of social change.

Part I

Legacies, encounters, continuities, misunderstandings

1 The current relevance of Basil Bernstein in the sociology of education in France

Roger Establet

I have been asked to discuss the reception of Basil Bernstein's work in France. However, I feel unable to treat this magnificent subject in its full scope, particularly because of the comparisons between those two "sacred" intellectual giants, Basil Bernstein and Pierre Bourdieu, that would inevitably arise and which would lead the discussion infinitely beyond my competence.

Therefore, I have considerably reduced my ambitions and will consider the reception of Bernstein's work as observed from my position in the Sociology Department of the University de Provence. In 1975, my colleagues had given my friend Roger Benoliel and me the shared responsibility for two optional university courses, at the bachelor's and master's degree levels, entitled, in "elaborated code", "The Sociology of Education", and retranslated in "restricted code" as "Soc Ed". In this chapter, then, I will confine myself to "The Reception of Basil Bernstein in Soc Ed".

In 1975, when we set up the curriculum for the undergraduate course, we were somewhat obliged to begin by addressing the upheavals that happened in the discipline at the end of the 1960s. These include the first INED (French National Institute of Demography) survey and systematic follow-up of a complete generation of students, beginning in 1962, which contained a particularly significant table (see Table 1.1) that reversed the economist vision that leftist organizations had held regarding class inequality in relation to schooling.

The table clearly demonstrated that, in terms of academic qualifications, income by itself does not determine schooling success but that the impact of academic qualifications on income is definitely significant. Paul Clerc, the author of the table, concluded that: "In reality, income has no particular influence on schooling success ... The effect of familial environment seems therefore almost exclusively cultural" (Clerc 1970).

The most recent demonstrations to date of the specific influence of parents' academic qualifications in France have been documented by DEP (French research centre on evaluation and policy) researchers Jean-Paul Caillé and Sophie O'Prey (2005) and, more broadly, in the countries constituting the OECD by the Program for International Student Assessment (PISA).[1]

Table 1.1 Entry ratio in first year of secondary school according to father's income and academic qualification in 1962

Father's diploma	Monthly income in French francs				
	400–1,000	1,001–1,400	1,401–2,000	2,001 and above	Average
No diploma	42	36	42		38
CEP	40	37	46	43	39
Technical	28	44	52	44	47
GCSE	55	63	60	54	63
Baccalaureate and above		65	68	65	68
Average	39	43	53	59	48

Between 1960 and 1970, French sociology of education was also marked by:

• The introduction of the concept of "cultural capital", based on very productive empirical analyses, by Pierre Bourdieu and Jean-Claude Passeron.
• The resurrection, following a seminar by Bourdieu and Passeron at the Ecole Pratique des Hautes Etudes, of Durkheim's *magnum opus*, *L'évolution pédagogique en France* (published in English as *The Evolution of Educational Thought: Lectures on the Formation and Development of Secondary Education in France*), which had become largely unobtainable before being reprinted in 1968.

As these events served to renew the discipline, a flowering of rich studies in the field of the French sociology of education followed and includes the work of Guy Vincent on school form (1980), Viviane Isambert-Jamati on secondary education, Luc Boltanski on primary education (1964), Alain Girard on school demography, Claude Grignon on vocational education (1971), and Claude Seibel and Jacqueline Levasseur on the inefficacy of repeating first grade (1983, 1984). Reference to Basil Bernstein is present throughout each of these works. And while the large INED anthology, *Population et l'enseignement*, does not include a bibliography, I can testify that Alain Girard grilled me for a long time about "restricted code" and "elaborated code" during the oral defence of my thesis.

Finally, the publication in 1975 of *Langage et classes sociales* (a French translation broadly in line with volume 1 of *Class, Codes and Control*) in the "Le sens commun" series edited by Pierre Bourdieu is perhaps the most noteworthy indicator of Basil Bernstein's presence in the French sociology of education.

Basil Bernstein was in a way, then, one of the main actors in the renewal of French sociology and thus he assumed the rank of a "classic" in the "Soc Ed" curriculum.

To follow in such limited space the meanderings and nuances of Bernstein's presence in these and other diverse works is a challenge that is out of my reach. Therefore, I will simplify my task and follow Bernstein along two tracks that have constantly inspired our undergraduate (bachelor's degree) curriculum: one opened up in *L'ordre des choses* by Claude Grignon (1971) on vocational education, and the other traced by Viviane Isambert-Jamati on secondary education. It was necessary, for strictly pedagogical reasons, to introduce these unique works into our undergraduate curriculum.

L'ordre des choses: the opening made by Claude Grignon

Durkheim's *The Evolution of Educational Thought: Lectures on the Formation and Development of Secondary Education in France* provided a royal red carpet to our undergraduate curriculum and brought our students to reconsider their own secondary studies with interest just prior to their review of Paul Clerc's statistical data (outlined above). However, these works were largely concerned with general secondary education. *L'ordre des choses*, by Claude Grignon, appeared at just the right moment to fill this gap in our undergraduate curriculum. Grignon, in his 1965 surveys, had mobilized all available conceptual and empirical resources to deliver a true sociology of what we could call, in Bernstein's terms, "the educational recontextualization of vocational apprenticeships". This book has become a classic, as those who undertook studies on the evolution of vocational education in the 1980s and 1990s, and even today, constantly refer to this work.

Claude Grignon's text is profoundly inspired by Basil Bernstein. The innovative work of Bernstein on the uses of toys is evoked, and the hypotheses of sociolinguistics are explicitly mentioned (1971, pp. 235 and 238), as Grignon describes the games of secondary school students in CET (vocational secondary school). It is in the acuity of the description of language codes that Bernstein's inspiration appears most evident. Grignon demonstrates how the "restricted code" can be used as a weapon against the "elaborated code" (1971, p. 235) that teachers in general education condescendingly attempt to instil in students (1971, pp. 231–2). Inversely, the sudden transition on the part of a teacher from scholarly language to the popular language of the students is revealed as an efficient way to measure their unworthiness. Additionally, vocational teachers and general education teachers are shown to employ distinct codes in their classrooms and with their students. Thus, when students go from the classroom to the workshop, the code changes. This variation in codes provided Grignon with an effective instrument for analysing speech gathered in interviews.

The similarity of the ideas of Bernstein and Grignon is also remarkable, as evidenced in *L'ordre des choses* by the implicit but very strong presence of analyses in terms of "classification" and "framing"; thus, Basil Bernstein's *Langage et classes sociales* (1975) can be viewed as contemporary.

If one does not want to give in to the "epistemic fallacy" of the precursors or the false coincidences, one could suggest to an undergraduate teacher in the Sociology of Education the following exercise: "find in *L'ordre des choses* all analyses that could enlighten Bernstein's concept of 'classification' and 'framing'". For the teacher's clever students, the harvest would be ample. The CET ideal type described by Grignon (1971, p. 217) is an example of strong internal classification: between vocational education and general education, between the workshop and the classroom, and between spaces occupied by distinct actors, including the dining hall. Such classification is well internalized because, while CET students know that their vocational apprenticeship is significant, it is the congruent portion of general education that bestows on them the relatively enviable status of secondary school student as they leave the institution. As for "framing", the CET appears, to all those who have followed the more flexible models of general education, as a direct prescription of all the details of all the performances expected from its students. Meanwhile, the detailed analysis of the functions of technical drawing, with the exemplary combination of moral virtues and technical precision that it instils, illustrates the blending of "regulative discourse" and "instructional discourse" and the embedding of the second within the first.

> The drawing is defined at the same time as a professional activity and as a cultural activity; as such it serves as a privileged mediator between "trade culture" and "learned culture", and, by that, a very efficient means of making trade culture more sophisticated. We judge a drawing as a material object and as a symbolic object at the same time: a successful drawing should be clean, neat, carefully produced, without erasures or deletions; but it should also be exact. The draftsman should possess "manual" qualities, such as dexterity, precision, neatness and meticulousness; but the draftsman's work opposes, by its modalities and objectives, that of a labourer: instead of large and heavy objects and tools, he manipulates and uses subtle instruments and quasi immaterial substances: paper, pencils, ink, straight edges, rulers, compasses, etc; he does not produce things, but signs, abstract equivalents of things and of their transformations. Thus, drawing opposes itself to manual labour; it aligns itself on the side of the impeccable, the discreet, of the "non nature": the white coat of a draftsman or PETT (professor of theoretical technical education) opposes itself to the dungarees of a labourer or the grey coat of a workshop teacher. Although it is distinct from an "art drawing" by its professional finality, by the rigour of the constraints that weigh on its execution, technical drawing is not without sharing in cultural and artistic values imparted to that person.... A number of apprentices execute sketches where the influence of professional drawing

is perceived; they gladly boast about the aesthetic qualities of some of their workshop drawings.

(Grignon 1971, pp. 253–4)

Finally, strong external classification (the hierarchy between general instruction and vocational education) is constantly present in curricular details. Three examples are provided.

We still remember the French teacher who proposed a "beautiful topic" that he would "like to study himself" but who warned that "it is a difficult topic that not everybody can tackle".

"You have witnessed a brilliant cultural manifestation; tell what your impressions were". Then, for the majority he reserves the command, "You have made for the first time a useful object: tell how rewarding your experience was".

Or, we remember the parenthetical and insidious remark of that vocational teacher:

> You will see the composition of the dissolved salts. I gave you the names and also the chemical compositions of them. That's chemistry; it may be a little bit complex for you and I am not asking you to memorize it, but it is good to have a look at it anyway.

The little undergraduate exercise suggested above does not have as its only objective the refutation of the proverb "traduttore, traditore". It also allows those who would attempt to carry out on contemporary vocational education a synthesis comparable to that of Claude Grignon's to equip themselves with conceptual tools that may be more indispensable now.

A measure of the evolution of vocational education in France is illustrated in Table 1.2 and Figure 1.1.

In Claude Grignon's analysis, vocational education is essentially centred on the CAP (certificate of vocational aptitude), the dominant and yet not

Table 1.2 Proportions (in %) of the different vocational and technical degrees awarded in 1965 and in 2004

1965				2004			
Level V	86	Including CAP:	76	Level V	46	Including CAP:	19
Level IV	12			Level IV	33		
Level III	2			Level III	22		
	100				100		
		% of success in the CAP by this generation: 21%				% of success in the CAP by this generation: 13%	

Sources: TEN retrospective (1958–69); Criteria statistical references (2005).

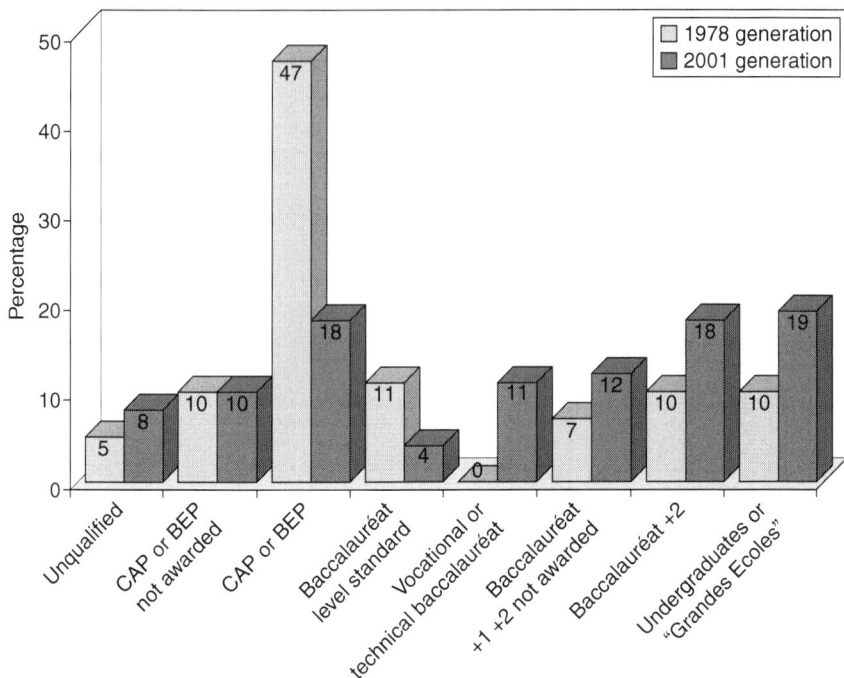

Figure 1.1 Proportion (in %) of the different level degrees among students having left the educational system in 1978 and 2001.

easily accessible diploma. The CAP consisted of a recontextualization of labour apprenticeships intended for prospective elite labourers. In today's formal curriculum, the place of the traditional training of workers is clearly diminished in favour of more ambitious curricula (the vocational baccalaureate and BTS (an advanced vocational diploma) or the DUT (a vocational university diploma)). In a situation where there is a shortage of jobs, the possession of a CAP no longer guarantees recognition of a qualification, though it somehow saves one from the severest forms of job insecurity or instability.

This institutional transformation has been accompanied by the less visible pedagogy of the hierarchy of diplomas. In 1965–6, the school year when Grignon conducted his research, only 5.3 per cent of vocational students went on to higher studies. Yet today, some vocational certificates, and the BEP (a vocational education diploma) in particular, are conceived within the formal curriculum as a means to continue one's studies. In Meirieu's 1998 questionnaire, all secondary school students were asked: "Do you envisage higher studies?" Although, by its wording, the question was not intended for vocational secondary school students, they answered it anyway and the systematic analysis of their replies across three local educational institutions reveals that,

Table 1.3 2001–4 generation of students having left the educational system in 2001

Level		%	Monthly income	Quick access to stable job (%)	Slow exit from unemployment (%)
VI	Non-qualified	8	1,000	31	33
Vbis	CAP or BEP not awarded	10	1,050	48	20
V	CAP or BEP	18	1,090	73	9
IV	Bac not awarded	4	1,080	64	11
IV	Vocational or technological Bac	11	1,120	74	7
III	Bac+1 or + 2 not awarded	12	1,180	64	9
III	Bac + 2	18	1,300	81	4
II	Undergraduates	9	1,320	74	7
I	Masters, "Grandes Ecoles"	10	1,930	79	10
		100	1,200	68	11

Source: CEREQ generation (2001).

most often, students studying for a CAP envisage obtaining a BEP; students studying for a BEP envisage obtaining a vocational BAC; and the secondary school students studying for a vocational BAC envisage obtaining a BTS. Rare are those who mention a faculty or the *Grandes Écoles* in comparison with their peers in general or technological courses of study. For, in spite of equal designations in terms of the level, there are still metaphoric glass walls which separate vocational education from the classical courses of study. In the first years of the twenty-first century, only a minority (7 per cent) of vocational BAC holders launched themselves into university studies and, of that minority, only a minority (11 per cent) attained their Bachelor's degree. This constitutes a less than a one-in-a-hundred chance that vocational BAC holders will move on to attain a Bachelor's degree.

These ambivalences – whether the vocational certificate is to be considered a qualifying final diploma or a passport to higher studies – necessarily have some consequences for the way in which teachers deal with the real curriculum.

This is in any case what Sandrine Wamain (2004) has demonstrated in a detailed qualitative survey (which resulted in her thesis) of vocational secondary schools in the Bordeaux region between 2001 and 2002. Some sections of the BEP, the ones that are less promising for employment and therefore chosen less often by students, are confronted with a recurring problem: the standards for certification are far beyond the scholastic capacity of the majority of the students studying for it. Faced with that challenge, Wamain identified three main ways in which teachers redefine the official curriculum:

- Some teachers keep to the letter of the "formal curriculum", counting on the continuation of their studies by a minority of the "happy few" and regretfully reminiscing about the "good old days" when the aptitude of their students was far higher. This hopeless and despairing respect for the formal curriculum is offered only by a minority. Other teachers demonstrate two opposed ways of redefining the formal curriculum.
- Some totally sacrifice the official objectives, devoting all of their teaching to the students' main weaknesses in French or in mathematics.
- The others take a different stand. From the beginning of the year, they identify each student's strengths, employing a differentiated pedagogy and, much like sports coaches, encourage everyone to become conscious of his or her assets and to use them more effectively.

Inspired by François Dubet's theses and basing her analysis on these contrasting real curricula, Sandrine Wamain is not far from concluding that we are witnessing the disappearance of the institution named "vocational secondary school". Personally, I would encourage the close study of all of the real curricula, from the less opaque to the more opaque, making full use of all of the instruments of Bernstein's sociology.

I do not know if today the project of writing a sociological synthesis comparable to that of *L'ordre des choses* is a reasonable objective or an impossible challenge. In any case, there is no lack of partial analyses which freely but explicitly employ the concepts of Bernstein or Young. Since the creation of CEREQ[2] in 1970, research on vocational education is often conducted by researchers within that organization or by university researchers who are associated with it. Each have an evaluative function and many of these researchers have found precious conceptual resources in *The New Sociology of Education*. They also give well-justified advice to representative commissions on certification about the creation, removal or reshaping of vocational diplomas. Keeping a close eye on the real curricula is part of their mission. At the same time, this task is made more difficult by the separation between certification and education. The experts' task is not to evaluate or redefine programmes, but to designate and assess the competences that can or cannot be the aim of education. Here, the relation between certification and education is extremely contradictory. On one hand, the standards for certification are created according to the competences required for a job; but on the other hand, the qualifying level is estimated according to the framework for the grading of schooling. The "level" does not function to denote the time necessary for education or training but as a hierarchic signal. Thus, we are far from a recontextualization of schooling for vocational apprenticeships.

Today someone updating *L'ordre des Choses* would have at their disposal very detailed studies on institutional transformations and very rich statistical data on the debates resulting from the creation or the removal of vocational diplomas. He or she would not be able to manage without Basil Bernstein's tool box.

Viviane Isambert-Jamati, sociologist of curricula

If the red carpet laid out by the resurrected Durkheim had spread as far as the table of Paul Clerc, who inaugurated our course of "Soc Ed" in Aix, one could nevertheless identify a second gap: in *The Evolution of Educational Thought: Lectures on the Formation and Development of Secondary Education in France* (Durkheim 1938), there is almost nothing on the evolution of secondary education during the nineteenth century. Of course, here and there throughout the work, Durkheim offers fascinating thoughts on the too-often-neglected formative virtue of the experimental sciences as well as one or two notes on projects of study initiated by the Ministry of Public Instruction. But the work contains nothing as systematic as or comparable to, for example, the pages dedicated by Durkheim to the medieval articulation of the *Trivium* and *Quadrivium*, pages that sparked Basil Bernstein's deep reflections in "Thoughts on the *Trivium* and *Quadrivium*: The divorce of knowledge from the knower" (see Bernstein 2000). Viviane Isambert-Jamati's thesis, published by the Presses Universitaires de France in 1971 under the title *Crises de l'école, crises de la société*, served to fill this gap and we included it in the course each year.

In the book, Isambert-Jamati reviews the evolution of the French system of secondary education from 1860 to 1965, its objectives and its guiding values, by analysing data collected from 2,000 speeches at academic awards ceremonies. The analysis is commendable for its rigour and methodological precision: it is one of the rare works of that era in which the content analysis is systematically applied to the entire corpus, with a transparent explanation of the categories and units of measure implemented. Basil Bernstein's presence is central to the work. In the bibliography, which contains headings in accordance with the framework that regulated the production of theses in France, Bernstein's article "Language and Social Class" appears under the heading "Works that served to establish categories of analysis".

In re-editing some of her earlier works and articles in a book entitled *Les savoirs scolaires* (1990), Viviane Isambert-Jamati strongly reaffirms her attachment and connection to the British school of *The New Sociology of Education*. The book is subdivided into two parts titled "Formal Curriculum" and "Real Curriculum". It is in the latter that an article from 1967 contains some findings of the thesis. In her introduction, Isambert-Jamati describes her relation to the British tradition. After citing the English sociologists who inspired her (Banks, Bernstein, Eggleston, Hargreaves, Lawton and Young), she sums up the lessons she had drawn from them:

> They strongly affirmed that nothing is simple, nothing goes without saying in the curriculum, in what we estimate to be worth communicating to different publics, at one particular historical moment or another. The contents prescribed by the authorities – the formal or official curriculum – are, as time goes by, the product of a whole process of selection within the accumulated culture, a work of reorganization, of changing the demarcations, of a shaking-up of the hierarchies between disciplines. As for the knowledge that is being transmitted, the program's authors, at least when not too far behind schedule, arrange it chiefly according to the perceptions they have of the schools' public. But their recommendations can only be suggestive. Every chapter of the program is open to many interpretations. We can also see teachers, in turn, selecting themes, highlighting various aspects, presenting knowledge in different ways. Thus, each class follows a real curriculum that, in the end, is different from the others.
>
> (Isambert-Jamati 1990, p. 9)

Striking parallels exist between the study of the real curriculum in Viviane Isambert-Jamati's work on French pedagogy and the multiple investigations undertaken on education, in direct relation with Basil Bernstein by the Portuguese researchers Ana Morais, Fernanda Fontinhas, Isabel Neves and their colleagues.

The 1976 work of Viviane Isambert-Jamati claims explicitly to be Bernsteinian. In 1976, the year of the survey, the formal curriculum for the teaching of French in secondary schools was again being redesigned. The work of the commissions responsible for this was largely public and thus teachers could anticipate the future formal curriculum. Isambert-Jamati always worked very closely with teaching professionals. Hence, she could develop a methodical procedure for observations meant to describe and evaluate the various real curricula as delivered by teachers. With the help of a methodical framework (with a battery of 24 indicators) for observations and interviews, she characterized the pedagogy of 24 colleagues teaching senior classes; then she collected the marks obtained at year's end on the baccalaureate exam in French by the 570 students of these 24 teachers.

In the interest of brevity, the results have been collated in Tables 1.4 and 1.5.

At my own risk and peril, I have added a Bernsteinian glossary at the end of each of the tables.

Isambert-Jamati offers a simplified summary of the pedagogical orientations of the teachers in the study:

- "Modernist" teachers are not concerned with the socioeconomic composition of their class. Their objective is to teach their students to master

Table 1.4 Proportion of students (in %), by social class, obtaining excellent results on the baccalaureate French exams

Excellence

Coding Isambert-Jamati:	Children			Recoding according to Bernstein
	Of workmen	Of middle class	Of management	
Modernist pedagogy	25	36	44	−Cli/+CAi
Libertarian pedagogy	35	45	63	−Cli/−CAi
Classical pedagogy	26	38	47	+Cli/=CAi
Critical pedagogy	25	24	7	+Cli/+CAi

Table 1.5 Proportion of students (in %), by social class, obtaining less than average results

Failure

Coding Isambert-Jamati:	Children			Recoding according to Bernstein
	Of workmen	Of middle class	Of management	
Modernist pedagogy	31	30	17	−Cli/+CAi
Libertarian pedagogy	31	22	23	−Cli/−CAi
Classical pedagogy	22	10	14	+Cli/=CAi
Critical pedagogy	11	18	27	+Cli/+CAi

information and communication with a view to their successful integration into a technically oriented society.

- "Libertarian" or "anarchist" teachers – true sons and daughters of 1968 – refuse to take social distinctions into account, addressing themselves to individuals whose creativity they want to awaken.
- "Classical" teachers are in favour of inherited culture, fear cultural levelling and strive to draw out an elite that is "up to" the classical culture.
- "Critical" teachers give priority to democratization and want to form individuals capable of fighting the exploitation constituted by "forced" assimilation into learned or scholarly culture.

Confining ourselves to a consideration of the failure of students from underprivileged social classes, Isambert-Jamati's data reveals that: "The rate of failure is not at all equal across the pedagogical methods adopted by teachers. Therefore teachers have more power than they generally imagine." The effects of invisible pedagogies feared by Basil Bernstein are evident in the case of libertarian pedagogy, which paradoxically allows few successes but generates numerous failures. Teaching methods that are more explicit about their contents (strong internal classification) and their requirements (strong internal framing) are most likely to promote success among students from underprivileged social classes.

Very similar results were reached, in the 1990s, by Morais and Neves, the Portuguese researchers introduced above in projects conceived directly in relation to Basil Bernstein's theory. For ordinary school tasks such as the understanding and definition of concepts, experimental work and problem solving, the researchers created distinct, well defined teaching practices, varying according to the strength of internal and external classification and framing, that teachers then applied in their instruction to their students. These teachers were familiar with the social and ethnic background of each student as well as the forms of authority and communication particular to each student's family. Their results are convergent with those obtained by Isambert-Jamati. Pedagogies that define more explicitly the pertinent knowledge (strong classification) and that inform students more explicitly of the performance expected of them (strong framing) are more effective in allowing children from underprivileged classes to succeed. These results allow not only for verification, but also for the concepts to be clarified and refined. Concerning teacher–student relations and the relations between students, those practices that are more open are often the most effective. I regret that these studies became known to me only after my retirement: they would have permitted me to improve the exercises I proposed to my own students.

It is not only the results that matter in these research studies. Their methodology is also precise, well conceived and executed, and remains very relevant today. In the "discipline(s)" of education, an orientation towards results has developed in the last few years that strives to measure the efficiency of particular regions, institutions or types of institution, and teachers. Such an orientation entails the creation of a black box: results are observed at the beginning and at the end of courses and the value added by the actor concerned is calculated. Increasing statistical sophistication allows this type of calculation to be carried out with precision and rigour. This type of measurement[3] was inspired by Alain Mingat's successful implementation of it in estimating the effects of teachers in the most important class of elementary school, the first grade. Thus, he was able to calculate the amount of progress made by each student over a year and to link it to each of their teachers. This confirmed the intuitions of *The New Sociology of Education*: that teachers exercise a great influence over students' results. While each teacher's influence is not the same and while there are no miraculous teachers who, like Jesus Christ or Mao, can make the last become first, we can distinguish between three types of teachers: those who raise the average results and reduce the gap between first and last; those who raise average results yet maintain the gap between first and last; and finally those who simply maintain (or perhaps even increase) the gap between first and last. If there is no Christ or Mao, neither is there the kind of teacher, often spoken about so willingly, who decreases the gap between first and last by lowering results across the board. The generally inefficient teachers do not produce equality in any sense.

By themselves these results are very interesting. They confirm the diagnoses put forth by Viviane Isambert-Jamati and Ana Morais: that teachers have more power than they imagine. What is deceiving, for the time being, is that, at the end of these analyses, we remain unsure of what explains the success of one teacher over another. To combine the inductive approach of the teacher-effect with the constructed approach inspired by Bernstein is without a doubt a way to escape this impasse. As long as the teacher-effect or institution-effect is observed without being explained, we have at best a management tool and not a lever to improve education and promote equality.

Basil Bernstein's concepts have their full place in the most recent work in the sociology of education.

Notes

1 PISA (2003, tables 4.2b to 4.2e).
2 CEREQ is a French public body working under the aegis of the Ministry for National Education, the Ministry for Economy, Industry and Employment, and the Ministry of Labour, Social Relations, Family, Solidarity and City. As a centre of public expertise at the service of key players in training and employment, CEREQ is involved in the production of statistics, in research activity and in providing support for the implementation of policies. It provides advice and counselling intended to clarify choices in the area of training policy at regional, national or international levels.
3 The establishment, by Claude Thelot, of a culture of evaluation within the Ministry of Public Education has served to acclimatize researchers and practitioners to a precise culture of results.

2 Why Bernstein?

Brian Davies

Bernstein in the Anglo-Saxon world

For all practical purposes, "the Anglo-Saxon world" refers to where English is predominantly spoken as a first language, that is to say, the UK and its former colonies/dominions, particularly the USA, Canada, South Africa, Australia and New Zealand. However, Bernstein scholarship in the sociology of education is vestigial in North America, while his ideas have had powerful appeal to some scholars in the Portuguese- and Spanish-speaking worlds. With few exceptions, the empirical and theoretical advances which Bernstein codified in successive volumes of *Class, Codes and Control* rest foursquare on the empirical work of Pedro, Diaz, Cox, Morais and the like. Moreover, while his sociolinguistic work has sustained lively academic progress in some centres in Australia and work of highest quality on pedagogic discourse has been sustained in Cape Town, the purchase of his ideas on the sociology of education in general in the UK has been limited; it remains more enclave than mainstream.

There have always been at least three audiences for his scholarship, in sociolinguistics, teacher education and the sociology of education. The former served as the origin of Bernstein's public reputation, providing the notion of "codes" which undergirded the structure of his thought throughout his work and continues not least in the work of former colleagues, such as Hasan (2004) who has sought, among other things, to relate it to Vygotsky, as have Daniels (2001) and other activity theorists. Yet we might do well to remember that, even in sociolinguistic circles, when Bernstein visited the USA his welcome was as an anthropologist. In the UK, a popular work such as Chambers' (2003) *Sociolinguistic Theory* has not a single mention or citation of Bernstein's work.

His sociolinguistic thesis set Bernstein in the consciousness of British teacher trainers in the 1960s and 1970s as the person who demonstrated the ineducability of the working class – those who could neither speak nor learn "properly" – rather missing the carefully nuanced theoretical delicacy of his Sociological Research Unit's findings on class-control relationships, consciousness, cognition and behaviours. The episode with Labov became a wonderful example of knowledge recontextualization, the re-forming, always ideological, of "new" knowledge into that which is regarded as safe and fit to teach, in this case, largely to intending teachers. "Cultural deprivation" served the interests of both political and school masters; blame for educational failure lay with the lower social orders themselves; pedagogy had no voice of its own. That these issues are not dead may be witnessed in relation to Nash's (2006, p. 550) claims.

Systematic misrecognition of his sociolinguistic thesis deeply wounded Bernstein and led directly to his decision that future empirical work would be carried out in the context of doctoral supervisions rather than funded team work. The agenda was portended by his famous 1971 "Classification and Framing" paper and its successive reworkings traced in the volumes of *Class, Codes and Control* published between 1971 and 1990, culminating in the eponymous volume V in 1996 and his final words in 2000 and 2001.

Bernstein "too difficult"?

I have never known a time when many students, teachers and fellow sociologists have not complained that Bernstein "was too difficult" even while they might, at the same time, be overdosing on the less than pellucid prose of one or more Grand Masters or more recent structuralist and post-structuralist circumlocutions. However, phenomena cannot be theorized at the level at which they arise and, notwithstanding Bruner, some things are not easily explained, requiring special and initially strange vocabulary and going to the edge of the familiar and hitherto unvoiced. In terms of prose style, exemplification and clarity Bernstein wrote at a number of levels of accessibility, at best in his prefatory introductions, less accessibly in initial formulations of his key conceptual claims. While he might talk brilliantly, even inspirationally to students, they found reading him difficult; he was not always his own best prose exegetist. Moreover, he has never been the focus of an army of commentators and sympathetic simplifiers, such as Foucault or, even more so, Bourdieu experienced. Indeed, in the 1970s, as he began to construct his sociology of education, many of his closest colleagues not only did not "teach him" but actively fomented root and branch opposition to his ideas under the banners of "new directions" (or relativism without a cause), neo-marxisms and combinations thereof[1] (Davies 1994). In the age of standpoint epistemology, Bernstein, who never argued other than that class, gender and ethnicity were, all three, the crucial, invidiously ranked social categories of his and others' societies, was accused of ignoring gender and neglecting ethnicity when, in reality, he was consumed by issues of their interrelation. The de-intellectualization of initial and in-service teacher education, which accompanied state-dominated, managerialist redefinition of curriculum and assessment from the late 1970s to the present, saw "silent" pedagogy fall into line. Not only do our teachers not answer back but they have lost the memory of doing so. Courses in management, assessment and evaluation, mentoring and neo-comic book approaches to learning and cognition – Mozart with mathematics, learning styles and metacognition provide the gruel of their non-school subject diet. In the wake of several decades of denial and oversimplification of pedagogic realities by a variety of others, it needs to be reasserted that Bernstein's oeuvre, as problem pursuit, is essentially a challenge to *do* things.

Bernstein too demanding?

In sociology of education, we have been on a low plateau of limited public interest in Bernstein's work for some time. Why has its considerable intellectual purchase made relatively little wider impact? In an intellectual field where perfecting positions has primacy over empirical warrant or theoretical purchase it may be that Bernstein's disinterest in what he considered was an ontological case has ruled him out of serious contention for some as a scholar of weight. He worried a good deal less about his position in social science eschatology than about delicacy of understanding. One upshot may have been that in the academic identity politics of horizontal knowledge structures selective attention is paid not to those concerned with "finding out" but to the exigencies of possessing the "gaze". Alongside limited attention to and poor dissemination, uptake and skewed recontextualization of his work and intentions, what is "too demanding" about his oeuvre is the character of the relation required between theoretical and research practice.

Insistence on problem primacy might appear seductive enough until we remember that education is prime territory for solutions seeking problems. Schools have become sites of policy excitation where teachers wearily do the next thing asked of them by politicians who see crucial, middle-class votes in being seen to be in charge of policies which serve their interests. While the *cri de cœur* is social inclusion and tackling inequality, policy outcomes tend to be otherwise, again, at least in the UK. In such a climate, as Bernstein recognized, research and inquiry on pedagogic practice tends to respond either overtly or covertly to official "reform" agendas in the new, official, research economy. Yet Bernstein's view of intellectual necessity was clear and severe; "problems" must be located within conceptual frameworks and their elements translated into researchable entities, where "findings" stood in open relation to theory.[2] Relatively few of our students or even more those who conduct funded research of the type that reaches our journals or the ears of policy-makers, succeed adequately in articulating internal and external orders or levels of description. There are many that pick up bits of Bernstein terminology as citational trinkets, sometimes ten to 30 years in arrears with their debt to the changing *oeuvre* and thoroughly tone-deaf as to its successive sustentions. However, I know of none that are so full of promise for understanding, penetrating and providing insight upon the possible grounds for modifying pedagogy in pursuit of more equitable outcomes.

Bernstein as action man

The complex journey that Bernstein undertook from sociolinguistic codes to pedagogic discourse and device in what he latterly referred to as Totally Pedagogized Society, aspects of which are referred to in a number of chapters in this volume, is depicted in *The Discursive Field Today: A Bernsteinian Framework* for which I am entirely indebted to Bill Tyler. The "meaning" of the framework lies in its juxtaposition of levels in the spheres of production and reproduction in relation to their forms of contestation. None of it makes sense except as the contrivance of arrangements designed to elicit certain types of identity in relation to economic, cultural and knowledge orders. Knowledge "types" (discourses, structures and grammars within intellectual fields) condition and are recontextualized in the formation of curriculum codes and design, struggle for control (of the pedagogical device) in terms of visibility/invisibility and performance/competence becomes expressed through national and local curricular formations, evaluation strategies, technologies of assessment and modalities of delivery in the hands of relatively autonomous agents, including teachers. Basic structural tensions inhere in regulative and instructional and vertical and horizontal discourses and visible/invisible modalities.

Given that policy regularly claims to be but rarely is "evidence based" and given that the notion of the latter is incoherent unless adequately theoretically founded, what would a Bernsteinian approach to "policy" look like (Fitz *et al.* 2006)? Do Bernstein's ideas give us a handle on the character of

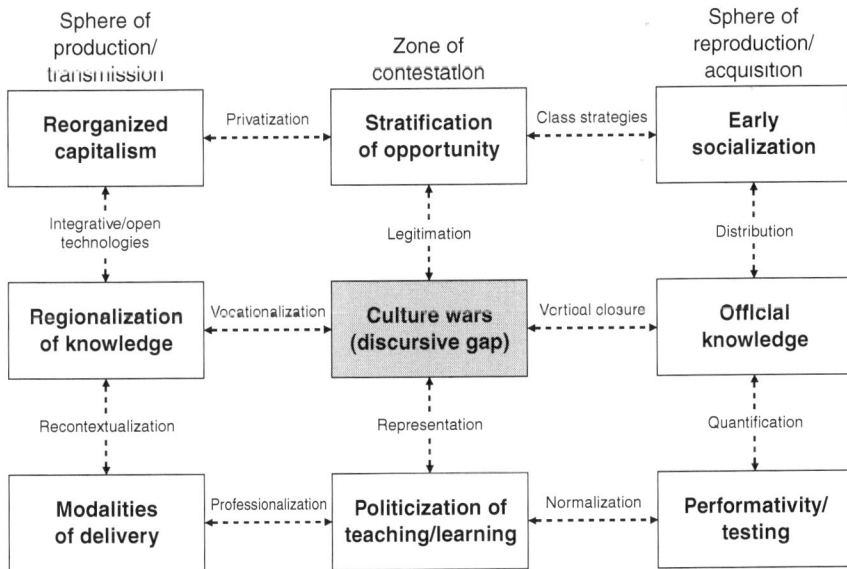

Figure 2.1 The discursive field today.

policy process, currently the home of the *bricoleur*, "flailing around for anything that looks as if it might work" (Ball 1998, p. 126)? It would be
mistake to picture it simply as the domain of wise people seeking clear and
just goals. Partiality, ideology and self-seeking are mixed with altruism and
pursuit of "public interest". There is a rich, dynamic interior to its processes
and the sites where they take place. Many ideologically accented voices
clamour for attention to their own causes. Institutions, whether departments
of state, "think tanks", official agencies, publishers, teachers' associations,
local education committees or school staffrooms all have "lives of their own".
Adequate ways of conceptualizing policy origins, processes and destinations
sociologically must be ones that allow us to stay in touch with their complexity and scope, while providing appropriate languages of description that
connect empirical and theoretical work.

Writing at the cusp of his shift from analyses of language and control in
families to school processes, Bernstein (1975) underlined that what characterized their continuity was their setting "against a broader canvas of
changes in forms of social control" that did not lose sight of "the grim consequences of class relationships". By 1996, he represented this work as
having been empirically mainly about "class inscription" and theoretically
"increasingly concerned with general questions of pedagogic communication
as a crucial medium of symbolic control" and prospectively about "understanding the social processes whereby consciousness and desire are given specific forms, evaluated, distributed, challenged and changed". In such quests
"policy" takes its place as one mode of attempting control of "pedagogic discourse", for which he offered an encompassing framework. Its key element is
"the pedagogic device" that "provides the intrinsic grammar of pedagogic
discourse" through its interrelated distributive, recontextualizing and evaluative rules. The scope allowed to pedagogic recontextualizers is the measure
of compulsory education's relative autonomy, reliant on education's systemic
relation to production, attempts to increase the tightness of which have been
shown to lead to paradox (Bernstein 1977; Vlasceanu 1976). Periods of its
loosening have been historically somewhat transient and recently[3] reframed
in recent years by converging, centrist parties in systems like the UK on the
basis of managed ignorance guaranteed by reliance on hired "research" hands
and inspection tied to policy imperatives.[4] Might we then expect to find an
empirical world subjected to intended policy change which is rife with
revanche, revision and backsliding rather than cool implementation? After all,
everything from the classroom nod and wink to evaluation by formal examination is involved in the reproduction by "teachers" of chosen content or text
that has originated with knowledge producers and has been recontextualized, turned into its "imaginary" school version, by specialized state and
educational agencies for transmission to "acquirers" categorized in particular
ways, particularly age, stage and gender. In Bernstein's language, teachers'
and students' experiences of such specializations of "text, time and space"
leave their marks "cognitively, socially and culturally" (1996, pp. 49–50).

Nothing is neutral, everything is weighed and valued, yet the adventitious, if not the serendipitous, rules. Skocpol's (1992) insight that the best predictor of any given policy is the character and content of the one that went before sits alongside Bernstein's judgement that education preserves structural relations between social groups but changes structural relations between individuals and the latter is sufficient to create the impression of general and probable movement (Skocpol 1992, p. 11). Patterns of educational success and failure have long been and continue to be strongly influenced by social class which, in turn, mediates patterns by gender and ethnicity, though it performs inconveniently as an overt electoral banner for policy-makers.[5]

By way of exemplification of Bernsteinian policy analyses, two far from mutually exclusive themes will now be briefly explored: the long trail that policies tend to follow from primary sites of inception, through processes of recontextualization, to attempted implementation; and attempts at anatomization of pedagogic discourse.

Long trail a winding

Many studies have revolved around the tribulations of introducing or sustaining competence modes. Al-Ramahi and Davies (2002), very much in the tradition of taking Bernstein's ideas to the analysis of planned change in state-dominated systems, showed how a Palestinian system with no discernible pedagogic recontextualizing field was sponsored by agencies from the developed world in attempting to capitalize on informal pedagogic modalities developed while formal schooling was intermittent or prohibited during Intifada. Bureaucratic in-fighting began what generally untutored, unwilling and unconvinced teachers in relation to what was required of them finished, as traditional Arabic, rather than Western new middle-class, pedagogy reasserted itself.

In a completely contrasting context, Thomas and Davies (2006) showed how contemporary change in Welsh nurse education presented an intriguing instance of where power and control actually lay in a policy process as between well defined official and pedagogic recontextualizing fields. Authoritative, officially required, new curricular formations with strong, ostensible competence orientation, in contrast with the didactic, subject focus that it replaced, was thwarted by slow staff turnover and ineffective preparation for the new, intended discourse among teacher educators fearing that the "new nurses" to be produced were likely to be less well prepared for hands-on tasks. University autonomy allowed them effective control of continuing pedagogic forms in face of requirements of an ostensibly strong official recontextualizing field to develop quite different practices

At the Welsh secondary school level, "performativity", a state-sponsored initiative, has imposed "restructuring" as a series of contradictory processes of decentralization though local management and funding and accompanying processes of centralization, including imposition of a National Curriculum and its associated assessment, then inspection, since the 1980s. James (2005) sought to locate the impact upon school target-setting and performance achievement of the latter, delegated to small teams of privatized "registered inspectors", intended shock troops of the official recontextualizing field, who relied greatly on school-prepared documentation. Despite lengthy preparation and post-inspection feedback, reflection and response, disciplinary design and collegial desire left most inspectorial judgements mired in necessity, with teachers feeling stressed and only fleetingly and, in some cases, inappropriately judged by others who they felt could not do what they did. Their managers felt that some benefit arose, not least in providing them with "levers" to realize their objectives but at quite disproportionate cost in terms of staff time, effort and angst.[6]

Much recent policy emphasis from Britain to Taiwan has concerned (re) specifying school subject contents. In Britain, officially telling teachers how, as opposed to what, to teach has been reintroduced, though largely confined to "the basics" in primary school in terms of literacy and numeracy initiatives. At the same time narrowing curricular time, focus and resource in favour of "core" subjects has created a range of policy casualties among more "peripheral" subjects, like PE and Music.[7] These conditions have ensured, for example, that Economics in UK schools has been shunned by students and parents, despite attempts backed by extraordinary amounts of corporate funding to redefine it in terms of "economic understanding" or "business enterprise", cross-curricular themes to be made available to all (Jephcote and Davies 2004, 2007). Music has also been reduced to an arcane curricular pursuit undertaken by less than 10 per cent of those in state schools after the age of 14 and a curricular grace note for most others, particularly after primary school (Wright 2006). Though its National Curriculum version aimed to combine a competence modality, focused upon skill acquisition, with emphasis on aesthetic response, nominally across "musics" of various genres, it was tied closely to Western Art Music in its delivery. In an age of increasingly abundant musical "access" among teenage students whose identities and tastes were closely bound up with "popular music" and instruments associated with its delivery, school music tended to signify to them the wrong habitus, wrong sounds and wrong emphasis on prolonged engagement with learning the wrong instruments for practical examination. In Wright's view, circumventing its substantially class-based unpopularity requires "more than a little discretion over numerous aspects of regulative and instructional discourse and the classroom expression of distributive, recontextualizing and evaluative rules" (Wright 2006, p. 275).

The shaping capacity of an external world can become literally a matter of life or death among the predominantly young women aged 12–18 experiencing "disordered eating" (Evans *et al.* 2008). Schools and other pedagogic agents ascribe values, meanings and potentials to "the body" that have particular characteristics in time, place and space. These reflect wider, national and global, socioeconomic trends increasingly celebrating particular virtues in terms of "flexible identities" and manifest aspects of "performance" and "corporeal perfection", usually defined as "the slender ideal". Schools have become sites of pervasive surveillance of "the body", reaching into and encoding every aspect of life, in effect, making "pedagogy" everyone's concern. Self-assessment and self-monitoring under the normalizing gaze of others are routine features of their performative cultures (Burrows and Wright 2006). Just as "performativity works from the outside in and the inside out" (Ball 2004, p. 145) and is capable of both building a "love of product" or belief in service provided and engendering individual feelings of pride, guilt, shame and envy that seem rational and objective, so "trainability" entails continuous dispositions of subjects to be made ready for the requirements of their entire lives (Bonal and Rambla 2003). The alluring call of the world outside to endless perfectibility almost literally gets under the skin of the "eating disordered".

Such policy studies at Cardiff and Loughborough have circled rather obsessively about what has been at stake along the trail that winds from policy production to recontextualization and reproduction. In the main they have been case studies which have asked how crucial social categories, particularly class and gender, form and are reformed by policy objects and processes and raise important issues as to the degree of insulation between primary, secondary and reproductive knowledge and policy contexts.

Anatomizing pedagogic discourse

Work of highly superior quality in two other centres in particular bears on many of the same issues. No one, for example, has yet approached the meticulous and fruitful detail with which Morais, Neves and their colleagues have anatomized pedagogic discourse, mainly in Portuguese science curriculum, working with teachers to show how intervening in pedagogic practice can alter subject understanding and achievement (see, *inter alia*, Morais *et al.* 2004). If there is a canon for empirical practice to which we might currently aspire and which has energized classroom investigation, this is it. Moreover, its relevance for policy *and* to teachers' perennial "Monday morning" question that transcends curricular sticking plaster, in terms of their notions, such as "mixed pedagogy", is extreme, as will be readily evident from their contribution to this volume.

An as yet less well publicized flow of research is coming out of Cape Town, among it a remarkably interesting investigation by Davis (2005) at UCT of pedagogic discourse in school mathematics, focusing upon notions intrinsic to "pedagogic texts structured by a South African, constructivist-inspired teaching methodology, referred to by its proponents as the *"Problem-centred approach"* (PCA) (Davis 2005, p. 17), that mathematics should be fun and "that the student does (and must) 'construct' the particular mathematics content" (p. 208). The problem that "the everyday is not the academic" is set against the "insistence on pleasure" in key, constructivist South African mathematics texts (*Mathematics at work*, Grades 1–4), set against the background of the boundary-dissolving propensities of contemporary utilitarianism. The issue concerns the taming of *jouissance* – how "Pedagogic discourse within competence pedagogies is obliged to engage the pedagogic subject in two ways: it must reproduce knowledge as apparently pleasurable as well as simultaneously negate the solipsistic pleasure of the pedagogic subject" (p. 79). He juxtaposes Bernstein's ideas with those of Lacan, Hegel, Freud, Althusser and Zizec as supporting cast. Among the original contributions of his investigation is detailed analysis of the relation between regulative and instructional discourse, where the former was asserted to be prior to and embedded in the latter by Bernstein but which Davis prefers to regard as "working in the service of instructional contents, but in accord with dominant ideological imperatives" (p. 2). He argues that Freud and Lacan's accounts of imaginary and symbolic identification appropriately supplement Bernstein's notion of the social logic of competence, serving "to produce a more theoretically informed reading of the type of pedagogic relations produced under the conditions of a society subjected to the demands of contemporary capital" (p. 73). It concludes that "the PCA succeeds for the wrong reasons", its originators having "generated a pedagogic modality that allows itself to be duped by the ideological call for the dissolution of boundaries" that "has simultaneously attempted to maintain its fidelity to mathematics", ending up constructing "a world of imaginary relations structured along the lines of utilitarian moral regulation" while disrupting it "in order to assert the Symbolic in the guise of mathematics" (p. 208). Once again, questions are raised "about the definition of competence pedagogies, especially around the feature of an evaluative focus on presences rather than absences in the production of the pedagogic subject" (p. 184).

If Davis' work is a thrilling glimpse of how to close the gap between "blue skies" research and policy imperatives, Hoadley's (2005) abiding problem is how to lay bare the mechanisms of social-class differentiation that schooling appears to be all too adept at engendering. The long haul to unpick the brute fact that "stuff happens" when teachers and students interact has passed through a succession of more or less unsatisfactory periods of emphasis, implicating families and their resources, cultures and attitudes, teachers and their expectations, knowledge and its class basis, teaching methods and their bearing on learning styles and, in our performative age, leaders/managers and their attachment of followers to goals. In the face of this passing parade, how the trick is induced has remained stubbornly elusive. In Hoadley's exemplary investigation, having precisely eviscerated effectiveness studies, the way out of the conceptual woods is via applications of Bernstein's theory of pedagogy by Dowling (1993, 1998) and Morais' ESSA group in Lisbon, adding a metric for setting classroom events against school and teacher characteristics. The latter are delineated in terms of social class and professional dispositions, particularly in relation to the part they play in the specialization of student voice with respect to the school code and "The potential for teachers, as sub-relays in the process of the reproduction of school knowledge, to interrupt the community or restricted code of learners in contexts where an elaborated orientation may not have been acquired in the home" (Morais *et al.* 2004, p. 270). While elements in the design attend to specifics of the South African primary school context, concentrate on Maths and Literacy only and contrast very stark class extremes in her four-school sample, this investigation produces results which are very striking, indeed, almost chilling.

Hoadley's work arises from a group working with Muller and Ensor whose collective contribution to our understanding of schooling has become very significant in terms of its intellectual intensity, integrity and policy relevance. Reeves (2005) sought to establish whether or not there was empirical support for the South African policy of promoting learner-centred pedagogy to improve academic outcomes in classrooms with learners from socioeconomically disadvantaged backgrounds. She concludes that teacher effectiveness in classrooms with predominantly low-SES learners relates to whether they confront principled as well as procedural knowledge adapted to their individual ability and progress, including their misconceptions and difficulties, delivered as a coherent entity underpinned by internal disciplinary principles, rather than as a series of fragmented and disconnected components within each grade. This is a finding loaded with policy implication pointing to the particularities of "mixed pedagogy" and involving issues both of teachers' subject competency and students' opportunities to learn in Maths. Bolton (2005), in her study of final year secondary school achievement in the "loosely bounded discipline" (p. 1) of school art, suggests similar issues, while Breier (2004, p. 204), in her study of postgraduate labour law students argues that "the recontextualization of segments of horizontal discourse (everyday knowledge) in the content of school subjects does not necessarily lead to more effective acquisition" but is usually confined to "less able" students and reduces vertical discourses (the hierarchical knowledge of academic disciplines) to a set of strategies to improve "their functioning in the every day world of work and domesticity". Gamble (2004), in her study of craft apprenticeship, pursues similar concerns.

Taken together, these studies suggest that it may well be that the rhetoric flowing from both pedagogic and official recontextualizing fields "about knowledge needing to be immediately relevant to the needs of economic production (the world of work) and the individual needs of citizens" may, indeed, be "the ideological expression in schooling of a more general political and economic demand for the dissolution of boundaries", reconfiguring "the pedagogic device at the level of the reproduction of knowledge", transforming educational policy, curriculum and pedagogic practice so as to align "the education system with the economic imperatives issuing from capital" (Davis 2005, p. 200).

Who wants to know better?

Where does all this leave us? I think with better, finer-grain detail of how policy simultaneously regulates, educates and controls; with firmer grasp of how it is recontextualized and enacted; and better understanding of how knowledge, ideology and morality are embedded in the actions of teachers, pupils and schools. Sharpened global, national and local historical and contextual notions matter if our mission is to better understand the "pedagogic device". It seems difficult to conceive of a more important conceptual seedbed for growing policy; we have now elaborated not only the conceptual tools and evidential base for doing things rather than simply talking about them but have hardly formed the basis of a mass movement. The characteristic of all big ideas, even when counterintuitive, in education, as elsewhere, is their ability to bring those who receive them to the point of exclaiming "Well, was *that all* it was really about?" We have several such ideas here which Hasan (2006, p. 212) exhorts us to use to provide not only the "motivation but also suggest the direction" of desirable social change.

Notes

1 What goes round comes round and former, major detractors, such as M.F.D. Young have now had their epiphany on the road to "critical realism".
2 He expressed this in a number of places, including his 1996 "Volume V" and contested it most fully in his 1999 *BJSE* article.
3 Bernstein's (1996) position suggested that the relative autonomy that we had come to esteem in the UK was sandwiched somewhere between the post-war "second wind" of the 1960s and Thatcher's politics of envy, a historically brief excrescence of the pedagogic recontextualizing field.
4 The favoured sons of the school effectiveness and improvement "movements", the media masters of the educational pantheon, have proved very congenial to "can-do" policy-makers, along with those offering management and leadership "solutions" for "failing" system parts.
5 Moreover, Ball's (2007) rather shocking study of the very rapid growth of private-sector involvement in English state education regards it as less than apocalyptic, judging that "there is no going back to a past in which the public sector as a whole worked well and worked fairly in the interest of all learners because there was no such past".
6 James concluded that:

> real teachers were not standing around waiting for the next well-founded piece of research or the next best way to pump up test scores but they did seem to suffer increasingly from governments fed bad research by compliant academics anxious to increase their mutual sense of control.
>
> (James 2005, p. 11)

7 Bernstein (1996) noted that one of the more striking contrasts between school and post-school (further and higher) curricular formations has been the remarkable resilience of "singulars" in school discourse, the growth of "regional" modes in higher education and the push for "generic" ones in further and vocational educa-

tion. The former are the narcissistic, strongly bounded subjects that figure in the school curriculum that come and go only at its margins. Regions like engineering, medicine, architecture, cognitive science or communications and media recontextualize singulars, weakening their discursive and political bases. They signal a change from narcissistic, subject-based, introjected identities to more externally dependent, projected ones that schools have hitherto resisted or rejected very well. Generic modes privileging "trainability", the heart of Bernstein's TPS, reflect three decades of blaming state education for what neither the economic system or the state itself have been able to deliver in terms of adequate levels of employment and skill formation. They have tended to meet stout resistance in schools, provided only for students deemed unsuited to the normal academic world of singulars.

Part II

The social and the psychic

The interdisciplinary debate

3 The message and the voice

Jean-Manuel De Queiroz

The landmark nature of the publication of Basil Bernstein's *Pedagogy, Symbolic Control and Identity* (2000) in French was recognized at an international conference ("Social issues, knowledge, language and pedagogy: The current relevance and usefulness of Basil Bernstein's sociological work") dedicated to commenting on the book and held in 2007 at the National Institute for Pedagogical Research in Lyon.

The book is a strange one. In fact, it is not really a "book" in the traditional sense of the term, rather a disparate collection of chapters adapted from journal articles, appendices, postscripts and interviews without a particular regard for chronological order. Bernstein's emphasis is on the presentation, development and clarification of his concepts as well as responses to criticism of his work, with empirical studies conducted by PhD students or other researchers forming a sort of "backdrop". In other words, the book constitutes what Umberto Eco might term an "open work". As such, the book can also be considered a labyrinth, within which it is quite possible for readers to go astray.

There are a few vital leads in approaching this labyrinth. Emile Durkheim is one of them. To discuss the links between Durkheim and Bernstein is to adopt a theoretical approach requiring both caution and modesty, particularly as Bernstein regularly mentioned the necessity of links between "theory" and "research", and between empirical tasks and the need for conceptualization. Any commentary such as this (a presentation from the conference mentioned above and converted into this chapter), without a conscientious discussion of the data, can result in the sort of misinterpretation to which Bernstein so clearly took exception.

Bernstein works throughout *Pedagogy, Symbolic Control and Identity* to clarify his analysis, particularly that which concerns cultural reproduction, to avoid such misunderstandings. I argue in this chapter that Bernstein actively and consciously employs Durkheim as a "weapon" in an effort to preserve the "open" character of his work and so to eliminate any possibilities for his work to be recoded and placed within a closed system. The purpose of this chapter is not to argue whether or not Bernstein is a Durkheimian but, rather, to demonstrate *how* he is and to explore the use he makes of this.

The message and the voice: what is a loyal reading?

It is essential to work to translate an awareness of the Durkheimian inspiration running throughout Bernstein's work into a more complex understanding of its precise nature. Analysing Bernstein's links with Durkheim must not become a meaningless exercise of erudition, a kind of abstract scholastics, particularly as Bernstein provides in his texts the means to avoid this type of dead end. In fact, in drawing together the variety of texts that constitute *Pedagogy, Symbolic Control and Identity*, Bernstein demonstrates an extraordinary degree of reflexivity, particularly as he works to apply the very standards and categories for analysis he has developed to his own work as well to the critical commentaries to which this work has given rise. Bernstein is well aware that his work belongs to the field of symbolic control and therefore must be submitted to the same type of critical analysis as the object he writes about. Consequently, the "theoretical" approach of his work is not far removed from "empirical research" but, rather, constitutes a sort of genealogical enquiry (an "enquiry" as it was considered by Hume, Locke and the most famous Anglo-Saxon empiricists) into the nature of this well hidden, enigmatic, yet so powerfully concrete object: the nature of understanding which enables human beings to work and to move, the functions and the rules behind the ways we generate our own principles of classification and which make humans "continuous creators" of the world.

This chapter presents the hypothesis that Bernstein fully understands that his work and various commentaries on it, and applications of it represent a pedagogical relationship and, as such, a struggle for control over the work, and that the "framing" of commentators – I am one of them – can alter the classification of the author or the relationship "between" him and us or others; it can modify the internal relationships present in his work.

Bernstein has found in Durkheim something useful to preserve his own voice from the dangerous possibilities of such a denaturation. He is not dogmatic; he does not submit to a doctrine. On the contrary, and particularly in *Pedagogy, Symbolic Control and Identity*, he works to demonstrate the renewability of his concepts, how his theory can constantly be revised and submitted to empirical tests. In this respect, Bernstein's work is "open" and does not need a protective orthodoxy or a strong shelter. Yet, he wishes to preserve the originality of his work even if this means that it is creatively transformed (but not distorted) by other voices. Frequently, Bernstein presents his message positively as a message of emancipation, of "disruption", or of change rather than as a message of reproduction. But (recognizing that we live in a world where the enemy can hide his or her hand) alternative interpretations also exist and at times have presented Bernstein's message as a conservative force that serves to attack free ones.

Bernstein, throughout his career, has often had to face up to such accusations. His "restricted code", for example, was classified (or, perhaps, reclassified) as representative of a sociocultural handicap or as a type of deficit theory.

To counter such distortions and, in the hope of ultimately avoiding them, Bernstein writes that: "My preference is to be as explicit as possible. Then at least my voice may be deconstructed" (2000, p. 126). By offering precise and consistent explication allowing for such deconstruction, Bernstein has sought to fend off what he believed were distortions of his work, diversions from the aims of his project. His use of Durkheim underpins his efforts to allow for what might be termed, then, "protective deconstruction". He ties his theory to a Durkheimian ground in an attempt to resist distorting, particularly structuralist, framings (and, among those who could be grouped loosely as structuralist, Bernstein is concerned especially with the orientations of Bourdieu, the "great reproducer"). Bernstein admits, then, that there is something tactical (perhaps even opportunistic) in his relationship with Durkheim; but this is justified. In attempting to present the foundations for this justification, I do not seek here to identify "influences" or "filiations"; this would be a non-productive work of erudition leading only to misinterpretation. Such an effort would lead inevitably to the sort of "heritage quarrels" already too common among sociologists. We work in what might be considered a "theatre of operations", where alliances are formed, tools are borrowed and weapons are used. With this in mind, I wish to avoid an exercise of classification; our hero has already undergone such exercises too often.

Bernstein states that, if it must be classified (an exercise that constitutes "external evaluation" and that can be considered a form of symbolic control), his work is often perceived as a sort of "structuralism with strong Durkheimian roots" (2000, p. 92). Such analysis and commentary separates the productivity of Bernstein's theory from the specific process of its creation, whose precisely inner opponents are sociological structuralisms of any sort. Bernstein specifies that concepts should not be used as theoretical "identifiers" (he gives the example of "subjectivity", though "structure" or "code" could just as easily suffice here) because this type of identification and classification annihilates by reduction the operativity of the theory. Thus, it becomes immobilized and frozen. A theory which is not imprisoned by an identifying label remains open. In other words, it allows for free or mobile thinking.

The interpretation I propose in this chapter, then, has nothing to do with a sociological "family romance". I recognize, rather, that what is at stake is the construction (involving displacements and reshapings) of a problem; an affair involving disparate alliances and a fair amount of "sizing up". So, what does Bernstein accomplish with his use of Durkheim? To gain a better insight we must return to the concepts of message and voice. Bernstein's obstinacy in fighting against the misinterpretation of his work, against false portrayals of it (whether these portrayals are mistaken or whether they are conscious acts of betrayal cannot always be discerned), is striking. He purports that the message can transform the voice, that framing can transform dominant classifications, that the form of transmission (the "manner") can upset the legitimate discourse (the "matter", i.e. borders, as they determine the relations between contexts; the curriculum). But the capacity for subversion that underlies any apprenticeship (to learn something is at the same time to learn how to unlearn it) can work both ways: there are some progressive subversions but, also, regressive messages which can stifle the voice. The battlefield of the social sciences is certainly one arena where the fight between the message of diversion and the message of emancipation is raging.

I like to think that one of the goals of the "Social issues, knowledge, language and pedagogy: The current relevance and usefulness of Basil Bernstein's sociological work" symposium was to ensure that Bernstein's voice should not be betrayed. But it would be too simple to present, in a dichotomic way, an opposition between a message of betrayal and a message of loyalty. In fact, there are two types of "voices" between which Bernstein does not draw particularly explicit distinctions. There is the concept of voice as it is opposed to the concept of message in a conceptual pair invented in 1981 and essential in his analytical framework. But Bernstein also often uses the word "voice" in speaking about "popular voices" which have been stifled. The meaning of the word "voice" varies according to whether it is a dominating or dominated voice; the relationship each type of voice has with the message is different and dissymmetric.

This asymmetry is not only a matter of power. Undoubtedly, there is always a balance of power which is favourable to some and unfavourable to others. But this is not essential: the asymmetry is qualitative. The "horizontal" voice indicates a way of life, a means to becoming a subject, a link to existence implying the development of singular potentialities. The voice which encodes the message – in other words, the pedagogical one – looks for its strength in power, in the mastering and hailing of singularities according to quite a different mode of subjectification. So, there is the voice of power but, also, voices of opposition, of resistance, which, most of the time, are exerted practically, tacitly and which implement other principles of classification and an understanding of the world in another relation with existence. This voice is multiple, local, immanent in its context of completion. It is the ordinary voice of ordinary language, always "inside" and not "practical", as we often write, but *before* the distinction between theory and practice, just like the distinction between object and subject. Yet, we have to understand such a "before" not only as a sort of past but, also, as another place always virtually present and offering possibilities for actualization under some conditions. In this sense, this voice is not "theorizable" but, rather, resists theorization (just as some groups of pupils "resist" school). In any case, it requires another mode of theorization which allows the voice to be heard, and a mode of writing that remains affected, altered by this notion of "before". This manner of theorizing and of writing can be termed "free reported speech". In short, it is a specific form of message, a singular modulation of communication (see Bautier's chapter in this book, which aims to locate the rules for generating a space of transmission crossed with a voice which enables pupils to appropriate the message and to learn it successfully). This is what is also at stake in the controversy between Bernstein and Labov. It is, likewise, the deep source of Bernstein's hostility towards Bourdieu. For Bernstein, theories such as those presented by Labov and Bourdieu misunderstand the possibilities for the transformation of popular voices; they fail to recognize what is specific in these voices and define them only as they relate to a context, a territory, an institution, a symbolic market, where they are always normalized, interpreted through criteria of perceptions which are not their own. Such theories produce a simplistic conceptualization of popular voices, deprived of their potentialities. They are unable to generate principles of description that apply to their own object and they are unable to account for and produce change. The entirety of Bernstein's body of work and his documentation of the process behind it bears witness to his effort to create another mode of theorization: a theory which does not deliver "scientific truths" or "dogmata" but, rather, which works to develop a descriptive language, a syntax of conceptual creation which is not isolated but which can generate an external language that can be transformed into something different. Bernstein works to make visible and audible what was previously invisible and inaudible: a whole, an open multiplicity, something like a people in a free state.

Not betraying Bernstein's message also means not merely repeating it. We can be loyal without simply becoming followers or epigones (contrary to Bourdieu, Bernstein did not seek disciples but, rather, cooperators who could become friends as long as they worked for themselves and at their own risk; in other words, "freelance thinkers"). Loyalty calls neither for reproduction nor for sheer repetition. Rather, it is a sort of creatively different repetition and, since Bernstein uses the word at least once, I will use it myself; it is a form of "deconstruction". To echo the voice of somebody with loyalty is to "deconstruct" it, i.e. to make it explicit, to "unfold" it, and to identify other areas of resonance and actualization.

As such, I shall next attempt to make explicit and to deconstruct a relation, a movement, and to demonstrate how Durkheim gives "a hand" to Bernstein and offers him something to take and to make something out of, but also something else very special, since, being completely at one with Bernstein, it is, more than ever, "durkheimian".

The "banner"

Durkheim's presence in Bernstein's work is global. This could perhaps be termed "labelling", even though Bernstein is suspicious of labels. Durkheim's is the theoretical tradition (among others, to which George Herbert Mead and those of an interactionist descent, particularly those interested in verbal interactions, must be added) with which Bernstein aligns himself, one among others. Durkheim comes first, constituting Bernstein's "roots". Bernstein tells us this primacy is "obvious". He even speaks about his Durkheimianism as a banner he unashamedly waved (2000, p. 124). While it may look as if, in doing so, he places himself under the protection of a patron, he warns in the same passage that any label is relative: it depends both on the moment it occurs and on the sometimes unscrupulous commentary which is bound to address it. So, for Bernstein (who, of course, knows perfectly well the passage from "The elementary forms of religious life" about the vital social meaning of this "piece of stuff" since it symbolizes a social link), what does it mean to claim a Durkheimian banner? First, it must be noted that Bernstein was the type of sociologist who did not work on his own but who was very conversant with the global scientific field to which he belonged and who was very knowledgeable of its history. What is more, Bernstein understands how Durkheim has been received historically. He is particularly aware that when he started his career, the sociological universe revolved largely around (if it was not dominated by) sociology as it was conceived of and practised in the United States and that the sociological "message" depended largely on this "voice". At that time, the prevailing (though not the only) interpretation of Durkheim was Talcott Parsons' typically "American" structural-functionalism and, more widely, statistical empiricism. This was a conservative interpretation depriving the Durkheimian voice of its subversive potential. Bernstein is very severe in his treatment of Parsons, claiming that his conceptual cathedral and system of variables is nothing but a falsifying reshaping of "mechanical and organic solidarity" (2000, p. 124); in other words, it is tantamount to plagiarism and misinterpretation. In placing himself under the patronage of Durkheim and in his footsteps, Bernstein is prepared to fight and to reappraise. He protects his protector. So, Durkheim's primacy in the mind of Bernstein is not at all mysterious. It is a sign of Bernstein's entry into intellectual life and into the conflicts and coalitions of the mind. Thanks to Durkheim, Bernstein can say "no" to structural-functionalism and "no" to conceptualizations of socialization as the internalization of a range of predetermined roles within a system of systems. This first battle enabled him to win others and to break with the reproductionist paradigm once he had recognized – under another semantics and under other masks – the Parsonian grid disguised as habitus: the internalization of exteriority, etc.

But it is this initial Durkheimian marking, this first battle to save the Durkheimian message from the Parsonian voice, this original dubbing, which allows Bernstein to unmask, with his acute sixth sense and in the texts most apparently oriented "against domination", the hidden presence of this theoretical poison, namely the image of a society doomed to reproduce itself without inventing something new, of a history incapable of undergoing real revolution, an arena of eternal damnation (how religious "reproduction" is ...).

So we must give Durkheim his voice back.

And what must be preserved at any cost? Not a doctrine ("It has always seemed to me that one's allegiance is less to an approach and more to exploring a problematic" (Bernstein 2000, p. 125)) but, rather the issues that Durkheim has addressed and raised. He is the one who discovered the social nature of education and began to analyse the historically variable links between educational systems and the moral, material characteristics of given eras. The common objective of Durkheim and Bernstein is to constitute pedagogical relationships as a genuine issue, as a crucial enigma to be clarified. Each of them has identified a conflictual space where different strengths are in direct opposition: the transmission of knowledge is not foreign to the exercise of power. In reaching this end, Durkheim did not content himself with generalities. He conducted a sociohistorical study of the French educational system, analysing not only its institutional construction but, also, the pedagogical discourses, the methods of teaching and the curricula within it. This is the orientation to be maintained.

The heritage they share, which Bernstein carefully lays hold of, consists of a community of objects. Bernstein clearly states this in an article translated in 1992 in *Critiques sociales* (1992, pp. 21–2). Durkheim provides Bernstein with a useful path to follow in tracing the nature of the relay that supports what is relayed (the relay that remains invisible and unrecognized in theories of cultural reproduction). So, they have the same empirical object: school, its functioning and its relations with the global society. They share also the same theoretical object: education as a conflictual process of construction and the imposition of a world (and of its correlate: a subject). For them, each type of objective world only exists "objectively" by involving a type of subjective modality, a mode of subjectification. These double communities of empirical and theoretical objects are very visible in *Evolution of Educational Thought: Lectures on the Formation and Development of Secondary Education in France* (Durkheim, 1977). In the succession of chapters within that work, some are devoted to pedagogical doctrines, some to curricula and discourses and others to institutions and practices. The real object is not addressed in some chapters as opposed to others but, rather, in their intertwining. We can attempt to discover this embrace either in the disciplines of the bodies and of their terms (this is what Michel Foucault has done, in a way Bernstein has not only not followed but, also, has not even really understood), or in the language disciplines of curricula. This is the common path followed by Durkheim and Bernstein.

Creative differentiation

Yet, even concerning this fundamental link, this community of objects and this exploration of identical territory, the question is not one of similarity. Bernstein's takeover of the Durkheimian project is at the same time a move towards a creative differentiation. As an exploratory outline, this differentiation can be qualified through three words: extension, reversal and radicalization.

1   First of all, because Bernstein never considered Durkheim's work as a closed corpus but considered it, rather, as an impersonal project extending beyond its author and capable of being continually enriched, he practises what could be called an "extensive Durkheimianism". Bernstein extends the concept of pedagogy. For him pedagogical relationships exist anywhere

learning occurs, even tacitly, and everywhere that "knowledge-power" is exerted. Doctors, social workers, prison staff, psychiatrists and virtually all wage-earners are included within this arena of confrontation (see Bernstein 2000, p. 101). Consequently, however, such a consideration also extends the field beyond the question of schooling. What is at stake in terms of pedagogy is also present in other social relationships where visible forms of oppression and repression are deployed (i.e. workplaces, prisons, etc.) as well as in the sphere of benevolent services where individual care based on specific skills is carried out (i.e. general medicine, social work, psychological support, etc.); in short, everywhere human beings strive to cure minds, souls and bodies. The mere association of these disparate parts of the social sphere must be recognized. Training, as it occurs in schools, still involves the formative action of strengths that can presently be found in other institutions. In all of them perhaps? A contemporary diagram of power? This is a prominent theoretical and political issue.

So, it is not surprising to find Cassirer included in this inheritance and involved in this adventure as a sort of Durkheimian, even if he is not aware of it. Cassirer, like Durkheim, was inspired by Kant and interested in researching a priori structures of particular eras as well as the links between symbolic forms and knowledge. It would be extremely instructive, in recognition of Durkheim's efforts at a bold sociogenesis of the basic, elementary categories that shape our knowledge, our reason, to compare how Bernstein and Bourdieu use Cassirer. Here, however, I will provide some more general remarks about Bernstein's "use" of his predecessors.

In every text there are moments when the author, by "raising" his or her "voice", invites the reader to prick up his or her ears. This is very much the case in a passage where Bernstein vividly protests ("I certainly disagree..." (2000, p. 123)) against the idea that his concepts, his most famous dichotomic pairs (restricted and elaborated codes, personal vs. positional, etc.) should be considered Weberian ideal-types. Bernstein understands that categories of thinking do not offer absolutely realistic pictures of things (if they did, he would not modify them so often). He stresses, however, that these categories are not "ideal-types" but, rather, that they are "forms" – generative forms capable of generating something more than themselves – and, even if their capacity to do so is low at the beginning, the progress of research serves to strengthen this capacity. It could also be surmised that the passage referenced above is inspired by Chomsky. It could be considered as a typical example demonstrating how Bernstein uses others as a real fencer; to put forward his concept he is, here, against Weber but with Cassirer and Durkheim. Bernstein's conceptualization of theory as a symbolic form in the progressive construction of a truth (i.e. something new) seems to entail elements of Cassirer's reinterpretation of Durkheim.

Bernstein's treatment of the work of the outstanding Durkheimian anthropologist, Mary Douglas, who died only a few days prior to the "Social issues, knowledge, language and pedagogy: The current relevance and usefulness of

Basil Bernstein's sociological work" conference, is no more surprising. As soon as he read her book, *Purity and Danger* (1967), which deals with the categories of "pure" and "impure" as they exist in African societies, Bernstein immediately reinvested them in a short article "making more explicit concepts of boundaries, insulations, social divisions of labour, with regard to the purity and mixing of categories of discourse and organization" (2000, p. 97). The vocabulary of Douglas is also present in an appendix to chapter 10 of *Pedagogy, Symbolic Control and Identity*, where Bernstein develops a humorous typology of the criticisms his work has attracted. The fighting spirit evident in Bernstein's "use" of his predecessors cannot be denied, but the consideration that the conceptual categories created by authors can be revised, renewed, reused and applied in other contexts reveals a sense of generosity as well. In a way, Bernstein is a wizard: he makes dead people speak (a "free reported speech"); he reactivates them and gives them life and a voice again. This theoretical and conceptual art (I term this form of theoretical work, which "frees" other voices, "spiritual") is reminiscent of the skills of the handy person who knows how to use worn out and "dead" things in a manner that revivifies them in new ways and contexts; it is the art of tricks and guiles embodied by Ulysses. Levi-Strauss revealed these skills among Indian artists in the Amazonian rainforest and Certeau uncovered them in the daily manners of the poor (1980). Whether the concepts are his own or borrowed from Durkheim or from other researchers and popular categories, Bernstein constantly affirms and reaffirms that he has found his banner in Durkheim and in many others close to him and that he has found it in what Durkheim has asserted and undertaken regarding the object "education". This involves a double proposal, inseparably epistemological and ontological.

Epistemologically, he extends beyond the dialectic opposition between realism and nominalism. He states that he is not a nominalist and that his concepts, just as Durkheim's, cannot be confused with Weberian ideal-types, stylized pictures of an impure reality. For all that, however, he states that he is not a realist in the sense that would require scientific theory to deliver loyal representations of what is given, of reality. For Bernstein, social science is not representative but, rather, generative; it produces something new: new truths. It means conquering a "new world", a "new outside".

Ontologically, he proposes the obverse of the same coin: that the social real (or the human real; they are one in the same) is ambivalent, open. It is a whole, an open multiplicity from which that which does not yet exist (or, at least, has not yet been recorded) can appear as an "event", "news" or as "fresh air" (the sudden appearance of a person crying out, a popular "voice"). Ideally, the aim of a "fighting" sociology would be to map such "events" and their possibilities, which would constitute a very powerful means to stopping history from becoming a closed and backward-looking chronicle of what are always the same things simply under different masks.

2   Second, Bernstein initiates a reversal of perspective. For Durkheim, the real problem of contemporary education was one of symbolic integration

(how can we foster the development of a *society* by educating *individuals?*). For Bernstein, on the contrary, the issue is one of symbolic control (how can people exist as individuals when education controls their borders and so defines the field and the nature of their relationships?). This reversal leads Bernstein to focus his work on different modalities of communication and the transmission of knowledge, to incorporate the heritage of G.H. Mead and interactionism and, especially, work in sociolinguistics and his successive encounters with different trends and authors addressed and integrated throughout *Pedagogy, Symbolic Control and Identity*. Still, it is quite noticeable that Bernstein uses Durkheim as a landmark and a mooring in his debates with the sociolinguists. For example, in Bernstein's conflict with Labov, what does the latter refuse? It allows the meaning of language differences between young black Americans and representatives of the school to be reduced to a dialectal difference exploited negatively by the institution. That is all very well. The parlance of young black Americans, asserts Labov (1978), has its own consistency and only loses its positivity when judged academically. The way young black Americans speak is a way of life, a product of and for socialization, serving to create a society. That, too, is perfect. However, such assertions only make sense under one condition: the condition of school failure. That is why, for Bernstein, Labov and Willis (1977) represent symmetrically the same mistake: Labov by focusing his work on the exploitation of language differences by the dominant institution (oppression); Willis by focusing on the exploitation of the same differences by the exploited "lads" of Birmingham who indulge in "having a laff" (resistance). Bernstein tells us that the one are "lames" and the other "deafs", because the only thing they can do it is to reproduce themselves as workers; here, by dropping out (Bernstein 2000, p. 147). So, for Bernstein, these two authors fail to address the real problem and the real question: how does the school curriculum prevent the "members" and "lads" from appropriating it? It is admittedly legitimate to give value to "street language" and to depict how future workers stand up for themselves against school by claiming the fully fledged value of their own world; still, the pupils concerned in each of these cases ultimately fail to use knowledge as a weapon. Labov's conceptualizations lead directly to a deficit conception and to the theory of sociocultural handicap; Willis', no better, to a theory of counter-handicap – a blurred mixture (not to say a poor mixture) of miserabilism and populism. Bernstein, on the contrary, issues the challenge of considering that a solution is possible and that popular languages and cultures are not doomed to express their possibilities only under the negative conditions that inevitably prevent access to formalized knowledge.

This point is essential sociologically as well as epistemologically. What is at stake is the status of "differences". For Bernstein, difference is not intended to be thought of as something lacking or to be negated. He viewed such negation as, simply, a reversed image, an instance of negativity (here, we are introduced to Bernstein the dialectician, or, the Hegelian!). Bernstein was sometimes considered, meaninglessly, as a "neo-marxist". Partly because of Marx, partly in spite of him, the marxist tradition has unfortunately dealt with difference in a dialectical way where the "moment of negation" has been granted a central place. Today, still, many theoretical (and political) aporias stem from such a yoke (Passeron has perceived this well in "Hegel or the Clandestine Passenger" (Passeron 1991), his retrospective and critical analysis of the concept of reproduction).

It is, in fact, impossible to analyse this reversal – if it is not limited to a dialectical one, where opposing differences simply change places to achieve a "synthesis" (the negation of negation, as Hegelians put it; a false movement, not a creative one) – without considering something else entailed by it. The reversal of a problematic of integration into a problematic of control does not bring together equivalent terms. The issue is not integration versus control. The term indicating these two dissymmetric perspectives are disparate. In order to tackle and to operate the reversal, the shift from one point of view to another, something special has to be done. Something, which remains latent in his theory of integration but which can be explicitly expressed in the Bernsteinian conceptualization of symbolic control, must be "snatched away" from Durkheim. This violent movement can be termed the "radicalization" of Durkheim and the moment when reversal and radicalization successfully meet can no longer be called "extensive Durkheimianism" but should be considered, rather, an "intensive" one.

3   So, where Durkheim thinks in terms of social integration, Bernstein reverses the vector of analysis and thinks in terms of symbolic control. This leads to a new question, one of identity and of modalities of the self. Here again, however, Bernstein remains Durkheimian in addressing this new question. Indeed, he states that: (1) the constitution of the self is formed through and can be located within specific social relationships and (2) the question of the nature of the symbolic control possesses a Durkheimian influence (Bernstein 2000, p. 97). This assertion, in particular, is somewhat enigmatic. As such, I wish to shed light on it by re-examining a passage (in fact, a lecture) from *Pedagogy, Symbolic Control and Identity* devoted to commentary on Durkheim's own commentary on the transformation of the medieval curriculum in *L'évolution pédagogique en France*. In fact, this (re)consideration of the *Trivium* and the *Quadrivium* serves precisely as an example of the operation of "creative differentiation" as it relates closely to the Durkheimian text. The blacksmith introduces us to his theoretical forge and demonstrates how a new weapon is manufactured, exploring with energy the theoretical apparatus employed previously by Durkheim and taking his question "further", crafting "a stronger version" (2000, p. 82). In his comments on the transformation of the medieval curriculum, Bernstein makes his conception of the subject strongly explicit, inseparable from the process of the production of a mode of subjectification. As a result, this text occupies a very special status since those reading it are direct witnesses to the birth of a new conceptualization of the subject.

This conceptualization is drawn from Durkheim's own words, which have been revised and even disjointed (in fact, creative differentiation or radical movements, always involve a disjunctive synthesis). Even if this concept is very rich and suggestive, I am able to focus here on one simple idea (but there are many others): in my opinion, Bernstein gets as close in this text as he can to a theory of the subject based upon a mode of subjectification (we could also say "forms of subjectification", since each mode produces specific subjective forms). What, wonders Bernstein, is the specificity of the Christian self? It is created through a very singular process of conversion (bearing in mind that "metanoïa", the Platonic conversion, is defined as a movement, a displacement of the whole soul), a subjective modality involving a distancing from the external world, culture and practices within which the first Christians were living: an inner life isolated from its initial world, "intrinsically an abstract orientation" (Bernstein 2000, p. 83). Indeed, according to Paul, Christians are not from this world, and they must live in it as if they were not in it. Their self-without-world has to be reconstructed, has to reconquer a world, and this was historically accomplished by developing the Greek elements of profane reason and abstraction based on a tension between faith and reason that Durkheim identified as the dynamic source of the medieval university. So, the first Christians went through an experience of distancing, of discontinuity between an "inner world" and an "outside world", through a form of "absence to the world", beginning the occidental movement towards the "rationalization" of, and disenchantment with, the world. This huge movement of Christian intellectual creation (a movement not entirely grasped by Durkheim), in the form of the neo-Platonic tradition and, particularly, of Thomas Aquinas' new Aristotelianism, involved a sort of "grabbing hold" of Greek thinking in the effort to, according to Bernstein, "colonize" and transmute it.

This movement draws its strength and its dynamism from a characteristic specific to the Christian God. Contrary to Judaism, where "there is no dislocation of inner and outer", Christianity "creates a special modality of language, an interrogative mode which splits the self from its acts, intention from practice" (Bernstein 2000, pp. 84–5). In the Jewish culture, any generalization is banned (it is "held in contempt") and thinking develops by working out one specific fact before moving to another. On the contrary, Christian culture involves a doubtful subject bound to question his or her faith and to speculate abstractly. Bernstein interprets the rupture between the *Trivium* and *Quadrivium* in a new and unique way, stating that it leads to the completion of the rupture between disciplines of "the word" and disciplines of "the world": there is "No World prior to the word" (Bernstein 2000, p. 82). The new sequencing of knowledge initiates the dislocation of the self necessitated by the Christian faith. Thanks to the appropriation and reinterpretation of the Greek voice, a new message is developed – one which finds its correlate of existence in an external, rational world and one which ensures the solidity and validity of the internal world. The new world that emerges, the modern world, began "nearly a millenary ago" with Christianity. Over the last five centuries – 500 years of humanism and of the humanities – the religious basis on which the original inside–outside rupture was developed and completed has given way to "a humanizing secular principle" (Bernstein 2000, p. 85). Bernstein concludes his commentary with a diagnosis, stating that this period is now over. A (neoliberal) dehumanizing principle has taken over, reversing the movement described above by creating a new gap between the world and the self, producing this time a self without a world and eliminating the possibilities for a habitable world, for creating "humanity", "society", a specific culture, or a "sociotope" (a distinct place with a certain composition of utility values and meanings). This evolution impacts directly on the organization of curricula and the process of academic transmission. This is where Bernstein's sociohistorical analysis presently ends. The question of academic knowledge leads Bernstein to seek to discover the deepest mechanisms of the genesis of a very special civilization: our own. He presents this search and discovery as an unfinished script "where the plot is not worked out, and half the characters are missing" (2000, p. 81) and he invites us to complete it by proceeding through "trial and error" as Celestin Freinet, a genuine resistor of pedagogy, expresses it. This is what I would like to do in concluding, employing again the concept of the mode of subjectification.

The term "mode" is essential. It indicates that the subject is a singular reality, simultaneously both modal and modular. It is, at once, a reality "tailor-made" as a type or a style of subjectivity shaped by an imprint (the imprint of education) and, at the same time, an active source of subjectification which consists of "objectivizing", i.e. of making a stabilized, habitable world of consistent objects exist (it could be said that the proper operativity of a subject is to build a sociotope; so, strictly speaking, the subject has a decisively sociotopic nature). The belief in sacredness and its keystone, God, indicates such a process of sociotopic "mapping", of the stabilization of chaos, of the springing up of a cosmos. We can define a cosmos as a system of pertinences, an intelligibility, a belief in the world which does not develop through explanation but, rather, through intuition or evidence ("evidence", in English, means proof: "evidence" is convincing and self-sufficient proof for which a journey through the detours of unfolding chains of reasoning and deductive sequences is unnecessary).

It is the invention of a type of organization able to produce an intuitive understanding of the world or, rather, an "evident", "objective" world. But this objectivity is not identical to the one proposed by the world of science and rationality. It is immediate and not mediated. It is based not on generalized abstraction culminating in the absolute domination of the "free market" but, rather, on the concreteness of shaping a habitable word, a "sociotope" or "society", another sort of "new world". This new world requires a fierce fight over borders, about the principles of classification, about the sequencing of official knowledge and the curriculum. School is altogether at the heart of this immense battle.

4 Subject position and discourse in Activity Theory

Harry Daniels

In this chapter I wish to explore the extent to which two approaches to the social formation of mind are compatible and may be used to enrich and extend each other. These are: Activity Theory (AT), as derived from the work of the early Russian psychologists, Vygotsky and Leontiev, and the work of the sociologist Basil Bernstein. The purpose is to show how Bernstein (2000) provides a language of description which allows Vygotsky's (1987) account of social formation of mind to be extended and enhanced through an understanding of the sociological processes which form specific modalities of pedagogic practice and their specialized scientific concepts. The two approaches engage with a common theme, namely the social shaping of consciousness, from different perspectives and yet, as Bernstein (1977, 1993) acknowledges, both develop many of their core assumptions from the work of Marx and the French school of early-twentieth-century sociology.

There has been much debate over the years about the effectiveness of schooling but relatively little about the effects of different modalities of schooling. The empirical work which is used to illustrate the theoretical argument of this chapter is drawn from a study conducted in British special schools. This sector of the state school system was selected as it is the one which exhibits the greatest diversity of institutional modalities of schooling. The empirical work in this chapter seeks to investigate the effects of different forms of institutional modality and the theoretical work seeks to develop a language of description which facilitates such research.

It is possible to track different approaches to the study of cultural historical formation in the early work of Vygotsky and Leontiev. The unit of analysis was word meaning in the case of Vygotsky (1987) and the activity system in which the individual was located in the case of Leontiev (1978, 1981). In both approaches, there is little by way of an explicit focus on institutional structure. In their attempt to develop an account of social formation their gaze fell first on the individual in dialogue and the object-oriented activity system. The notion of the object of activity – the problem space or raw material that was being worked on in an activity – is central to the work of Leontiev.

Bernstein developed a theory and descriptive categories that oriented researchers' gaze towards the social, cultural and historical nature of institutions and the principles of discourse that shape the possibilities for individual and collective thought and actions. The rules regulating processes of cultural historical formation of mind rather than the object of activity are the focus. That is not to say that the social, cultural-historical formation of mind is not important in the theories of Leontiev and Vygotsky, rather that they do not focus on the explication of wider social principles which regulate this formation. It is as though they were starting from opposite "ends". Thus in this chapter a focus on the rules which shape the social formation of pedagogic discourse and its practices (Bernstein 2000) will be brought to bear on those aspects of psychology which argue that object-oriented activity is a fundamental constituent of human thought and action (Cole 1996). Crucially an attempt will be made to hint at the possibilities for the development of a language of description which will enable macro-constraints to be made visible in their power to shape interactions. The institutional level of analysis was all but absent in much of the early Vygotskian research in the West (see Daniels 2001). There was no recourse to a language of description that permitted the analysis of object-oriented activity in terms of the rules which regulate the micro-cultures of institutions. Recent developments in post-Vygotskian theory (most notably Activity Theory) have witnessed considerable advances in the understanding of the ways in which human action shapes and is shaped by the contexts in which it takes place (Daniels 2001). They have given rise to a significant amount of empirical research within and across a wide range of fields in which social science methodologies and methods are applied in the development of research-based knowledge in policy-making and practice in academic, commercial and industrial settings.

In the course of a workshop which forms part of a large scale ESRC TLRP-funded research project entitled "Learning in and for Interagency Work", a community paediatrician remarked that her biggest learning challenge was "to learn to *be and talk* like a multi-agency person when I am not in multi-agency meetings". The theoretical challenge implicit in this short statement is as to how we can understand the relations between the social organization of work, discursive practice and social position. This is the challenge that I will try and address in this chapter. I will discuss the way in which the concept of social position can be used to promote theoretical development in Activity Theory. In so doing, I will consider the way in which the cultural artefact, discourse, is deployed in relation to the social position of the subject. Thus the chapter is primarily concerned with the analysis of subject positioning and discursive practice within activity systems. My key points of departure are to be found in three areas of academic endeavour:

- Post-Vygotskian and Activity Theory-based approaches to the study of artefact-mediated, object-oriented human activity as exemplified by the work of Yrjo Engeström (1999) and Michael Cole (1996).

- Recent attempts by Dorothy Holland and colleagues (1998) to synthesize the work of the Russian linguist, M.M. Bakhtin, Vygotsky and the French social theorist Pierre Bourdieu in an account of identity and agency in cultural worlds.
- The theory of the social structuring of discourse in society developed by Basil Bernstein (2000) and discussed in relation to the work of Halliday (1973, 1975, 1978) and Vygotsky by the linguist Ruqaiya Hasan (2001a, b).

Activity Theory

Within the post-Vygotskian theoretical framework there is a requirement for a structural description of social settings which provides principles for distinguishing between social practices. Descriptions of this sort would be an important part of the apparatus required to carry out empirical investigation and analysis of the psychological consequences for individuals of different forms of social organization. I am not treating the social organizational context as some kind of independent effect rather as a constraint on the scope for what Mike Cole calls the weaving of context (Cole 1996). Description of the institutional setting itself would not be enough. Vygotsky's writing on the way in which psychological tools and signs act in the mediation of social factors does not engage with a theoretical account of the appropriation and/or the production of psychological tools within specific forms of activity within or across institutions. However, some writers in the field have recognized the need for such a form of theoretical engagement (e.g. Hedegaard 2001).

In the same way that psychological studies of learning which ignore contextual constraints will confound and confuse the interpretation of results, the absence of an appropriate theoretical framework that includes wider social institutional factors will reduce Vygotsky's theory of appropriation of psychological tools to partial levels of explanation. Vygotsky's approach lacks a theoretical framework for the description and analysis of the changing forms of cultural transmission at the level of the institution. Activity Theory makes an approach to the institutional level of analysis but lacks a language of description which permits the production of artefacts (such as speech) in the institution to be studied in a manner which coheres with the principles which regulate that institution.

Vygotsky's (1987) distinction between scientific and everyday concepts and his account of the interplay between these two forms in the process of concept development provides an important insight into the psychology of activity within the zone of proximal development. Bernstein provides a sociology of pedagogy which allows the study of such psychological formation to proceed within a framework that articulates the formation of the scientific concepts which inhabit specific modalities of schooling. There is no account of the sociology of the formation of scientific concepts in Vygotsky's writing.

In this chapter, I will propose that there is a need to extend the analysis of the production of cultural artefacts in Activity Theory. I will also suggest that when the cultural artefact takes the form of a pedagogic discourse that we should also analyse its structure in the context of its production. My starting point will be taken from Vygotsky's (1987) insistence on the importance of both mediation and externalization. I will then move to consider the collective historical production of artefacts and raise questions about the way in which we can analyse this form of cultural-historical production.

In Figure 4.1 the subject is the individual or group whose actions are the focus of analysis. The object is the focus of the activity, the issue or thing that is being acted upon. In Engeström's hands this basic Vygotskian semiotic model of activity has been transformed.

In order to progress the development of Activity Theory Engeström expanded the original triangular representation of activity systems that was used in the first generation (see Figure 4.2). He did this to enable an

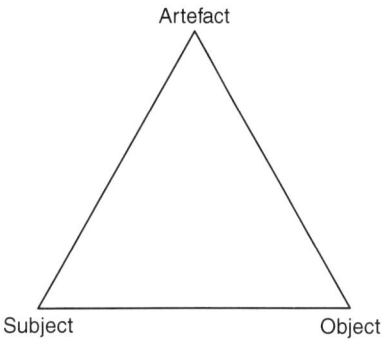

Figure 4.1 The basic triangular representation of mediation.

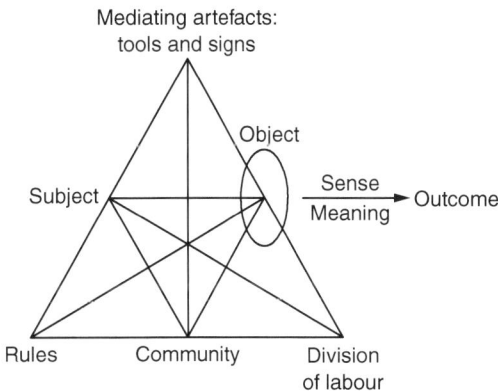

Figure 4.2 Second generation Activity Theory model.

examination of systems of activity at the macro level of the collective and the community in preference to a micro-level concentration on the individual actor or agent operating with tools. This expansion of the basic Vygotskian triangle aims to represent the social/collective elements in an activity system, through the addition of the elements of community, rules and division of labour while emphasizing the importance of analysing their interactions with each other. The community is the collections of individuals or groups who are all concerned with the same object. Here the division of labour refers to both the division of tasks and the status relations between actors. The rules are the principles of regulation of action and interaction. Engeström (1999) acknowledges the methodological difficulty of capturing evidence about community, rules and division of labour within the activity system.

The third generation of activity theory as proposed by Engeström intends to develop conceptual tools to understand dialogues, multiple perspectives, and networks of interacting activity systems (see Figure 4.3). He draws on ideas of dialogicality and multivoicedness in order to expand the framework of the second generation. Bakhtin (1981) provides some insight into how the processes by which multiple voices may serve a mediational function. His suggestion that language is "over populated with the intentions of others" reminds us that the processes of mediation are processes in which individuals operate with artefacts (words/texts) which are themselves shaped by, and have been shaped in, activities within which values are contested and meaning negotiated. In this sense cultural residues reside in and constrain the possibilities for communication. Thus the mediational process is one which neither denies individual or collective agency nor denies social, cultural, historical constraint. What Bakhtin does not provide is means of describing and thus analysing the regulation of agency and constraint.

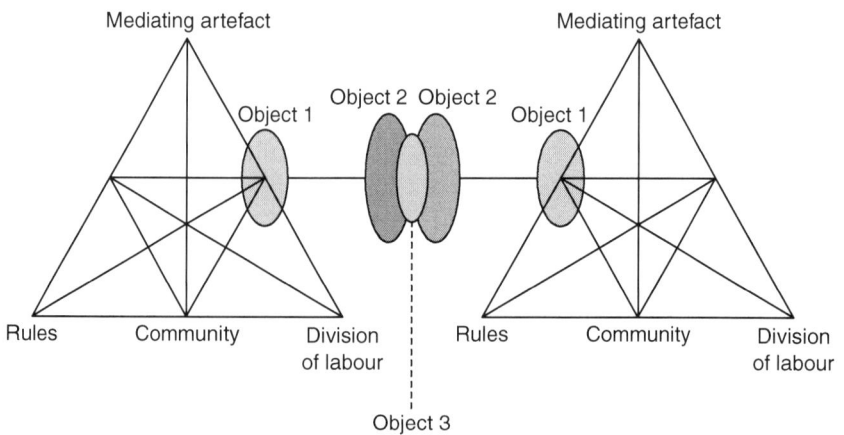

Figure 4.3 Two interacting activity systems as minimal model for third generation of Activity Theory (source: Engestrom 1999).

The idea of networks of activity within which contradictions and struggles take place in the definition of the motives and object of the activity calls for an analysis of power and control within developing activity systems. The minimal representation which Figure 4.3 provides shows but two of what may be myriad systems exhibiting patterns of contradiction and tension. Engeström's emphasis on the analysis of the activity system(s) is directed towards contradictions and tensions with specific emphasis on the object of the activity and the outcomes. The production, distribution and selection of artefacts tend not to be highlighted in the analysis.

Bakhurst (e.g. 1995) has done much to clarify the contribution of the Russian philosopher Ilyenkov to our understanding of the framework within which so much of the Russian perspective on mediation may be read. He outlines processes by which meanings are shaped and embodied in things. His contribution leads us some way towards a better understanding of the production of artefacts. A starting point from which to untangle some of the ramifications of his philosophical position is with reference to the concept of "objectification". It is with this concept that connection can be made to the cultural historical production of the artefacts which humans use to order and construct their lives. The idea of meaning embodied or sedimented in objects as they are put into use in social worlds is central to the conceptual apparatus of theories of culturally mediated, historically developing, practical activity.

Engeström (1999) sees joint activity or practice as the unit of analysis for Activity Theory, not individual activity. He is interested in the processes of social transformation and includes the structure of the social world in his analysis while taking into account the conflictual nature of social practice. He sees instability (internal tensions) and contradiction as the "motive force of change and development" (Engeström 1999, p. 9) and the transitions and reorganizations within and between activity systems as part of development. It is not only the subject, but the environment, that is modified through mediated activity. He views the "reflective appropriation of advanced models and tools" as "ways out of internal contradictions" that result in new activity systems (Cole and Engeström 1993, p. 40).

In our study of learning for and in interagency work we are drawing on this third generation of Activity Theory as we model networks of interacting activity (Daniels *et al.* 2005). The project is concerned with the learning of professionals in the creation of new forms of practice which require joined-up solutions to meet complex and diverse client needs. We are studying professional learning in services that aim to promote social inclusion through interagency working. Working with other professionals involves engaging with configurations of several, diverse social practices and the development of new forms of hybrid practice. The implications for notions of expertise have been explored by Hakkarainen *et al.* (2004):

> Expertise in a certain domain may also be represented in a hybrid expert who is able to translate one expert culture's knowledge into form that

participants of another expert culture can understand ... innovation emerges in networks of these kinds of communities. Creation of innovations supports gradually developing division of labour and increased specialization as well as combination of existing dispersed resources for novel purposes.

(Hakkarainen *et al.* 2004, p. 17)

Pirkkalainen *et al.* (2005) have argued that such hybrid practice is different from collaboration, cooperation or networking in which the constituent activities remain distinct. They suggest that hybridization involves change in positional relations *between* the agents of different activity systems and positional change of agents *within* some activity system. Such changes involve shifts in relations of power (in the division of labour) and control (within the categories established by the division of labour) within and between activity systems. The work of these shifts in the division of labour may well be discursive work. It is here that a present theoretical weakness is revealed by the introduction of the notion of hybridization and the focus on positional relations instead of object formation and historically generated forms of social relation instead of historical forms of work and organizations (Pirkkalainen *et al.* 2005). How do we develop a theoretical account of the discursive regulation of interpersonal relations which is compatible with the assumptions of activity theory?

Hasan (1992a, b, 1995) and Wertsch (1985, 1991) note the irony that while Vygotsky developed a theory of semiotic mediation in which the mediational means of language was privileged, he provides very little if anything by way of a theory of language use. In an account of the social formation of mind there is a requirement for theory which relates meanings to interpersonal relations. The absence of an account of the ways language both serves to regulate interpersonal relations and its specificity is in turn produced through specific patterns of interpersonal relation and thus social regulation constitutes a serious weakness. This absence has carried through in the development of Activity Theory. As Engeström and Miettinen (1999) note, it has yet to develop a sophisticated account of discursive practice which is fully commensurate with the assumptions of Activity Theory itself. At the same time, Engeström acknowledges the methodological difficulty of capturing evidence about community, rules and division of labour within the activity system (Engeström 1999). The theoretically powerful move would be to understand the discursive regulation of interpersonal relations in terms of processes of social, cultural and historical regulation as witnessed in Activity Theory by the notions of rules and division of labour. I have used the term "witnessed" because I argue that there is theoretical work to be done here. As Pirkkalainen *et al.* (2005) note at the end of their paper, the study of hybridization raises key questions such as "How do we understand division of labour?", "How do we understand rule in any given activity system?" (p. 7). They also suggest that there is a need to differentiate/unify concepts of agency, subject and actor. In the rest of this chapter I will attempt to address some aspects of these questions.

Engeström (1999) offers the suggestion that the division of labour in an activity creates different positions for the participants and that the participants carry their own diverse histories with them into the activity. This echoes the earlier assertion from Leontiev:

> Activity is the minimal meaningful context for understanding individual actions ... In all its varied forms, the activity of the human individual is a system set within a system of social relations ... The activity of individual people thus *depends on their social position*, the conditions that fall to their lot, and an accumulation of idiosyncratic, individual factors. Human activity is not a relation between a person and a society that confronts him ... in a society a person does not simply find external conditions to which he must adapt his activity, but, rather, these very social conditions bear within themselves the motives and goals of his activity, its means and modes.
>
> (Leontiev 1978, p. 10)

In activity the possibilities for the use of artefacts depend on the social position occupied by an individual. Sociologists and sociolinguists have produced empirical verification of this suggestion (e.g. Bernstein 2000; Hasan 2001a, b; Hasan and Cloran 1990). The notion of "subject" within Activity Theory requires expansion and clarification. In many studies the term "subject perspective" is used which arguably implies subject position but does little to illuminate the roots or formative processes that gave rise to this perspective.

Identity and agency in cultural worlds

Holland *et al.* (1998) have studied the development of identities and agency specific to historically situated, socially enacted, culturally constructed worlds. They draw on Bakhtin and Vygotsky to develop a theory of identity as constantly forming and person as a composite of many, often contradictory, self-understandings and identities which are distributed across the material and social environment and rarely durable (Holland *et al.* 1998, p. 8). They draw on Leontiev in the development of the concept of socially organized and reproduced *figured worlds* which shape and are shaped by participants and in which social position establishes possibilities for engagement. They also argue that figured worlds:

> Distribute "us" not only by relating actors to landscapes of action (as personae) and spreading our senses of self across many different fields of activity, but also by giving the landscape human voice and tone. Cultural worlds are populated by familiar social types and even identifiable

persons, not simply differentiated by some abstract division of labour. The identities we gain within figured worlds are thus specifically histor- ical developments, grown through continued participation in the posi- tions defined by the social organization of those world's activity.

(Holland *et al.* 1998, p. 41)

Thus this approach to a theory of identity in practice is grounded in the notion of a figured world in which positions are taken up, constructed and resisted. The Bakhtinian concept of the "space of authoring" is deployed to capture an understanding of the mutual shaping of figured worlds *and* iden- tities in social practice. They refer to Bourdieu (see 1977) in their attempt to show how social position becomes disposition. They argue for the develop- ment of social position into a positional identity then into disposition and the formation of what Bourdieu refers to as "habitus". It is here that I feel that this argument could be strengthened through reference to a theoretical account which provides greater descriptive and analytical purchase on the principles of regulation of the social figured world, the possibilities for social position and the voice of participants.

When faced with the empirical task of distinguishing between one habitus and another, a researcher is left without any analytical or descriptive research tools.

If we take a popular concept *habitus*, whilst it may solve certain episte- mological problems of agency and structure, it is only known or recog- nized by its apparent outcomes. Habitus is described in terms of what it gives rise to, and brings, or does not bring about ... But it is not described with reference to the particular ordering principles or strat- egies, which give rise to the formation of a particular habitus. The for- mation of the internal structure of the particular habitus, the mode of its specific acquisition, which gives it its specificity, is not described. How it comes to be is not part of the description, only what it does. There is no description of its specific formation.... Habitus is known by its output not its input.

(Bernstein 2000, p. 133)

Thus the study of processes of hybridization would be left without a means of distinguishing between key aspects of the activity systems in play. Hasan (1992a) also contends that the same problem is to be found with attempts which refer to Bakhtin's concept of speech genre:

Though Bakhtin's views concerning speech genres are rhetorically attractive and impressive, the approach lacks – both a developed concep- tual syntax and an adequate language of description. Terms and units at both these levels in Bakhtin's writings require clarification; further, the principles that underlie the calibration of the elements of context with the generic shape of the text are underdeveloped, as is the general schema for the description of contexts for interaction.

(Hasan 1992a, p. 48)

Linehan and McCarthy (2000) develop a strong argument in favour of the deployment of a notion of positioning in communities of practice as an approach to studying participation in social settings. They outline a problem space which echoes some of the concerns raised by Holland *et al.* (1998) but the problem of theorizing social and cultural position in such a way that the analytical and empirical engagement with the figured world becomes visible remains elusive.

Basil Bernstein

Bernstein (1990, p. 13) used the concept of social positioning to refer to the establishing of a specific relation to other subjects and to the creating of specific relationships within subjects. This seems to me to concur with the analysis outlined by Holland *et al.* (1998). He relates social positioning to the formation of mental dispositions in terms of the identity's relation to the distribution of labour in society. It is through the deployment of his concepts of voice and message that Bernstein forges the link between division of labour, social position and discourse and opens up the possibilities for a language of description that will serve empirical as well analytical purposes. In what follows I will provide a very brief presentation of the essence of this argument. Full details may be found in Bernstein (2000).

Bernstein's work is concerned with interrelations between changes in organizational form, changes in modes of control and changes in principles of communication. His language of description is generated from an analysis of power (which creates and maintains boundaries in organizational form) and control (that regulates communication within specific forms of interaction). Initially he focuses upon two levels: a structural level and an interactional level. The structural level is analysed in terms of the social division of labour it creates (classification) and the interactional level with the form of social relation it creates (framing). The social division of labour is analysed in terms of strength of the boundary of its divisions, that is, with respect to the degree of specialization. Thus within a school the social division of labour is complex where there is an array of specialized subjects, teachers and pupils, and it is relatively simple where there is a reduction in the specialization of teachers, pupils and subjects. Thus the key concept at the structural level is the concept of boundary, and structures are distinguished in terms of their boundary arrangements and their power supports and legitimations (Bernstein 1996). The interactional level emerges as the regulation of the transmission/acquisition relation between teacher and taught: that is, the interactional level comes to refer to the pedagogic context and the social relations of the classroom or its equivalent. The interactional level then gives the principle of the learning context through which the social division of labour, in Bernstein's terms, speaks.

He defines modalities of pedagogic practice in terms of principles for distinguishing between contexts (recognition rules) *and* for the creation and production of specialized communication within contexts (realization rules). Modalities of pedagogic practice and their discourses may then be described in terms directly referenced to the theory. Features of cultural artefacts may be described in terms of the cultural context of their production. Bernstein (1993) argues that much of the work that has followed in the wake of Vygotsky "does not include in its description how the discourse itself is constituted and recontextualized".

For Bernstein power relations regulate the degree of insulation between categories. Boundaries are established and challenged in relationships of power. For him power establishes "voice" in that it demarcates that which is legitimate within categories and thus establishes the rules by which voice may be recognized. The distinction between what can be recognized as belonging to a voice and a particular message is formulated in terms of distinction between relations of power and relations of control. Bernstein (1990) adapted the concept of voice from his reading of *The Material Word* by Silverman and Torode (1980). He grounds the concept in the material division of labour, thus allowing for the move between the analysis and description of the social order and that of the practices of communication.

> From this perspective classificatory relations establish "voice". "Voice" is regarded somewhat like a cultural larynx which sets the limits on what can be legitimately put together (communicated). Framing relations regulate the acquisition of this voice and create the "message" (what is made manifest, what can be realized).
>
> (Bernstein 1990, p. 260)

In his last book he continues:

> Voice refers to the limits on what could be realized if the identity was to be recognized as legitimate. The classificatory relation established the voice. In this way power relations, through the classificatory relation, regulated voice. However voice, although a necessary condition for establishing what could and could not be said and its context, could not determine what was said and the form of its contextual realization; the message. The message was a function of framing. The stronger the framing the smaller the space accorded for potential variation in the message.
>
> (Bernstein 2000, p. 204)

Thus social categories constitute voices and control over practices constitutes message. Identity becomes the outcome of the voice – message relation. Production and reproduction have their social basis in categories and practices; that categories are constituted by the social division of labour and that practices are constituted by social relations within production/reproduction; that categories constitute "voices" and that practices constitute their "messages"; message is dependent upon "voice", and the subject is a dialectical relation between "voice" and message (Bernstein 1990, p. 27).

One may speak with the "voice" of psychology but the particular identity as a psychologist is revealed in the actual messages produced/spoken. Change occurs when "new" messages are produced and give rise to changes in voice/classification/power relations. Identity may be studied in terms of utterance and the principles of social regulation through which it is generated and transformed. The rules of activity theory include what Bernstein refers to as framing and the division of labour (hierarchical and vertical) refers to classification. Hasan (2002a, b) argues that Bernstein paid very close attention to invisible semiotic mediation – how the un-selfconscious everyday discourse mediates mental dispositions, tendencies to respond to situations in certain ways and how it puts in place beliefs about the world one lives in, including both about phenomena that are supposedly in nature and those which are said to be in our culture. She asserts that discourse is not treated as simply the regulator of cognitive functions; it is as Bernstein (1990, p. 3) states also central to the shaping of "dispositions, identities and practices".

Hasan (2001b, p. 8) suggests that Bernstein's analysis of how subjects are positioned and how they position themselves in relation to the social context of their discourse, offers an explanation of hybridity in terms of the classification and framing practices of the speaking subjects. The invisible semiotic mediation is to be found in the relations of power and control which give rise to voice message relation in which identities are formed and social positions are bequeathed, taken up and transformed. In Hasan's empirical work she has evidenced this effect: "What the mothers speak, their selection and organization of meanings is a realization of their social positioning" (Hasan 2002b, p. 546).

There is a need to incorporate the institutional level of regulation and analysis into the post-Vygotskian account of mediation. The advances that have been made within recent developments in Activity Theory may be supplemented through a more detailed discussion of the modalities and structure of one of the central means of mediation within schooling, pedagogic discourse. Following the suggestion that specific forms of discourse may be associated with specific forms of activity, I argue that there is a need to develop an analysis of the production of pedagogic discourse within specific social institutions. Bernstein's work allows a connection to be made between the rules that children use to make sense of their pedagogic world and the modality of that world. This is done through taking measures of school modality. Depending on the research question relevant aspects of discursive, organizational and interactional practice are measured. The connection between these measures and measures of pupils' recognition and realization rules may then be analysed (see Daniels 1995).

The analysis of pedagogic relays involved in the processes of social, cultural, historical formation within schools should not be constrained to the study of speech. A study of wall display suggests that a more broadly based form of semiotic analysis may be beneficial as we seek to understand processes of mediation in schooling (see Daniels 1989).

A study of the institutional regulation of emergent masculinities[1] and femininities suggests that the complexities of the processes of identity formation require very delicate models of the discourses of pedagogic practice if they are to be made available to scrutiny and thus change (Daniels *et al.* 1999). These studies suggest that such processes are of relevance in the study of learning (see also Daniels *et al.* 1996).

A model of pedagogy which reduces analysis to pupil–teacher interaction alone results in a very partial view of processes of social formation in schooling. Schools are organized institutions within which specific forms of pedagogic practice arise. They are institutions which give rise to the production of specific cultural artefacts such as curriculum formations and their associated modalities of pedagogic practice and discourse which mediate the teaching and learning process.

Schooling may be understood as an elaborate form of sociocultural activity. This understanding invokes a broadly based conception of pedagogy. Vygotsky's work provides a framework within which support for pupil learning and the positioning of pupils within specific discourse structures may be explored. It may also be used to consider the developmental implications of different aspects of knowledge and knowledge-producing activities. Social relations which serve to mediate processes of individual transformation and change are pedagogic relations. As yet we know too little about the nature and extent of those social, cultural and historical factors which shape human development.

Conclusion

Subject–subject and within-subject relations are undertheorized in Activity Theory. It requires a theoretical account of social relations and positioning. Holland *et al.* (1998) bring Bakhtin's notion of the "space of authoring" into play as they outline the processes of mutual shaping of figured worlds *and* identities in social practice. They also argue that multiple identities are developed within figured worlds and that these are "historical developments, grown through continued participation in the positions defined by the social organization of those world's activity" (Holland *et al.* 1998, p. 41). This body of work represents a significant development in our understanding of the concept of the "subject" in Activity Theory. For my point of view there remains a need to develop the notion of a "figured world" in such a way that we can theorize, analyse and describe the processes by which that world is "figured". However, the theoretical move which Bernstein makes in relating positioning to the distribution of power and principles of control opens up the possibility of grounding the analysis of social positioning and mental dispositions in relation to the distribution of labour in an activity. Through the notions of "voice" and "message" he brings the division of labour and principles of control (rules) into relation with social position in practice. This theoretical stance suggests that Activity Theory should also develop a language of description which allows for the parameters of power and control to be considered at structural and interactional levels of analysis. A systematic approach to the analysis and description of the formation of categories through the maintenance and shifting of boundaries and principles of control as exercised within categories would bring a powerful tool to the undoubted strengths of Activity Theory. This would then allow the analysis to move from one level to another in the same terms rather than treat division of labour and discourse as analytically independent items. Given that, in Bernstein's terms, positioning is in a systematic relation to the distribution of power and principles of control, it is argued that this approach to our understanding the notion of social positioning is the underlying, invisible component which "figures" practices of communication.

> [A] specific text is but a transformation of the specialized transactional practice; the text is the form of the social relationship made visible, palpable, material ... Further the selection, creation, production, and changing of texts are the means whereby the positioning of the subjects is revealed, reproduced and changed.
>
> (Bernstein 1990, p. 17)

My argument is that there is much to be gained through a sustained theoretical engagement with the notion of subject in activity theory and that Holland *et al.*, Hasan and Bernstein provide rich sources of inspiration for such an endeavour. Such theoretical work would, hopefully, provide tools for engaging in the empirical study of the processes of hybridization which abound in the cultures of our everyday worlds.

My argument in this chapter is that the research presented here is suggestive of benefits that may be accrued from bringing a Bernsteinian perspective to bear on Activity Theory. The three questions (mentioned above) which drive the development of Bernstein's thesis present a challenge to Activity Theory. His work seeks to theorize the ways in which the dominating distribution of power and principles of control generate, distribute, reproduce and legitimize dominating and dominated principles of communication which in turn regulate relations within and between social groups and thence produce a distribution of forms of pedagogic consciousness. This account of social formation seeks to understand semiotic mediation in terms of the cultural formation of discursive practice. Activity Theory seeks to analyse contradictions between rules, community and division of labour and cultural artefacts but does not appear to benefit from a language of analysis and description that permit a cultural artefact (such as discourse) to be analysed in terms of the cultural specificities of its production. In one sense the artefact is not easily seen as a cultural product. Bernstein could help us to "see" institutions in talk as we study activity in institutions.

Note

1 It was with some amusement that I discovered that my spell check does not have a check for masculinity while it does for femininity. It would appear that masculinity remains a singularity in some circles!

5 The work of Basil Bernstein

A non-"sociologistic" and therefore non-deterministic sociology

Jean-Yves Rochex

I would like to take my cue from Johan Muller's introduction to a collection of essays entitled *Reading Bernstein, Researching Bernstein* (2004). In "The Possibilities of B. Bernstein", Muller makes two observations with which I fully concur. First of all, in his discussion of the political implications of Bernstein's work (which extends the Bernsteinian project), Muller situates these implications within the framework of the descriptive and analytical power of the theory as a whole, inasmuch as the theory is capable of revealing and helping to conceive possibilities for political action and choice. Second, Muller insists that, unlike in Bourdieu's work, the category of *possibility* is not external to the theory and to the conceptual architecture of Bernstein's sociology. For Bourdieu, while a knowledge of the most probable (reproduction) is construed as helping to reveal other possibilities, such possibilities are not granted any status within the theory (see, among others, Terrail 1987). This is not the case with Bernstein's theory, which, in Muller's view – a view that I share – is an attempt to capture the real dynamically rather than merely statically, and thus to capture and interpret what I shall call the realized real (that which is noted, observed, analysed in the first analysis), as the realization of just one of the logical possibilities which the theory helps to describe and analyse. The real cannot be reduced to that which is realized; the analysis of the realized or dominant real is also designed to make it possible to construe and detect virtual or devalued possibilities, i.e. alternatives to the realized real. The theoretical framework, concepts and categories thus devised, used and ordered need to enable this or at the very least must be designed to enable this.

It is precisely to this extent that Bernstein's sociology may be viewed as a non-deterministic sociology. If this is the case, it is because Bernstein's work is a non-"sociologistic" sociology both in the conception of its object, attentive as it is to what Bernstein calls "the ambiguity which lies at the heart of the social" (Bernstein 1994, 2000, p. 92), and in its relations with that which it is not, especially Bernstein's desire to combine different disciplines and to foster a dialogue between them (in his latest book Bernstein references engage, among others, Durkheim, Bourdieu, Garfinkel and the ethnomethodologists, Vygotsky and Luria, "sociolinguistics", or Cassirer and

Foucault). In other words, the non-determinism of Bernstein's sociology is based jointly and severally on its "relations within" and its "relations to" other authors or theories, to use Bernstein's own categorizations. This chapter, relying for the most part on his latest work, *Pedagogy, Symbolic Control and Identity*, will largely follow the thread of Bernstein's critical dialogue with the authors and theories with and against whom he has tended to conceive and elaborate his own work.

The plurality and specificity of fields, devices and institutions

We know that Bernstein criticizes the dominant theories in the sociology of education, especially the theory of Reproduction (though the issue deserves to be raised in the context of other sociologies of education conceived as alternatives; see Rochex 1993, 2001) for remaining overly general and for eschewing an internal analysis of the structures of the pedagogical field, which they are therefore unable to describe or analyse precisely:

> The major theories of cultural reproduction which we have, essentially of the Parisian version, ... are unable to provide strong principles of description of pedagogic agencies, of their discourses, of their pedagogic practices. This, I suggest, is because theories of cultural reproduction view education as a carrier of power relations external to education. From this point of view, pedagogic discourse becomes a carrier for something other than itself.
>
> (Bernstein 2000, p. 4)

Or again:

> I clearly have gained much from reading Bourdieu; in particular, the concept of field. But there is a considerable difference which emerges out of my development of the importance of exploring within/between relationships. I would still hold that, certainly with respect to reproduction, and with respect to features of production, Bourdieu is not interested for conceptual reasons in "relations within" ... What is exposed is the game [power games and their strategies]. This necessarily follows from Bourdieu's relational analysis of fields. There is no need to show how a *specific* should have a determinate content.
>
> (Bernstein 2000, pp. 188–9)

Hence, Bernstein's critique of the overly general and, above all, homogenizing nature of Bourdieu's concept of habitus.[1]

Bernstein's interest in the plurality of fields that constitute the social space – an interest he shares with Bourdieu – is not guided by an essentially relational approach (Bourdieu),[2] but by an attempt to take account of the specificity of these fields and of the social functions which they perform, by considering them not only as *fields* but also as *agencies* (see Diaz 2001), as a matrix of activities inscribed within its own inherent order and contributing to the production of this inherent order. Hence the adoption and interest of the terms *discourse* or *device* (despite the broad, imprecise or disconcerting nature of their definition) as notions or categories capable of reflecting both the specificity of a form of social activity and the heterogeneous nature of the processes and objects (both material and conceptual) through and by which they are realized. In his own words, "pedagogy is the focus of my theory to the extent that pedagogic modalities are crucial realizations of symbolic control, and thus of the process of cultural production and reproduction" (Bernstein 2000, p. 201). The object of both his theoretical and his empirical work will therefore be to provide a descriptive and analytical account of "the potential colonizing/complementary/conflicting, privileging/marginalizing relations between local and official pedagogic modalities" (p. 201), between what he refers to as official pedagogical modalities (specific to institutions such as education) and local pedagogical modalities (specific to family, peer or "community" regulations) without ever separating this analysis from the issue of the inscription of social subjects and the institutions in question within social relations and the social division of labour.

The pedagogic device is therefore defined as "[a site] for appropriation, conflict and control" (Bernstein 2000, p. 28). This object, which pertains to a wide range of disparate fields and institutions (family, school, leisure and youth or child sociability...), and therefore the description, study and analysis of potential relations of conflict, colonization or complementarity between fields and institutions which it helps to describe and analyse between fields and institutions, nonetheless require the elaboration of a grammar and of general principles to which the concepts of discourse, device, code, classification and control contribute. The grammar and general principles need to be capable of accounting (here the ambitious and even immoderate nature of the project is in full view) both for the relations of relative autonomy of fields and institutions such as education (but also the family, which is not, however, Bernstein's main focus) and the heterogeneity of their components and the processes through which their own order is realized, maintained and transformed – thus resulting in an internal heterogeneity for which the concept of device borrowed from Foucault perhaps provides a better account than the notion of discourse (as Anne-Marie Chartier noted during the conference from which this book was conceived) and which, allied with the heterogeneity and the contradictions relating to the relations between different fields, is a source of historicity, both for social formations and for subjects.

An exacting sociologist for other disciplines

In comparison with other sociologists, Bernstein pays significantly more attention to the nature and specificity of the practices and knowledge that are constructed, deployed and transmitted in different areas of the social space. Yet Bernstein remains a sociologist, and, as such, his objective is still to describe and conceive their rootedness in the actual living conditions of social subjects, connected with their inscription within social relations and the social division of labour. The consistency of this sociological questioning is the source of the criticisms (contrary to those levelled by Bourdieu) which he levels at the various authors or theoretical trends with which he has tended to have relations of greater or lesser proximity. Bernstein criticizes what he refers to (perhaps in overly general terms) as "sociolinguistics" for failing to consider seriously the prefix (*socio*) of the word and instead focusing, in line with the ethnomethodological approach, on interactions and micro-encounters without sufficiently elaborating the principles that "should facilitate descriptions of the relations between micro encounters and their macro contexts, where appropriate" (2000, p. 149). This focus considerably limits the possibilities for dialogue and common elaboration between linguistics and sociology: "the 'socio' of sociolinguistics seems to be very narrowly focused, selected more by the requirements of linguistics than developed by the requirements of sociology" (p. 149).

The same kind of criticism is also applied to Foucault and to the tendency, common to Foucault and to many of his followers, to separate the analysis of discourse from social analysis:

> To a very great extent the foregrounding of discourse as the centre of gravity of social analysis by Foucault and other Parisians had made these authors the new definers of the social. Thus the concept of the "social" is being rewritten by non-sociologists and taken over by sociologists. It is not simply the evacuation from the use of social class but the evacuation from *sociological* analysis.... The privileging of discourse in these analyses tends to abstract the analysis of discourse from the detailed empirical analysis of its basis in social structure. The relationships between symbolic structures *and* social structures are in danger of being severed.
>
> (Bernstein 2000, p. xxvi, n. 2)

The same criticism of a non (or insufficiently) sociological definition of the social is also at the heart of the ambivalent relations between Bernstein's sociology and the work of Vygotsky and the uses of this work in what Bernstein refers to as "post-Vygotskyism", the theoretical and institutional success of which can by his reckoning be accounted for at least in part by the fact that it "enabled the salvation of the liberal/progressive position in the new performance culture" (2000, p. 62, note 2). Bernstein claims to have discovered the work of Vygotsky in the late 1950s as a result of reading an extract from *Thought and Language* published in English in the journal *Psychiatry* in 1939, and also through fruitful meetings with Luria. Bernstein frequently refers to Vygotsky's work as one of the major references upon which he founded his own thought, particularly by contrast with Piaget's theory (which he describes as "abstract structuralism") and with all the theories that tend to converge towards the "idealism of competence" achieved at "the price of abstracting the individual from the analysis of distributions of power and principles of control which selectively specialize modes of acquisition and realizations" (2000, p. 43). The major Vygotskian thesis of a social genesis of thought and consciousness through activities carried out in common with others certainly reflects his own theoretical and empirical interests, even if he was no doubt less sensitive to the variation of the procedures and processes of the semiotic mediation of social genesis, as Ruqaiya Hasan (1995) remarks. It is precisely sociological questions which gave rise to Bernstein's interest in language, in the role of categorizations or classifications, and in linguistic forms and practices as an intermediate register between the social division of labour and forms of communication and thought; hence Bernstein's use of Vygotsky's theory as a stepping stone for his own work. In fact, Bernstein is one of the few sociologists to have taken language seriously, and to have criticized as early as 1965 the relative indifference of his fellow sociologists, as well as their reluctance to "study … language as a social institution" (Bernstein 1975, p. 119): "the patterning of speech is allocated no independence in this theory nor in the behaviour which this theory illuminates" (p. 120).

Yet, for Bernstein, the reference to Vygotsky's theory remains critical. According to him, the Russian psychologist was unable to infer all of the sociological implications of his thesis because of his overly restrictive conception of development, which exposed him to the risk of linguistic or instrumental determinism:

> Vygotsky appeared to have a restricted view of development, essentially cognitive, and a practice which appears to privilege the acquisition of the "tool" rather than the social context of acquisition … The metaphor of "tool" draws attention to a device, an empowering device, but there are some reasons to consider that the tool with its internal specialized structure is abstracted from its social construction.
>
> (Bernstein 1994, p. xvii)

The issue here is not merely the need to take account, between history and the development of individuals, of the specific histories and unequal development of the various social formations, as Sylvia Scribner (1985) has already insisted in a critical discussion of Vygotskian theory, but also the need to take account of the inherent heterogeneity and inherent potential for conflict in every social formation, as Ruqaiya Hasan insists in writing that "where Vygotsky appears to see homogeneity, Bernstein, from the very beginning, sees heterogeneity" (2004, p. 36). Hasan underlines the complementary nature of Vygotsky's and Bernstein's approaches, but also emphasizes what she sees as the more heuristic and more elaborated character of Bernstein's study of the relations between family socialization and school socialization and between "local" and "official" pedagogical modalities, and the possibility of giving them their full sociological dimension:

> The school is where the business of learning is "institutionalized" but, as Vygotsky pointed out, "any learning the child encounters in school has a previous history" (Vygotsky 1978, p. 84). Bernstein's message on this issue was more elaborated: he tried to show us what previous histories of discursive participation different groups of children bring to the school and how this history might impinge on learning in school given the nature of the official pedagogic systems.
>
> (Hasan 2002b, p. 547)

I will argue that, as far as certain aspects of the relations between family socialization and school socialization are concerned, it is also reasonable to assume that Vygotsky's work allows for considerations that extend beyond those offered by Bernstein, or rather for questions other than those addressed by Bernstein to be raised.

A mode of sociological thought mindful of contradiction

I remarked above that Bernstein's sociology may reasonably be viewed as a non-determinist sociology because of a particular concern (a concern to which Bernstein's theory is more attentive than most sociological theories) for what he calls "the ambiguity which lies at the heart of the social". According to Bernstein, this ambiguity needs to be reflected in sociological theory, which he explicitly claims as one of the chief objectives behind his definitions and uses of the concepts of classification and code. But it also needs to be reflected more generally in what appears, outside of a handful of exceptions which will be referred to here, as a dialectical conception and usage of the numerous conceptual dichotomies which he develops, often in reference to one another, from one work to the next. This is especially true of the notions or concepts of boundary and classification.

Bernstein insists on the dual dimension (relational and specific) and on the dual orientation (external and internal) of insulation and classification (reflecting the permanent focus on the necessary dialectics of *relations to* and *relations within*):

> A can only be A if it can effectively insulate itself from B. In this sense, there is no A if there is no relationship between A and something else. The meaning of A is only understandable in relation to other categories in the set; in fact, to all the categories in the set. ... We can say, then, that the insulation which creates the principle of classification has two functions: one external to the individual, which regulates the relations between individuals, and another function which regulates relations

within the individual. So insulation faces outwards to social order, and inwards to order within the individual.

(Bernstein 2000, pp. 6–7)

There follows a reminder of Durkheim's analysis of the separation of the *Trivium* and the *Quadrivium* in medieval universities. For Bernstein, the issue at stake – irrespective of the relevance which historians may grant to Durkheim's argument or indeed to Bernstein's commentary – is not merely the separation of the *Trivium* (logic, grammar and rhetoric) and the *Quadrivium* (astronomy, music, geometry and arithmetic), but also the fact that the constitution of the former, which pertains to the order of the word, contributes to the related construction of "a particular form of consciousness, a distinct modality of the self" (2000, p. 83), in other words a regime of individuation or subjectification (see De Queiroz in this volume), and proves to be the condition making possible the latter, which "is concerned with abstract formulations about the fundamental structure of the world, the physical world": "it is socialization into the word that makes the abstract exploration of the world safe ... The *Trivium* establishes a legitimate form of consciousness which can then be realized in other explorations" (2000, p. 8); "Durkheim was concerned to show how the discourse of the medieval university contained within itself *a tension, even a contradiction*, which provided the dynamics of the development of the university" (2000, p. 81).

This approach to insulation and classification in terms of tension and contradiction appears to warrant greater attention than it commonly receives in most analyses and commentaries on Bernstein's work. It is also reflected in Bernstein's analyses of the two classes of knowledge, i.e. thinkable and unthinkable knowledge (or the profane and the esoteric ones in Durkheim's work), which can be likened to Vygotsky's distinction between everyday knowledge and scientific knowledge, or to Bakhtin's distinction between primary genres and secondary genres (the focus of Elisabeth Bautier's chapter in this volume) or of the two discursive modes, the horizontal and the vertical modes. Bernstein initially emphasizes the need to guard against a substantialist and ahistorical use of these categories and of their distinctions: "The line between these two classes of knowledge is relative to any given period. What is actually esoteric in one period can become mundane in another. In other words, the content of these classes varies historically and culturally" (Bernstein 2000, p. 29). It can be argued that Bernstein's views on social history apply equally to individual development and the schooling process of social subjects, during which the realm of the esoteric or of the unthinkable at a given time could pertain to the ordinary in another period, thus repeatedly activating a process of reconfiguration and subservience of pupils' relation to the world and to language that is required of them without such forms of knowledge being explicitly taught (see Bautier's chapter in this volume).

Yet it appears that Bernstein's theoretical elaborations (and the results of empirical research designed to put them into practice) entail another necessity that is perhaps less visible and more implicit: the necessity not to conceive of the relations between the two classes of knowledge and these two orders of discourse as being or having to be relations of mutual exclusiveness, but rather as being or having to be relations of reciprocal elaboration, mediation and development. I am alluding here not only to what Georges Canguilhem argued concerning the relations between ideology and rationality in the history of science and scientific theories and problems (Canguilhem 1977), but also to the dialectical conception of the relations between daily concepts and scientific concepts in the writings of Vygotsky. This is especially the case when he observes in Chapter 6 of *Thought and Language* that: "What constitutes the great force of scientific concepts is also the great weakness of everyday concepts, and vice versa.... Scientific concepts prove to be just as inconsistent in a non-scientific context as everyday concepts are in a scientific context." Both types of concepts require one another in order to develop: "Scientific concepts emerge and develop downwards through the medium of everyday concepts. Everyday concepts emerge and develop upwards through the medium of scientific concepts" (translated from Vygotsky 1985). In Bernsteinian terms, the specific meanings and strategies of horizontal discourse and "ordinary" or "profane" knowledge "are local, they are organized segmentally, are specific to the context and dependent upon it, in order to maximize the encounters with people and habitats". Those that characterize vertical discourse and "esoteric" or "scholarly" knowledge are isolated from these encounters and contexts and seek to establish relations among themselves to build a specific order, unthinkable in only one context and thus likely to be "a site for alternative possibilities, for alternative realizations" (Bernstein 2000, p. 30). Both types of knowledge and discourse are uniquely efficient within their specific orders and contexts.

Radical visible pedagogy versus pedagogic populism

The descriptive, theoretical, epistemological and axiological complexity of the issue of the relations within classes between school knowledge and school subjects, and "ordinary" knowledge and practices, which are at the heart of the work of many sociologists who have sought to use Bernstein's theoretical framework to guide and conduct their empirical research, is evident in light of the discussion above. Hence also the difficulty (though possibly also the very possibility) of acting upon the modes and constraints of classification and framing, a possibility explicitly claimed by Bernstein in pleading for a pedagogy which might weaken the connections between social classes and school "performance", which should be, according to the terms used by Jill Bourne (2004, p. 65), a "radical visible sociology", i.e. the "the radical realization of an apparently conservative practice". Bernstein writes:

> It is certainly possible to create a visible pedagogy which would weaken the relation between social class and educational achievement. This may

well require a supportive pre-school structure, a relaxing of the framing on pacing and sequencing rules, and a weakening of the framing regulating the flow of communication between the school classroom and the community(ies) the school draws upon.

(Bernstein 1990, p. 79)

The work carried out from this perspective, especially by Harry Daniels (1995) and Ana Morais and Isabel Neves (2001), shows that the attempts to weaken the framing and classification constraints and to recontextualize modes and fragments of ordinary experience and segments of horizontal discourse in the contents of school disciplines and activities are often presented as being concerned with and desiring to facilitate and democratize access to specialized knowledge. Yet, in their results, they are far from tending invariably in this direction, and may lead to pupils from underprivileged backgrounds becoming even more disadvantaged. Bernstein himself raises this issue when he remarks that what he refers to as horizontal discourse (and the blurring of the distinction between horizontal discourse and vertical discourse) can be "a crucial resource for pedagogical populism" (Bernstein 2000, pp. 169–70) and may contribute to a shift in the focus of sociological analyses and political debates "away from equality of opportunities towards a recognition of the diversity (of voices)" (Bernstein 2000, p. 170). Far from the ideologies of the "openness" and the "impermeability" of education to the outside world, "life", the "community" or the neighbourhood, commonly conceived in very general terms, far from pedagogical populism or legitimacy, these writings suggest the conception and application of a "mixed pedagogy", to use the phrase coined by Morais and Neves (2001). Beyond such dichotomies as open versus closed schools, visible versus invisible pedagogies, weak versus strong classifications and framings, or a pedagogy of discovery versus a pedagogy of transmission, the concept of "mixed pedagogy" plays subtly on the possibilities and necessities of maintaining and even strengthening or conversely of reducing and weakening the framing and classification constraints according to the different components of the pedagogical apparatus or discourse, but also according to the moments and modalities of the work over the time during which it is deployed.[3]

All of the questions that I have just evoked pertain not merely to the necessity and difficulty of a joint interpretation of relations within and relations to, but also to the necessity and difficulty of construing dialectically the relations between pedagogical or epistemological reason and sociological reason (Forquin 1987, 1989). Bernstein can be seldom faulted on this issue, except perhaps in certain passages that address the relations between two components of pedagogic discourse, i.e. instructional discourse, "transmitting specific forms skills and their relations to each other" and regulative discourse, "transmitting the rules of social order" (Bernstein 2000, p. 102). A close analysis of *Pedagogy, Symbolic Control and Identity* uncovers a number of shifts in the way in which Bernstein describes (or rather conceives, since the statements which he makes in this respect do not appear to be based on any empirical research) the relations between the two discourses or modalities of pedagogic discourse. In some passages, Bernstein claims that these discourses and the rules which they implement "can vary independently" (2000, p. 38), and that it is therefore possible to examine framing "in respect to each discourse, separately" (2000, p. 158). Yet the relative autonomy of the two discourses in relation to one another appears to be belied by other passages, such as the following in which Bernstein states (once again rather than demonstrating or arguing) not merely that "regulative discourse is the dominant discourse", but also that "regulative discourse produces the order in the instructional discourse", in such a way that we may say that "the whole order within pedagogic discourse is constituted by regulative discourse" (2000, p. 34), as if the order of instructional discourse or even of pedagogic discourse owed nothing, and perhaps *could* not owe anything, to the intrinsic order of scholarly discourse which pedagogic discourse serves to recontextualize (or to transpose, as didacticians would say), to what would thus pertain to an epistemological order enabling a reflection (without however being capable of determining them outside any context) on the most relevant constraints of classification, framing, sequencing and progress.

Symbolic control and the inherent ambiguity of the social

Besides this particular example and the changing views concerning the relations between instructional discourse and regulative discourse, it appears that Bernstein fosters throughout his latest book an open or dynamic tension for thought, between *relations within* and *relations to* and between epistemological reason and sociological reason, thus suggesting a process of keeping alive (in the sense of keeping a fire or conversation alive) required to avoid closing down the questioning and to avoid the double pitfall of legitimacy and populism. It is this concern for contradiction and for "the ambiguity which lies at the heart of the social" that Bernstein seeks, unlike most of his fellow sociologists, to represent within his conceptual apparatus and categorizations. It is a concern that leads him to claim that "control is double faced for it carries both the power of reproduction and the potential for its change" (Bernstein 2000, p. 5), that "the concept of code, which at the same time as it relays ordering principles and their related practices necessarily opens a space for the potential of their change" (2000, p. 92), and that "code acquisition necessarily entails both acquisition of order and the potential of its disturbance" (2000, p. 203). The result of this paradoxical character or the dynamic contradiction inherent in the concepts of code and control and in the concepts of pedagogic discourse and device is a resolutely non-deterministic sociology at the very heart of Bernstein's conceptual elaboration and apparatus. This is one of the reasons (an internal reason) why "the device is not deterministic" (2000, p. 38). According to Bernstein, this non-determinism is the result of two reasons, or rather two orders of reason:

The effectiveness of the device is limited by two different features: 1. *Internal*: ... although the device is there to control the unthinkable, in the process of controlling the unthinkable it makes the possibility of the unthinkable available. Therefore, internal to the device is its own paradox: it cannot control what it has been set up to control. 2: *External*: The external reason why the device is not deterministic is because the distribution of power which speaks through the device creates potential sites of challenge and opposition.

(Bernstein 2000, p. 38)

We might say that the relations which the pedagogic system has with the social world, conceived in terms of its heterogeneity and conflictuality, are internally a source of creative (or necrotizing) tensions, contradictions and discordances between its various components. These contradictions and discordances never cease to foster and renew the ambiguity at the heart of the social and to enable it to become loaded with new contents in a highly complex dialectical relation in which specific processes and generic processes, internal relations–contradictions and external relations–contradictions, are a source of potential transformations in relation to one another.

Yet the issue of the relations between the educational system and pedagogic discourse or device, on the one hand, and social conflictuality, on the other hand, is only present in a very general form and for essentially heuristic reasons in Bernstein's work (even if some who have been inspired by his work have gone further than Bernstein in this respect). It is reflected in his interpretation of the "conflict" between visible and invisible pedagogies, or between competence and performance models, as the reflection or refraction of an ideological conflict between different fractions of the middle classes (fractions located in the field of production and fractions located in the field of symbolic control) concerning the forms of control. Bernstein focuses on the working classes when he addresses the issue of the relations between differential class socialization, modes of communication, sociocognitive and sociolinguistic aptitudes and their treatment by the various official pedagogical modalities by way of better understanding the production of social inequalities in educational performance. Yet his interest in this issue is considerably weaker when he seeks to account for the evolutions of the educational system and pedagogical ideologies, which by his account are reducible merely to conflicts and rivalries between the different fractions of the middle classes. Sally Power and Geoff Whitty (2002) lead to the conclusion that Bernstein is making "the history of educational systems the history of the middle classes" at the risk of underestimating the significance of popular working-class milieux, aspirations and practices. A sustained comparative analysis of the relations between the evolution of educational systems and the different classes and fractions of social classes in Britain and France would certainly be an extremely fruitful avenue to explore, given the differences between the role of education within the political space and social conflictuality within these social formations.

Michael Apple also underlines what he sees as being a limitation of Bernstein's use of social class, which is founded on an overly static and even taxonomic (and insufficiently dynamic or historical) conception of the different social classes, conceived and described more in terms of their internal structures and characteristics than in terms of their relations (Apple 1995). Bernstein rightly responds that Apple's criticism has more to do with an appeal for an empirical research programme than an actual instance of such research, while remarking that future research in the field should be based on an "empirical base which should be more detailed and less homogenized" than that presented in *Learning to Labour* (Willis's work cited by Apple), and calling for a renewal of theoretical and empirical analyses in terms of social classes that might take account of the evolutions of the social world since the end of the twentieth century (Bernstein 1995, p. 387). Yet in a passage of *Pedagogy, Symbolic Control and Identity* Bernstein does acknowledge (though without referring explicitly to Apple's critique) that, in his theory of the various forms of symbolic control as regulatory forms of cultural reproduction and change, he "became more interested in the more general question of symbolic controls than in their class specifics" (Bernstein 2000, p. 123).

A strong conception of the social cannot do without a strong conception of thought and personality

I would like to conclude with a defence of the following hypothesis: Bernstein's thought can be extended beyond the confines of his own work on the issue of conflictuality not only concerning the relations between the social world and the educational system, but also concerning the relations between social processes and psychic processes, which will return via another route to the dialogue between Bernstein and Vygotsky.

In a study of Bernstein entitled "Subject, power and pedagogic discourse", Mario Diaz (2001) underlines the usefulness of Bernstein's work for elaborating a social theory of the human subject which only relies on a conception of the subject as decentred and non-solipsistic. Diaz rightly insists that, for Bernstein, "neither meanings nor the subject are *a priori* categories", and goes on to say that even if there is no explicit theory of the subject in Bernstein's work, his theoretical developments suggest that "the subject is produced by the setting of differences, oppositions, and locations, displacements and substitutions through which meanings are also produced" and that the subject is therefore "an inscription in the discontinuity of meanings drawn from oppositions within and between fields" (Diaz 2001, p. 88). Extending the argument, we need to take better account than Bernstein does, not merely of the inherent heterogeneity and conflictuality of the social, but also the inherent heterogeneity and conflictuality of thought and personality.

Bernstein refers frequently to his dissatisfaction in the 1950s over the dominant theories of socialization which "relied on some mystical process of 'internalization' of values, roles and aptitudes" (Bernstein 2000, p. 89). He claims to have remained concerned from the 1950s to the end of his life: "Theoretically, with what was then conceptualized as the outside → inside → outside problematic and, empirically, with problems of the class specialization of the cultures of schools and families which gave rise to different access and acquisition" (Bernstein 2000, p. 145). This is another reason for examining both questions (i.e. the theoretical and empirical questions) in his work, and their relations, which I shall do by appealing to Vygotsky and by hypothesizing that, on this point, the "advantage" which Hasan attributed to the British sociologist could be reversed in favour of the Russian psychologist.

To the best of my knowledge, and despite the passages quoted above, the issue of internalization is rarely discussed and conceptualized in Bernstein's work, probably for the same reasons that there is no explicit discussion of the question of the subject or even of subjectification (despite his evident interest in Foucault and the frequent references to Foucault's work). Such is not the case with Vygotsky, for whom development moves from interpsychic activity and functions to intrapsychic activity and functions. Through a process of internalization, language – conceived as an instrument of exchange and action upon others – becomes an instrument of action upon the self, of control over one's own activity, and thus an instrument of thought, while the dialogic discursive space instituted by interlocution becomes a mental space and consciousness becomes "a form of social contact with the self" (translated from Vygotsky 2003; see also Vygotsky 1997). Yet this movement is not a simple matter of internalization; it is a movement of development and transformation, and the internal language, a language for the self, differs from socialized and externalized languages not merely by virtue of its function but also as a result of its structure (Vygotsky 1997; see also Schneuwly 1985, 1987). More generally, in Vygotsky's work, internalization is never synonymous with reproduction at the internal level of activities and structures elaborated externally; the shift from the interpsychic to the intrapsychic is invariably a production process of development and transformation:

> The transformation of an interpersonal process into an intrapersonal process is the result of a long series of developmental events ... [External processes] take on the character of internal processes only as a result of a prolonged development. Their transfer inwards is linked with changes in the laws governing their activity; they are incorporated into a new system with its own laws.
>
> (Vygotsky 1978, p. 57)[4]

Unity and discord: thus might we characterize the relations between interpsychic and intrapsychic processes, unity being the fruit of their common instrumental and semiotic nature and discord arising out of the differentiation of their functions in systems regulated by their own laws.

Vygotsky is also particularly attentive to the plurality of psychological functions and of the components, forms and registers of psychological activity, and thus to the question of their relations. These relations, according to Vygotsky, cannot be conceived as being constant or invariant or as relations of unilateral dependence. They need to be construed both as relations of unity and as relations of discord. Vygotsky insists, for instance, on the need to consider intellectual and cognitive development on the one hand and affective and subjective development on the other, in terms of their unity, without however confusing them, and on the need therefore to consider and elucidate their relations and the development of their relations throughout the activity and history of the subjects in question. In other words, the proposed unity and discord between both registers of development suggest a conception of their relations as subject to development throughout which every function or every register may in return exert effects upon the others (on this point, see Vygotsky 1994 and Rochex 1999).

Bernstein appears to be less attentive to this relative autonomy and to the relations of discord between the different psychic functions, the various components of thought and personality, which leads him to views or claims that might be deemed to be incautious or imprudent in view of their all-embracing generality, in particular when he addresses the difficult issue of the relations between codes and change. In *Pedagogy, Symbolic Control and Identity*, Bernstein observes that:

> As Cs [classifications] and Fs [framings] change in values, from strong to weak, then there are changes in organizational practices, changes in discursive practices, changes in transmission practices, changes of psychic defences, changes in the concepts of teacher, changes in the concepts of the pupils, changes in the concepts of knowledge itself, and changes in the forms of expected pedagogic consciousness.
>
> (Bernstein 2000, p. 15)

The passage implies a generalization that appears to overlook the precautions taken for example in Bernstein's critique of theories of reproduction, so that the consideration of the social relations of power and domination do not lead to the occlusion or underestimation of the specificity (and therefore the relative autonomy) of the different registers and their internal relations, and which does not make decipherable the processes of recontextualization and reappraisal of what might occur within one such register in and through the inherent constraints of others. The quote is an echo of statements made 30 years earlier when, insisting on the relations between language and socialization, Bernstein wrote that "It would seem that a change in this mode of language-use involves the whole personality of the individual, the very character of his social relationships, his points of reference, emotional and logical, and his conception of himself" (Bernstein 1975, p. 54). In my view these quotations are indicative of the risks entailed in making an excessively dichotomous use of Bernstein's categories and concepts, in particular the categories of change and development, which he uses (in an argument that unfortunately remains underdeveloped) for the purposes of reflecting on the relations between codes, family socialization and educational experience:

> It is thought that the theory might throw some light on the social determinant of educability. Where a child is sensitive to an elaborated code the school experience for such a child is one of symbolic and social development; for the child limited to a restricted code the school experience is one of symbolic and social.
>
> (Bernstein 1975, p. 136)

While a perspective such as this may appear to be relatively fruitful for the purposes of reflecting on the relations between social class and educational inequalities, between family socialization and educational experience or between child or adolescent and pupil, we may nonetheless question the meaning that needs to be given to the opposition between change and development, the difference being construed here in terms of discontinuity versus continuity, or even incommensurability versus commensurability.

Yet many clinically based studies show that, from a psychological point of view, any development is an experience of ipseitic change, in Ricoeur's sense of the term (Ricoeur 1990), in so far as it preserves and helps to elaborate a relation of continuity between permanence and change enabling the subject to recognize what he or she was in the subject he or she is becoming or is expected to become by integrating activities and social relations that require reaching beyond the established confines of the self (see Aulagnier 1986, 1988). Some studies of statistically minor cases of educational success among children from working-class backgrounds show that their educational experience may be just one such experience of development or ipseitic change, while, conversely, a representation or sense (of which the subject is likely to remain largely ignorant, and even unconscious) of educational experience as an injunction for radical change that would not enable the preservation of the relation of continuity between permanence and change proves to be a source of serious cognitive and/or subjective difficulties that may give rise to active behaviours of educational failure or refusal (see Rochex 1995, 2000).

The issue at stake is both empirical and theoretical. It involves a reflection on cultural, linguistic and subjective change, which educational experience does indeed represent, particularly the education of children and teenagers from working-class backgrounds, as something that cannot constitute a process of eviction and/or of disqualification of their social and family experience, and creating its pedagogic (in Bernstein's sense of the term) and institutional conditions. At the subjective and symbolic level, the radical visible pedagogy which Bernstein's work helps to outline pertains to an ipseitic pedagogy that might contribute to the efficiency of the three "pedagogic

rights" which he defines, in particular "the right to individual enhancement", which he describes thus:

> I see "enhancement" as a condition for experiencing boundaries, be they
> social, intellectual or personal, not as prisons, or stereotypes, but as
> tension points condensing the past *and* opening possible futures....
> [E]nhancement has to do with boundaries and experiencing boundaries
> as tension points between the past and possible futures.... [I]t is the
> right to the means of critical understanding and to new possibilities. I
> want to suggest that this right is the condition for *confidence*.
>
> (Bernstein 2000, "Introduction", p. xx)

At a more general sociological level, the issue with which we are confronted
here is the thorny theoretical and empirical question of the homogeneous,
coherent (or plural and contradictory) nature of the systems of schemes and
devices constituted, to use Bourdieu's term, by the social habitus which, by
his account, serve to unify the different dimensions of the practice of social
agents. Bourdieu's postulate of the cohesion and homogeneity of the modes
of constitution of habitus and schemes, and of the resulting devices and practices, is currently the object of a number of theoretical and empirical criticisms. Nevertheless, can the heuristic usefulness of the notion of habitus (or
of code in the case of Bernstein) that grants and helps the agent to recognize
a "family resemblance" really be discarded, and may we assume that schemes
and devices might be stocked and juxtaposed side by side and coexist in a
state of mutual indifference or simple competition, without establishing
between them multiple (potentially conflictual) relations of interdependence
and intersignification? Can the issue of the unity of habitus or (at a more
subjective level) the unity of thought or personality, by virtue of the (well-
founded) criticism of the postulate of their coherence and their homogeneity,
really be discarded? I do not think it can, and I would argue that one possible way of going beyond this aporia would involve a holistic approach (to
be distinguished radically from the contextualist "constructivist" approaches)
to thought and personality that construes thought and personality simultaneously as an integrative (though not homogenizing) unity and as a product
of the plurality of modes of determination and therefore as a heterogeneous
unity constituted by differentiated though interdependent internal components, the relations and contradictions of which are a source of development for the subject, in the same way as the relations fostered between the
subject and the world.[5]

In my view an approach such as this is necessary for analysing (in a non-
prophetic – catastrophist or irenic – mode) the contemporary transformations of the forms and processes of subjectification, which Jean-Manuel De
Queiroz refers to in this volume and which Bernstein himself alluded to on
several occasions. Vygotsky's work, as well as the work of Wallon or of the
still largely unknown work of psychologists such as Ignace Meyerson and

Philippe Malrieu, appears to me to be incontrovertible in this respect in so far as, within the various disciplines of thought, they appear to be the most likely candidates for enabling a fruitful exchange and dialogue with sociologists. This is tantamount to saying that if we can follow Bernstein when he invites, if not Vygotsky himself, then at least the post-Vygotskians, to found their work and their theoretical elaborations on a stronger and fully sociological conception of the social, we might in turn invite, if not Bernstein, then at least post-Bernsteinians to find their own work and theoretical elaborations on a stronger and purely clinical conception of thought, personality and subjectification.

Notes

1 A similar criticism is levelled at Foucault's conceptualization of discipline, which Bernstein contrasts with Durkheim's use of the concept:

> It may be of interest here to contrast Durkheim and Foucault's concept of discipline. For Foucault, discipline equals the death of the subject through the annihilation of transgression in whose act the subject lives. For Durkheim discipline equals life for without it there is no social, no coordination of time, space and purpose. Transgression through its punishment revivifies the social. *Foucault homogenises discipline: there are no modalities each with their own consequences.* Durkheim in *Le suicide* shows the pathologies which inhere in different discipline regulations and the social basis of this variation. My work follows this approach.
>
> (Bernstein 2000, p. 206, emphasis mine)

2 Bourdieu explicitly claims that his aim is to use sociology for the purposes of a "social topology" and to interpret the social space as a pure space of positions occupied by "strictly relational entities", definable "precisely by the reciprocal externality of the positions" (translated from Bourdieu 1989, p. 9).

3 The question of the temporality of the pedagogic device and discourse would no doubt merit a more detailed analysis extending beyond the strict confines of this chapter.

4 The process of "externalization" is also a process of transformation requiring thought or affect (for example) not to "express themselves" but to "realize" themselves in different genres of discourse or different classes of works, and therefore to confront the specific norms that govern their specific order.

5 I have myself argued in favour of this type of approach at greater length elsewhere, in particular in a critical discussion of the theoretical views of Bernard Lahire (1998a, b) in Rochex (2000).

Part III

Language and the transformations of pedagogic discourse

6   Linguistic handicap, social handicap and intellectual handicap

Claude Grignon

Starting from the notion of linguistic code, I will develop in this chapter some ideas about the social hierarchy of cultures, which I first introduced in my work on vocational training. I was inspired to pursue this line of research after translating some of Basil Bernstein's work from English to French (Grignon 1971; Bernstein 1975; Grignon and Passeron 1989). I will refer here mainly to one of Bernstein's classic articles, "Elaborated and Restricted Codes: Their Social Origins and Some Consequences", from a 1964 issue of *American Anthropologist* which, interestingly, also included "Phonological Correlates of Social Stratification" by William Labov and "The Neglected Situation" by Erving Goffman.

An experimental criterion: predictability

Bernstein takes up the Saussurean distinction between language and speech. In this respect, language is all the possibilities or choices "theoretically" available to one speaker. It represents "what can be done". Speech "symbolizes", in turn, "what is done", what is said by a distinctive speaker in a distinctive situation. Between language and speech, linguistic codes determine the specific principles that serve to shape the choices a speaker makes from the range of options offered by the language spoken. These principles of choice determine "the planning procedures which guide the speakers in the preparation of their speech and which guide the listeners in the reception of speech" (Bernstein 1964):[1] the expectations and predictions of the listeners.

A language is therefore a structure, which exists apart from its uses and actualizations. One could theoretically write or draw a schema of the whole set of options, possibilities and rules which constitute it; in short, one could model it. On the contrary, speech is a process, which takes place across a period of time, occurring in a series and in a series of series. The notion of linguistic code refers to speaking and not to writing. One can browse a book, skim through it, summarize it, skip pages, etc. The table of contents and the index allow direct access to specific contents within it. Conversely, oral speech is a perpetual present. Unless it has been recorded, one cannot go back to the past of an oral speech (a previous sequence or section); one can only ask the speaker to repeat it. Likewise, one cannot hear in advance what will be said. It is somewhat like music, which is the art of time:

> The understanding of a musical work is subjected to its development during a given time. It is not instantly apprehended like a painting or a piece of architecture. One can say the same thing about literature or films, but – as far as they address the intellect – they are reducible, they can be summarized and so ignore the duration initially expected. Music, on the contrary, cannot be reduced.
>
> (Honegger 1996, p. 1026)

Hence the significance of the notion of *predictability*, which occupies a central position in the work of Bernstein; the degree of predictability of a speech, for the listeners as well as for the linguist, is the objective criterion which allows what Bernstein conceptualizes as "restricted code" to be distinguished from what he terms "elaborated code":

> If it is difficult to predict the syntactic options or alternatives a speaker uses to organize his meanings ..., this system of speech will be called an elaborated code ... with a restricted code, the range of alternatives, syntactic alternatives, is considerably reduced and so it is much more likely that prediction is possible.
>
> (Bernstein 1964, p. 57)

With this, Bernstein confers an experimental characteristic to the observations of the ethnolinguist; by allowing speech analysis not to be exclusively a matter of interpretation, he chooses an epistemology that submits theoretical propositions to empirical verification.

Moreover, by distinguishing between the two codes according to their unequal degree of predictability, Bernstein defines them not substantially and separately but comparatively. The theoretical definitions of restricted and elaborated code refer to a systematic set of oppositions where each code constitutes one of two poles. As I demonstrate later in this chapter, any comparison between the two codes is likely to be detrimental to restricted code; as soon as it is defined by its relation to elaborated code, restricted code is likely to be defined in terms of gaps and deficiencies.

Codes, classes and cultures

Linguistic codes (or speech systems) are "the consequence of the form of the social relationship" or, more generally, a "quality" or a "function" of the social structure that Bernstein inserts between language and speech:

> Between language in the sense defined and speech is social structure. ...
> Changes in the form of the social relationship can affect the planning

procedures an individual uses in the preparation of his speech and it can affect the orientation of the listener.

(Bernstein 1964, p. 56)

The "form of the social relationship" on which the linguistic code depends can be situated at the institutional level. It is the case of the ideal type of the restricted code (restricted code, lexicon prediction), when "the organization and selection of all signals is bound by rigid and extensive prescriptions", for example when "religious, legal and military social structures" impose on speakers and listeners an impersonal, ritualized and routine speech that must be reproduced verbatim. Here, prediction and predictability concern not only syntactic choices but also the choice of vocabulary and leaves no room for verbal expressions of personal differences. In this case, Bernstein states, each actor speaks or listens according to the social status to which they are assigned; "the individual is transformed into cultural agent". The code reinforces the form of the social relationship by restricting the verbal signalling of differences.

The same limits on the verbal expression of personal differences are also present in more widely employed restricted codes, where high prediction concerns only syntactic options (restricted code, high structural prediction). These codes can be found particularly in closed (most often dominated) groups – which are highly integrated and which demand from their members a high level of adherence and conformity – and are based on a strong and "sectarian" opposition between "in" and "out", "them" and "us". This is the case for "closed communities", such as prisons or combat units, for peer groups of children or teenagers, and even between married couples of long standing. These codes can be observed also in social interactions more or less linked to those groups such as close friends in a bar or youth "on a street corner".

The development and the use of codes depend on the social origin – that is on the position in the social hierarchy of the milieu in which an individual learns to speak. Linguistic codes are not only a way of speaking. They result also, through speaking, in a way of thinking; mental habits and intellectual connections are acquired and fixed as soon as the child begins to speak and discovers at the same time their surroundings, the way people and things which surround them answer and react to their tests, propositions and provocations, and the sanctions sent back. The learning of linguistic codes is a process of socialization, the formation of the social personality; each time they speak, the child:

learns the requirements of his social structure ... The identity of the social structure ... is transmitted to the child essentially through the implications of the linguistic code which the social structure itself generates. From this point of view, every time the child speaks or listens, the social structure of which he [*sic*] is part is reinforced and his [*sic*] social identity is constrained.

(Bernstein 1964, pp. 56–7)

The use of the restricted code is not a distinctive attribute of the working class. Bernstein maintains the sociological observations that show that working-class speakers are more likely to be relegated to the exclusive use of the restricted code while speakers from the middle and upper middle classes have access to and, depending on context, employ both restricted and elaborated codes:

> Children socialized within middle-class and associated strata can be expected to possess both an elaborated and a restricted code while children socialized within some sections of the working-class strata, particularly the lower working-class, can be expected to be limited to a restricted code.
>
> (Bernstein 1964, p. 66)

This is "very broadly" what can be said; it is possible to add some nuances, to go into particulars here. It remains, however, that this scheme associates restricted code with the working class. In the topology Bernstein proposes, the restricted code is located at the bottom along with the working class and the dominated.

This social positioning is itself associated with the limitation of the linguistic possibilities of restricted codes. The axis of the technical characteristics and of the practical possibilities the two types of code offer are superimposed upon the vertical axis representing social hierarchy; the social "inferiority" of the restricted codes corresponds with their technical inferiority (Figure 6.1).

Indeed, restricted codes:

- reduce the capacity of personal expression and of improvisation (hence the high degree of predictability of speech); the liberty of speech of the speaker limited to a restricted code is reduced. Speakers cannot express their "self" by varying their verbal selections; rather, they have to use an extra verbal channel by varying their gestures, their tone of voice, their mimics or their "physical set". This is what Bernstein calls "the vitality of the speech" but it can be said it is a regression behind the language and therefore the extra-verbal channel can be termed an *infra-verbal* one;
- present an obstacle to analytic and abstract thought; speech produced in restricted code is likely to be concrete, narrative and descriptive;
- present an obstacle to the logical organization of speech. They allow the speaker to speak with great fluency, but this hasty and continuous flow of words and meanings lacks clarity and consistency: "there might well be logical gaps in the flow of *meanings*." A speech delivered in a restricted code is less articulate than a speech delivered in an elaborated code: "In fact, the observer might find that the meanings were strung together like beads on a string rather than being logically ordered."

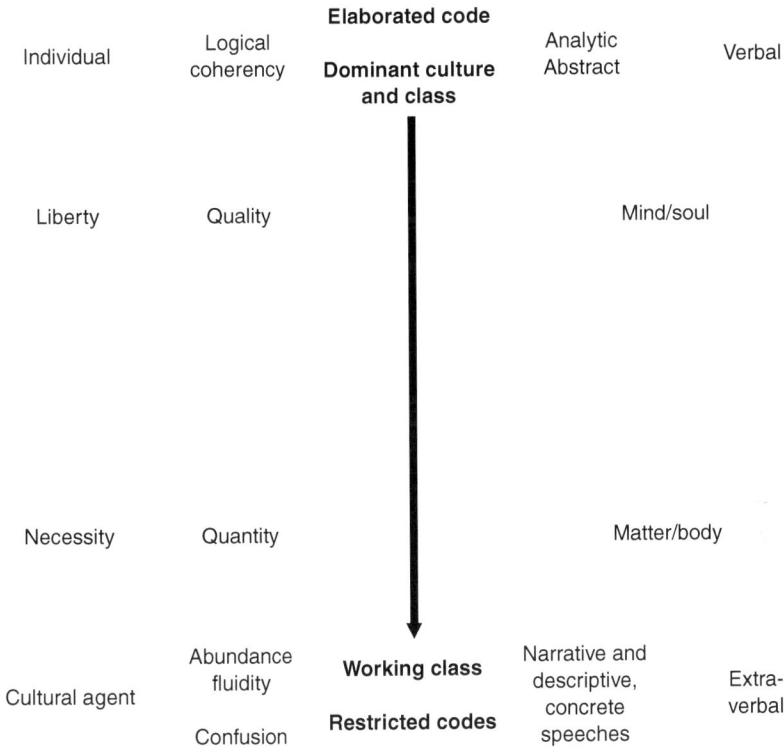

Figure 6.1 Oppositions and connotations.

This system of oppositions and associations, explicitly expressed in Bernstein (1964), asks a set of questions, which could be considered, to various degrees, objections.

There are restricted codes that are socially neutral. The most restricted codes (lexicon prediction) can be thought of as the most neutral because they are the most technical. They can be found in situations of emergency, when one must act quickly to prevent or to remedy a risk; when one has to execute listed and planned "manoeuvres" or manipulations by conforming to unambiguous instructions obtained by giving equally unambiguous information, by conforming to a protocol without any possibility of interpretation. These situations are perhaps never absolutely neutral (e.g. the dialogue between a male surgeon and his female assistant); but to forget their practical and technical dimension, the requirements for a successful operation, the degree to which they are submitted without delay to the sanction of reality, would lead to sociologism. Besides, the social relation between the one who gives instructions and the one who gives information and executes orders can be inverted (e.g. the case of the chief pilot and the air-traffic controller).

These protocols are technical routines. But the most predictable speech and the most restricted codes are also found in religious or political rituals, in the honorary ceremonies characteristic of the culture of the ruling classes, in the "higher" forms of social comedy (not only in the bar or on the street corner); here, in the symbolic (rather than the technical) order, in the order of decorum, the term "protocol" takes another meaning, it stands for "etiquette". Restricted codes are therefore to be found among the upper classes, indeed, among the ruling part of them. Speeches at receptions of the Académie française or the first address of a newly elected politician are highly predictable. Moreover, there are some "anthropological" invariants which can be observed at every level of the social hierarchy: in the functioning and the constitution of groups, in their relation with the out-group and, especially, in the demands they make of their members. In a way, there is no difference between a village society and a Grande Ecole; both are closed groups, locally based societies (Ecole Normale Supérieure of rue d'Ulm, École centrale of Lyon, etc.). Personalities who confront each other inside the groups from which the ruling classes recruit are bearers of status in the competition for superior status; membership inside this group gives to the certificated, titular individual a social status, which authorizes them to take the floor and seize power.

The most outstanding "products" of the literary Grandes Ecoles, those who appear on the political and intellectual stage, stand for and are perceived as exceptional personalities, original (even strongly peculiar) "selves". However, despite their super-sized egos, these personalities are at the same time "characters" that play a role in the repertoire. They produce exemplary speeches, that is to say speeches in conformity with the culture of which they are natives and with the orthodoxy they contribute to building and to maintaining. One can mimic and reproduce these speeches because they are predictable. Like caricatures, *pastiches* identify and amplify the distinctive features of a writer because these features are part of his expected originality and are likely to be found in his texts (see *A la manière de* or *Le petit Barthes sans peine*).

By drawing a correspondence between restricted codes, vernaculars and working-class cultures, one runs the risk of reactivating a restrictive conception of those cultures that defines them negatively, with reference to middle-class cultures, and therefore in terms of deficiencies and what they lack. Thus, the variety of working-class cultures is often forgotten; one ignores their positive aspects, that is to say the resources and possibilities they offer as far as practical knowledge is concerned, *savoir-faire* (the fitting in with living conditions) and *savoir-vivre* (the fitting in with social relationships). Besides locally based cultures there have been (until now) technical cultures, craft cultures linked to craftsmen or skilled workers, and household cultures (linked to odd jobs, gardening, sewing, etc.). Technical culture is partly theoretical and partly practical; the knowledge and processes it requires can be learned in books, at school, in training courses, and can be transmitted through speech.

However, its processes can be learned and accomplished, if not without speaking, at least with little speaking. Manuals and directions for use are rarely read comprehensively; drawings and schemas are preferred, even for computers or software. As such, technical activities can be linked to the use of restricted code; they often correspond to emergency situations, where communication is reduced to an exchange of information and instructions. But one can say equally that speech is not (always) needed to learn and practise; they are learned also and, above all, through mimesis and practice by observing and handling. Socialization proceeds not only through the learning of language and relations with others; it proceeds at the same time through the exploration of material surroundings and the manipulation of things (which generally do not speak, except for talking toys and devices). At the same time as one learns to speak, one has to develop knowledge of the basic know how of everyday life and to learn elementary body techniques. Knowledge of technical activities and actions upon things is transmitted mostly through the extra-verbal channel; but so far as they do not deal with a relationship with other speakers they are not a lower form of verbal communication. In this case the extra-verbal channel, defined as a set of efficient gestures, is not infra-verbal. Technical activities allow the development a particular form of sensibility, of gentleness of touch, even a sort of manual intuition, which allows one to guess how to use a tool when manipulating it.

Symmetrically, drawing a correspondence between elaborated codes, the upper-middle-class and dominant cultures risks obliterating the diversity as well as the negative aspects of the latter. We tend to think spontaneously that the richer and more learned a language, the more possibilities for choice in terms of vocabulary or syntax. The most learned and elaborated languages would therefore demand the most elaborated codes, the only ones able to provide access to the set of choices they contain. Indeed, whereas the restricted code requires the use of the extra-verbal channel, the elaborated code allows for oral speech to resemble the written language; one can then "speak like a book". But there is a need to distinguish among learned languages, between specialized scientific languages, which are (unequally) formalized, and the literary language, which is an elaborated variant of what is called "natural" language (and could also be called "ordinary" or "current" language). If literary language offers more possibilities for choice, it is because of its greater complexity but also because of its useless complication. French language, for example, is full of archaisms. Continuing to assign a gender to clothes, vegetables or stars may favour the expression of feelings and personal emotions and be useful to poets; but it is useless, if not awkward, when one tries to develop logical reasoning. The flexibility, which gives "natural speech" its power of evocation entails semantic anomalies: homonymy, synonymy, allotaxies, homotaxies, etc. (Gardin 1974, p. 83).

Conversely scientific languages are simplified and impersonal languages that offer their speakers reduced possibilities for choice and, as a rule, leave no room for subjectivity. This is particularly the case for formalized languages where, for example, a mathematician or a physicist applies an elaborated code to a restricted language. Bernstein (1964) suggests distinguishing between two modes of elaborated code: "one mode facilitates relations between *persons* and the second facilitates relations between *objects*." For the working class, this opposition corresponds probably to the opposition between local culture and craft culture and, for the middle class, to the opposition between literary culture on one side and scientific and technical culture on the other; an opposition fostered by the dualism of the French educational system.[2]

Social inequalities or intellectual inequalities?

These explicit oppositions cannot but evoke implicit ones for the learned reader. This occurs each time sociological realism is conducive to a hierarchical classification. It may induce one to reintroduce not only value discriminations but general and ultimate oppositions, dualisms that draw their intellectual authority and power of persuasion from the philosophical tradition.

So the idea of restriction calls for the idea of constraint. The greater predictability of speech in the restricted code; its greater conformity to group expectations, and its lesser ability to express the individuality of the speaker leads to the conclusion that those employing restricted codes are less free. From the statement that the life of members of the working class is actually in every field limited by the scarcity and insufficiency of the resources at their disposal leads to ideas that the life of members of the middle class is freer, less submitted to the "laws" of economy and history, that their opinions and tastes are less subjected to social determinisms. This goes back to the philosophical opposition between Necessity on the side of those who suffer domination and Liberty for those who exert domination.[3] The idea that restricted codes produce more abundant and more fluent speech that is less punctuated, less articulate and therefore more confused refers to the opposition between quantity and quality. The idea of quantity calls for the ideas of vitality and generosity but also rudeness and voracity; witness the literary stereotype of the overabundance of appetite and food among the working class (Grignon 1988). Quantity is spontaneously placed on the side of the *Populace*, that is to say the Many, the undifferentiated mass in opposition to the Few, the strongly differentiated "personnes de qualité", polished, with delicate tastes. Through its vitality, the Populace represents and embodies Nature when Culture is necessarily on the side of the elite and the ruling classes. The opposition between speech and the extra-verbal channel, the latter referring to messages delivered by the body, refers to dualisms which are themselves associated and more or less intertwined as Mind (or Soul) versus Body or Mind versus Matter (the latter opposition being very common in sociology and anthropology under the opposition between "symbolic" and "material").

These implicit oppositions do not withstand the presentation of objections and counterexamples. This is the case for the couple liberty/necessity. As I have demonstrated, the speeches of the leaders who occupy dominant positions in the intellectual milieu are highly predictable and conform to the expectations of the opinion that they contribute to shaping. The "Maîtres à penser" improvise only within the constraints on vocabulary and prescribed figures in a repertory upon which the literary intellectuals, along with the groups from which they originate and to which they address their speech, agree. This is also the case for the opposition between quantity and quality. The speech produced through elaborated code may be, and often is, prolix. So it is with texts: like the speaker, the learned writer has a wide knowledge of the wide range of possibilities offered by the learned language. A legacy of the pedagogy of the Jesuits, amplification is an essential element of literary education (Durkheim 1969); to deal with a subject, in a dissertation or a lecture, one must develop it by exploiting all the resources of the "natural language" including its anomalies, its ambiguities and its incoherencies. As a consequence, prolixity is closely associated with obscurity, more or less deliberate and elaborate, with confusion, indetermination of the terms, with a lack of precision and with a lack of logical consistency.

Besides these connotations, one piece of evidence remains: relegation to an exclusive use of restricted code prevents working-class children from being successful at school and, thus, from being socially successful. Bernstein states: "As a child progresses through a school it becomes critical for him to possess or at least to be oriented toward, an elaborated code if he is to succeed." Moreover, to what extent does the linguistic handicap that penalizes working-class children result in an intellectual handicap? Does the impossibility of access to the elaborated code generate inhibitions and blockages in learning? Does it prevent working-class children from crossing some thresholds? Does it prevent them from acquiring and learning to handle the most efficient tools of thought? More particularly, does it prevent them from gaining access to abstract thought? Does it eventually relegate working-class schoolboys and girls to the less elaborate levels of thought?

To what extent does this intellectual handicap contribute to poor achievement at school? To what extent does it explain and somehow justify dropouts? Conversely, to what extent do achievement problems and failure at school strengthen and reinforce this handicap? To what extent do these two mechanisms contribute to and mutually reinforce one another? For Bernstein it is social rather than biological heredity which determines one's orientation towards one type of code or the other. Children limited to the restricted code are inherently neither less gifted nor less clever than children who have access to elaborated codes; but using only restricted code induces in the long run a diminution of intellectual performance and of performance at school.

This deterioration in verbal IQ, discrepancy between verbal and non verbal IQ tests and failure to profit from formal education on the part of

> working-class children ... is thought to be closely related to the control
> on types of learning induced by a restricted code.
>
> (Bernstein 1964, p. 67)

By ranking the linguistic codes according to the level of thought and intellectual performances they allow, one thwarts a relativist (and populist) mood
and dogma that denies in every domain the existence of hierarchies. One
takes the risk of being mocked for naive evolutionism and suspected of
legitimism:

> How can you talk about different levels of thought unless you reintro-
> duce the notion of primitive thought? Can you distinguish between dif-
> ferent levels of culture, knowledge, of intellectual practices, and even
> tastes, unless you adopt the categories and the criteria of classification of
> the dominant culture and class?

Since cultural relativism does condition the parting from the dominant ethno-
centrism that is the basis of sociology and anthropology, such a suspicion is
particularly daunting for sociologists and anthropologists. But, on the other
hand, cultural relativism is also the starting point and cornerstone providing
support for a general and absolute relativism. By extending it to a linguistic
relativism, one transforms it into cognitive relativism. To lay down as a principle that all languages are equal, that they offer the same possibilities, the
same resources, the same equipment, that oral language has the same value as
written one, that it is inconsequential whether one knows several languages or
is restricted to a vernacular, is not only an obvious dismissal of realism; it is
also a choice in favour of a purely symbolic conception of languages which
leads to consideration of them not as tools of thought but rather as ornaments.
On the contrary, one drifts into legitimism when one forgets that the technical
definition and hierarchy of the kinds of thought are never completely independent from the arbitrariness of social hierarchies and of academic classifications. But one drifts into sociologism, and by the same token one gives a
handle to relativism, when one only says and repeats that intellectual hierarchies are so closely linked with social hierarchies that they blend into them
and that the idea of disentangling the two must be abandoned. On the contrary, this relationship must be examined and clarified as far as possible.

To conclude, let us consider the example of abstraction. The organization
of the French educational system transforms into a social fact a hierarchy of
intellectual activities that, as Durkheim (1977) has noted and regretted in
*Evolution of Educational Thought: Lectures on the Formation and Development of
Secondary Education in France*, privileges the more abstract types of knowledge: formerly, ancient languages and grammar; nowadays, mathematics (as
success at mathematics conditions access to scientific and medical studies in
the current French educational system). Hence, one can say that this organization promotes and rewards abstraction. However, by the same token, it

imposes a peculiar definition of it, one that is restrictive and even negative. Vocational learning and, even more, apprenticeship and preparation for working-class trades, occupy the lowest rank in the hierarchy of school subjects and types of learning institutions (from academic on top to technical education at the bottom); thus, this hierarchy keeps reproducing the old opposition between intellectual activities assimilated to the professions and the servile tasks and the fulfilment of material needs through material means and action on matter still more or less associated with the so-called "manual" trades. At the top of this hierarchy are the fields of knowledge deemed most abstract and thus of less use, more distant from reality, and less oriented towards labour and action on things. Abstraction, then, is defined as something without content. Such a social definition of abstraction differs greatly from the technical ones, such as the definition given by Piaget: "the power of forming operations on operations", of "elaborating relations between relations", a power:

> that allows knowledge to pass beyond the real and opens the endless way of the possible by the mean of the *combinatoire*, setting the knowledge free from the gradual, step by step constructions on which the concrete constructions continue to depend.
>
> (Piaget 1996, p. 53)

Predominant in the French literary educational system, the social definition of abstraction fosters the taste for general ideas, i.e. for the ideas that seem general only since they do not correspond to anything specific and thus are impossible to define, lending themselves to endless developments and debates. This definition diverts pupils from scientific education represented only by mathematics; it discourages the mind of observation and the experimental curiosity which are essential elements of the scientific mind, and which no doubt are to be encountered among working-class pupils as well.

Notes

1 The forthcoming quotations, with no references, refer to this same article.
2 As Bernstein notes, "it may have some relevance to the present problems of C.P. Snow's *Two Cultures*".
3 Regarding the opposition between "tastes of necessity" and "tastes of liberty", see *Le Savant et le Populaire* (Grignon and Passeron 1989, pp. 138–41).

7 The analysis of pedagogic discourse as a means of understanding social inequalities in schools

Elisabeth Bautier

For more than 40 years, the work of Basil Bernstein has provided vital insight into the relationship between schooling and social inequality. With the emergence of new theoretical developments that draw a close connection between language (in all the complexity of its uses in school) and recent shifts in prevailing educational objectives, values and practices,[1] the relevance of Bernstein's work has increased. Bernstein's dual (cognitive and sociological) perspective on language fosters an understanding of how schools often confront pupils from working-class backgrounds with situations that prove difficult and may even discourage them from learning and, particularly, from developing and using forms of language which can activate and enable access to new forms of (previously "unthinkable") knowledge and cognitive aptitudes.

In retrospect, it is surprising that the debates generated by Bernstein's work (particularly his work in the sociology of education and the sociology of language) have tended to focus so little on his conception of language (which was particularly innovative at the time). They have focused rather on issues that are chiefly ideological or, indeed, on the relatively secondary (though often pertinent) critique of the relations drawn between certain linguistic elements and thought operations in Bernstein's description of sociolinguistic codes.

In the context of education, language cannot be reduced to its value as an instrument of social domination and marking or to its function as a symbolic and cognitive "tool" that cannot be mobilized equally by pupils in so far as it is largely connected with their primary socialization in the home and community. Nor can language be reduced merely to its pragmatic functions, which may be studied through the analysis of conversational exchanges – even if, in view of current pedagogical practices, the construction of knowledge in schools and classrooms depends on these exchanges. Yet it is precisely by considering together the various and constantly interacting dimensions of language that we can gain an understanding of the processes through which language can undertake one of the most important roles in the construction of educational difficulties for some pupils and, hence, in the construction of educational inequalities. This is particularly the case if it is assumed that the enunciative possibilities encountered by pupils play an integral role in their construction as individual and distinct subjects, i.e. as social subjects and subjects of educational and non-educational learning.

The democratic challenge (i.e. the democratization of education and access to knowledge) is at the heart of the issue addressed in this chapter. In short, I aim to explore the extent to which the evolution of educational practices examined in their social context and within the context of the effective practice of teaching tends to favour the individuation and school acculturation of a socially situated subject.

A greater understanding of these issues may be gained from considering the theoretical similarities between Vygotsky's psychological conceptualizations of the relations between language and thought and Bernstein's sociological theories of language and language use in the context of socialization. The connection between Vygotsky and Bernstein is useful for theorizing and analysing teaching practices and pedagogic discourse as well as the resources that are thus constructed and that are (or are not) made accessible to students. More specifically, it makes possible an understanding of how intersubjective productions (i.e. the discourse generated between different actors within the classroom) are liable to become intrasubjective resources fostering new linguistic (and, consequently, cognitive) possibilities for pupils. These resources and possibilities are required by pupils in order to learn, to conceive of knowledge and learning, and to produce reflexive discourses or texts that demonstrate this knowledge. For some pupils, these resources and possibilities do not reflect the language they already know and use in the ordinary everyday context of non-educational life. Therefore it is the proximity between psychological and sociological conceptualizations, and what this proximity offers to an analysis of the language and linguistic conditions of class work, which help to make clear why certain class practices may be inadequate for the purpose of developing new linguistic and cognitive aptitudes.

Bernstein's analyses and concepts are useful for examining jointly issues surrounding the practical use of knowledge, forms of control and, therefore, pedagogy, as well as the role of language and its connection to the two former domains. Bernstein's latest book (2000) focuses more specifically on the inherent connections between the cognitive and social significance of issues – such as educational forms, the conception of knowledge (and, in particular, the transition from "knowledge" to "competence"), and the nature of the "pedagogic" discourse and types of interaction generated in the classroom – that are usually approached by each of these perspectives separately and without recognition of the inherent connections between them. The connection Bernstein draws here, then, is both innovative and heuristic. In making this connection, he provides crucial insight for understanding not merely the heterogeneity of the factors contributing to inequality but also, and perhaps above all, for understanding the significant cohesion of the forms and components of the pedagogic situation in terms of their effects of cognitive and cultural domination, particularly when these forms and components are implemented by and on pupils from working-class backgrounds. The different elements constituted by forms of discourse, classification and framing (in other words, the formal articulation of knowledge and the objects of knowledge, the mechanisms by which they are there to be seen and worked upon, the language exchanges that "carry" them, etc.), as they relate (or not) to the ordinary and "everyday" practices of some pupils can serve to distance them from the targeted knowledge. The opacity of the resulting situations (i.e. the classroom learning situations thus constructed) takes no account of the linguistic and cognitive skills, habits and attitudes of these pupils that may hinder learning and access to discourses of knowledge as sites of the "unthinkable" (i.e. knowledge of what is not "already there") and to new cognitive possibilities and the elaborations and re-elaborations of knowledge necessary for realizing them.

Based on my research findings, I hypothesize in this chapter that the cohesion outlined above plays a determining role in the construction of inequalities.

In short, by highlighting the interactions between cognitive, sociological and pedagogic perspectives, Bernstein's theoretical framework provides the basis for a close analysis of linguistic issues in (and of) the school and, therefore, of the issue of the democratization of education and access to knowledge. The different models developed by Bernstein are particularly helpful in illuminating the role of schooling in constructing social inequalities, where education is effectively carried out in alignment with certain class practices on a daily basis and where the school is conceived as an institution responsible for shaping and diffusing values and conceptions of social subjects, knowledge and learning. The heuristic value of Bernstein's work is clearly all the greater in light of his conception of "enhancement". He states: "Enhancement is not simply the right to be *more* personally, *more* intellectually, *more* socially, *more* materially, it is the right to the means of critical understanding and to new possibilities" (Bernstein 2000, p. xx). This conception confers significance to school learning and to the acquisition of new linguistic and cognitive aptitudes, and it is precisely from the perspective of the supposed functions of school outlined here that the following analyses need to be understood.

In continuing these introductory remarks, I would like to emphasize another (and not the least) of Bernstein's contributions: the possibility his theoretical framework provides for giving a general and generic value to descriptions of data drawn from particular situations. This dimension is rare in current research in the human and social sciences. Bernstein inscribes micro-level (situational) data within a macro-sociological framework and his analyses thus acquire the substance which the significant contextualization of current qualitative research tends to remove. Because of a constant oscillation between empiricism and theory, his work stands as an example of what research in the social and human sciences needs to amount to in order to construct and incrementally develop knowledge pertaining in particular to the social and educational world.

This epistemological observation implies another that is one of the major interests of Bernstein's work as it applies to the question of education in France today. Namely, a Bernsteinian approach serves to "re-sociologize" issues of inequality in the processes of the transmission and appropriation of knowledge. I say "re-sociologize" because, in the 1970s, educational and social inequalities and educational difficulties experienced unequally by different groups of students were sociologically conceived, on the basis of the work of Bourdieu and Passeron, as being connected to the reproductive function of education. Yet, since the 1980s, a process of de-sociologization has tended to favour analyses which emphasize cognitive difficulties and deficits, a lack of motivation and psychological issues (i.e. reasons which serve to individualize both the educational difficulties and failure experienced by some students as well as the "diagnoses" and remedies "prescribed" in addressing them)[2] in explaining these educational and social inequalities and the educational difficulties experienced by some students. Far from reducing pupils' educational difficulties to their cognitive or subjective dimensions, when they are attributed to pupils (and even, as is often the case, to causes external to schools, such as family or community situations), or to their didactic or pedagogic dimensions, when they are attributed to teaching methods, Bernstein's perspective conceptualizes and accounts for school interactions well beyond strictly pragmatic or didactic dimensions. Pedagogic discourse and class interactions are conceived, from the point of view of a sociology of language that is now largely ignored in favour of a generalized pragmatics, as social constructs in situations that have a bearing on the sociological register. Bernstein's theory implies that language and learning situations are co-constructions connected with the reciprocal adaptations of pupils and teachers, though which most often operate at the expense of pupils (see below).

The process of "re-sociologization" implies construing what happens in classrooms, in language interactions, in educational forms and in school practices more generally as an effect of social and historical conditions. Since Bernstein's theoretical framework and empirical descriptions are capable of accounting for the situation of French education (and, beyond, of situations in other European or South American countries), even though schools there have different histories and environments than the British schools to which he most particularly refers, these schools appear therefore not to be immune to the influence of the dominant values and conceptions or the social and political contexts of so-called developed countries. Neither can they be deemed to be immune to the forms of power relations, knowledge and the constitution of educational inequalities which these create. This tends to reinforce the view that educational inequalities are not a matter of "simple" pedagogic or didactic issues, which is precisely what current forms of school support for pupils still often appear to suggest. As such, analyses aimed at understanding the processes underlying the production and reproduction of inequalities and, furthermore, the reasons why practices which may contribute to this are commonly unrecognized by both teachers and pupils, need to take account of the sociohistorical context shaping these practices. This is the precisely the object of the next section.

The influence of school discourse on the co-construction of inequalities

This section of the chapter focuses on the impact of the dominant form of school discourse on inequalities in learning and access to knowledge. It examines:

- the use or application of the current form of school discourse (described below) as constituted by its forms, the enunciative sites it constructs and makes possible, its contents and objects, and what it implies in terms of pupils' interpretations, particularly regarding school work and the issues at stake in class situations;
- the conception of the role of language and its implementation in learning – a conception which, by its very nature, gives a predominant role to interactions in class;
- the impact of the current school discourse, in practice, on the effective work carried out by pupils who, since they do not mobilize the same register as the teacher thinks they do, or as other pupils do, tend to learn and construct knowledge differently.

The claims that follow are based on practical observations conducted and collected over the course of several years within my research group.[3] My argument will only be illustrated by a handful of examples since the object of this chapter is primarily theoretical, focusing on research programmes and their results.

Two contemporary and concomitant phenomena, which may combine and create obstacles to learning, tend to legitimate institutionally, and indeed account for, the predominant role of language interactions in class and their role in the production and reproduction of inequalities in education and learning.

One of these phenomena is specifically French and has a paradoxical function. In the last 15 years, language (in the different dimensions of its use and as necessary for learning, debating, explaining, narrating, representing and evoking) and communication have been placed at the heart of recommendations for educational curricula and activities from nursery school onwards. It appears therefore that all French pupils and the speech and enunciations they produce have been, or are bound to be, granted a place in the classroom. This may represent a step in the direction of increased access to learning and the formation of democratic subjects, which Bernstein views as positive aims of educational enhancement. In this respect, in "chatty" classes where pupils intervene throughout lessons and talk about work-in-progress and where the teacher speaks out loud to every pupil (and therefore to everyone), the words that are articulated, in the same way as the words which circulate, are not the object of specific work *in situ* or of a particular task resulting in educationally identified and objectified language and linguistic learning. However, in soliciting pupils' involvement, the interventions or enunciations offered by a pupil are not considered in cognitive and social terms, nor are they construed even in pragmatic terms. Rather, they are conceived as spontaneous expressions or, to use Bernstein's term, "*spontex*". This means that any intervention or enunciation by a pupil may not always be relevant to the particular situation at hand – and may even be highly *irrelevant*. Because of the freedom granted to pupils, the ability to intervene and speak results in significant disparities between them. Some pupil interventions are directly related to the task at hand. Yet, since the situation allows them to be spontaneous, other pupils express themselves outside the framework of their specific work objectives. Still others comment on the mere execution of work. The construction of inequality is thus a gradual process. Pupils' erroneous interventions, in terms of form or content, or irrelevant interventions, in terms of the cognitive objective of the given situation, are rarely the object of a reappraisal, evaluation or request for correction or justification by their teachers. Teachers' interventions may thus seem irrelevant to pupils since the language they produce is not the object of any specific work or evaluation that might make them aware of the necessity of calling upon, and therefore constructing, linguistic resources which apply specifically to (and indeed beyond) the situation at hand. Rather, the aim is to enable every pupil to intervene within the group, to sense that they are an actively participating member within the group (which some pupils deem to be sufficient in terms of "being" a pupil and responding to the expectations of the teacher and the institution; see Bonnery 2007), and even to foster a convivial work atmosphere.

Language learning (reasoning, debating and using the language of representation, of evocation, etc.) as represented in the French syllabus is, therefore, something that is not voluntarily solicited in other school situations.

A second phenomenon resulting in the omnipresence of the production and circulation of language in classrooms is only rarely mentioned in Bernstein's work. It concerns the current role of language in prevailing learning practices and in the conceptions of learning inspired by social constructivism and the equally prevailing conception which holds that it is important to encourage pupils to articulate their initial knowledge and understanding of, as well as their experiences with, the objects of knowledge before the teaching sequence actually begins. Through interactions *in situ*, pupils are expected to participate in the construction of the objects of knowledge and are expected to learn through reflexive thinking about these objects. A recent study carried out by the French Ministry of Education (see DEPP 2007), which focused on teachers of history, geography and civic education, provides a significant illustration of this trend. The study found that, while "traditional" transmission practices are still observed, these are considered by most teachers as belonging to another time. Some 91.4 per cent of history teachers claim that they "put their pupils in a situation to elaborate their knowledge based on the analysis of documents", while just 43 per cent claim that they transmit the knowledge that needs to be learnt. This trend is indicative of the changes called for by the institution, the ministry itself, i.e. the weakening of what Bernstein calls instructional discourse, the weakening of framing discourse and its embedding within a regulative discourse favouring pedagogical devices that encourage pupil interventions in the construction of knowledge.

The importance accorded to pupils' construction of knowledge raises the crucial issue of the very nature of the knowledge constructed in relation to the kind of discourse available to be produced in class. Whether this knowledge is formulated in terms of knowledge content (a currently minor view) or whether, as the (over 1,000) participating teachers claimed, the objective is instead to lead pupils towards an understanding of their work, to enable the elaboration of a critical point of view, to encourage an appropriation of concepts and to foster the ability to draw connections between different documents (a task deemed to be particularly difficult by 60.6 per cent of teachers), the question arises as to which language and which discourses pupils are able to use to produce the expected knowledge and thought operations. In other words, who produces the linguistic and discursive resources that will help them to carry out these thought operations, which are essentially unrelated to the ordinary non-educational uses employed by pupils?

This research uncovered a contradiction (or at least an apparent contradiction) between the knowledge and new aptitudes to be constructed and the rules of pedagogic discourse – i.e. discursive and control rules – that govern this construction. In Bernstein's terms, the objective described above (which currently prevails as the objective of the educational system from primary level onwards) is directed towards shaping the prospective identity of future adults, conceived in terms of a cognitive socialization that tends to value the development of pupil initiative, logical reasoning and reflexive habits more than it values an official body of established and formally constituted knowledge. Yet the pedagogic discourse that is assumed to accompany and construct cognitive socialization and classroom exchanges is increasingly enacted and conducted largely in the language of daily, non-educational interactions. This again raises the question of the resources which the school situation does or does not provide and allow pupils to develop, both through the construction of the thought categories produced by language and through the appropriate forms of thought realized as a result of pupils' familiarity with various discursive forms, in the shift from intersubjective exchanges to intrasubjective resources that may be employed in educational activities beyond the given situation. The classes observed and the high number of recorded teaching hours reveal very little in terms of pupils' successful development of resources and, more often than not, those that are developed in accordance with the conception of the language of school communication referred to above.

It is precisely this contradiction – a non-conscious contradiction of which both teachers and pupils remain unaware but one that tends to penalize pupils from working-class backgrounds on account of the language and repertoire available (or not available) to them – which Bernstein's concepts serve to highlight and analyse from a sociological point of view and from the point of view of curriculum change and the practices designed to implement it. This is certainly the case with the notion of competence, an invasive concept in classroom and work situations that is examined in the next section.

Bernstein and the issue of competence

Mirroring the emphasis placed on language and its uses in the school from nursery school onwards, and to secure its legitimacy within theories of the development and construction of knowledge, the application of social constructivist conceptions is usually accompanied by the effective demonstration of the competences acquired as a result of learning or task performance in the classroom. We need to understand what underpins the current significance of the notion of competence on both sides of the Atlantic, as it has played a significant role in the recent reform of primary education in Quebec and is included in evaluation handbooks as early as nursery school in France. It is also used widely as a criterion for the evaluation of the relevance and efficiency of education and training systems. It is equally important to understand how the concept of competence serves to shape and contribute to educational inequalities, an issue illuminated by Bernstein's analysis of the social logic of what he terms the "competence model". His analysis reveals both the ideological assumptions underlying the model and the "misappropriated" theoretical presuppositions which render the contradictions referred to above fully comprehensible. I will therefore quote at length Bernstein's "analysis of the social logic of competence".

I would suggest that an analysis of the social logic of competence reveals:

1   an announcement of a universal democracy of acquisition. All are inherently competent and all possess common procedures. There are no deficits;
2   the subject is active and creative in the construction of a valid world of meanings and practice. Here there are differences but not deficits. Consider creativity in language production (Chomsky), creativity in the process of accommodation (Piaget), the *bricoleur* in Lévi-Strauss, a member's practical accomplishments (Garfinkle);
3   an emphasis on the subject as self-regulating, a benign development. Further this development or expansion is not advanced by formal instruction. Official socializers are suspect, for acquisition of these procedures is a tacit, invisible act not subject to public regulation;

4   a critical, sceptical view of hierarchical relations. This follows from (3) as in some theories the socializer's function should not go beyond facilitation, accommodation and context management. Competence theories have an emancipatory flavour. Indeed in Chomsky and Piaget creativity is placed outside culture. It inheres in the working of the mind;

5   a shift in temporal perspective to the present tense. The relevant time arises out of the point of realization of the competence, for it is this point which reveals the past and adumbrates the future.

> Summarizing, broadly, according to competence theories there is an in-built procedural democracy, an in-built creativity, an in-built virtuous self-regulation. And if it is not in-built, the procedures arise out of, and contribute to social practice, with a creative potential. However, this idealism of competence, a celebration of what we are in contrast to what we have become, is bought at a price; that is, the price of abstracting the individual from the analysis of distributions of power and principles of control which selectively specialize modes of acquisition and realizations.
>
> (Bernstein 2000, pp. 42–3)

The assumption under this "democratic" and generous theory (since everyone has resources within them that merely need to be mobilized in any given situation) that participation in pedagogic dialogue and exchanges is possible for all results de facto in the (linguistic and, therefore, cognitive) exclusion of certain pupils. Indeed, it is not enough to solicit language use in order for it to be realized or indeed even merely realizable.

Note, as Bernstein does (speaking of the "price of abstracting the individual..."), that the prevailing theory of competences and skills contributes to the process of de-sociologization referred to above. The possibility of the differentiating dimension stemming from pupil contributions and interventions in class, or at least the way in which they might be indicative of differentiated work and levels of knowledge, is not analysed by competence theories.

It appears that pupils are universally and spontaneously competent in their ability to participate in the construction of the text of knowledge in the classroom. Yet this is not the case for several reasons that can be analysed using the Bernsteinian concepts designed to describe the dominant form and function of school discourse. I will therefore borrow Bernstein's descriptions of the effects of the logic of competences in pedagogical forms (or models, in Bernstein's work), since they highlight the social and cognitive coherence which it produces and, therefore, the accumulation of educational difficulties and inequalities referred to at the beginning of this chapter.

Bernstein contrasts the competence model with what he terms the "performance model"[4]

[Briefly, a performance model of pedagogic practice and context places the emphasis upon a specific output of the acquirer, upon a particular text the acquirer is expected to construct and upon the specialized skills necessary to the production of this specific output, text or product.

(Bernstein 2000, p. 44)]

based on their different components (i.e. the categories of time, space and discourse, evaluation, control, pedagogic text, pedagogic autonomy and economy as present in each model). I will focus here on discourse, evaluation and control, as they serve to mobilize language. The descriptions provided below account for the dominant characteristics of school practices, especially at the primary level and, paradoxically (given the attendant consequences), in schools where a majority of pupils come from working-class backgrounds. Yet this is merely an outward paradox since the practices are in conformity with the ideological presuppositions or conceptions outlined above.

In competence models,

> Pedagogic discourse issues in the form of projects, themes, ranges of experience, a group base, in which the acquirers apparently have a great measure of control over selection, sequence and pace. Recognition and realization rules for legitimate texts are implicit. The emphasis is upon the realization of competences that acquirers already possess, or are thought to possess. Differences between displaces stratification of acquirers.
>
> (Bernstein 2000, p. 45)

In the performance model,

> Pedagogic discourse here issues in the form of the specialization of subjects, skills, procedures which are clearly marked with respect to form and function. Recognition and realization rules for legitimate texts are explicit. Acquirers have relatively little control over selection, sequence and pace. Acquirers' texts (performances) are graded and stratification displaces differences between acquirers.
>
> (Bernstein 2000, p. 45)

Concerning evaluation in competence models,

> The emphasis is upon what is *present* in the acquirer's product. Consider a competence classroom where an acquirer has made an image. The teacher is likely to say "What a lovely picture, tell me about it". Criteria of evaluation of instructional discourse are likely to be implicit and diffuse. However, regulative discourse criteria (criteria of conduct and manner, and relation) are likely to be more explicit. [In performance models], ... the emphasis is upon what is *missing* in the product. Consider a performance

classroom where the acquirer has completed a painting of a house. The teacher is likely to say "What a lovely house, but where is the chimney?" Or if the acquirer has drawn a figure, the comment may well be "Very good, but your man has got only three fingers!" If the emphasis is upon what is *absent* in the acquirer's product, then criteria will be explicit and specific, and the acquirer will be made aware of how to recognize and realize the legitimate text.

(Bernstein 2000, pp. 46–7)

Since they are often expressed verbally, the modes of control exercised by teachers also constitute a significant object of analysis for the purposes of this chapter. The mode of control associated with the competence model is personalized or individualized, and emphasizes the intentions, aptitudes and reflexivity of the pupil. In the performance model, control is located in instructional discourse; it is constraining and explicitly identifies "deviances" and therefore refers to a collective norm that is external to the task itself.

In the competence model, which prevails in many classes, control is equated with regulative discourse – in other words, with a form of management of pupils' work that is relational rather than cognitive. The resulting confusion penalizes pupils who value the relational model in learning.

A return to the dominant form educational discourse (in the double sense of being apparent today and participating in domination)

The concepts of pedagogic, vertical and horizontal discourse and of control and classification appear therefore to be of particular heuristic value in addressing the question posed here regarding the role of the nature of language interactions in the classroom and its impact on learning. Despite shifts in the object of Bernstein's focus (the issue of the differentiated language and cognitive socialization of pupils is no longer central in the relevant studies here), discourse as a social construction (and not language as a human attribute, a significant "nuance") and the language that realizes it within the constraints imposed by the dominant form of pedagogic discourse remain at the heart of his theoretical construction.

Pedagogic discourse (and school discourse more generally) thus defined:

- constructs meanings and knowledge through recontextualizations that are necessarily performed linguistically;
- constructs relations of domination and control;
- constructs the nature of pedagogic exchanges (horizontal discourse versus vertical discourse) and their function (instructional discourse versus regulative discourse);
- and, therefore, regulates the knowledge that is thus constructed as well as the conditions for its realization.

The pedagogic configuration emerging from these different dimensions of classroom discourse helps in the identification of the dominant form of school discourse, especially in French priority education areas, or Zone d'éducation prioritaire (ZEP), a form of discourse closely related to the educational practices and educational devices which it constructs and accompanies, and which produces an accumulation of educational difficulties and disadvantages for certain pupils. As noted above, the prevailing form of discourse is related to the general evolution of educational conceptions and ideologies, including the social logic of competence. It is also connected with the conception of pupils and of what is currently deemed to constitute knowledge. Pedagogical devices and support also contribute to the nature of the form of discourse produced in the context of school work. The discourse is effectively realized in its more radical forms and in pre-elementary and elementary education, and produces a school socialization in young pupils that has a long-term effect on their interpretations and educational expectations. Of course, the concern here is not to postulate a priori a form of pedagogic discourse that is homogeneous in its functions and characteristics. More often than not, classroom discourse is heterogeneous and demonstrates constant – and necessary – shifts between regulation and instruction, between the language of ordinary and everyday exchanges and the language of knowledge. In this respect, pedagogic discourse manifests dominant characteristics, and its heterogeneity is open to question on account of the largely implicit articulations and the potential confusion which it tends to generate, particularly for pupils from working-class backgrounds who do not always identify these shifts or who only recall familiar elements from these changes of register.

We may thus fruitfully reintegrate within this theoretical and empirical framework the distinction which Bernstein draws between elaborated code and restricted code (EC and RC), and which current theoretical and epistemological thought does not invalidate. In connection with the oppositions drawn between competence and performance models, instructional and regulative discourse, and horizontal and vertical discourse, the notions of EC and RC, conceived as the familiarity with one and/or the other codes and the situations that elicit them, are the product of non-educational socializations and thus enable an understanding of some factors behind the educational difficulties experienced by certain pupils, particularly those from working-class backgrounds.

Based on these notions, we can demonstrate how the currently dominant form of discourse acts to leave some pupils unaware of the nature of institutional expectations as well as how it spurs them to develop neither the knowledge nor the resources necessary for constructing the expected aptitudes, and how it may even turn them away from participating in the process of the construction of knowledge. Based on over 100 hours of classroom observation, my research helps to categorize currently dominant educational methods in general or generic terms. These largely correspond to the social and pedagogical changes described by Bernstein.

Despite the educational changes referred to above, current educational practices still rest on the elaborated code, whether regarding the expected realization of texts of knowledge (texts articulated in the logic of written culture) or the cognitive mechanisms and meanings which it helps to activate. However, the pedagogic discourses and exchanges which tend to frame classroom work situations classify knowledge and accompany tasks and ways of organizing work pertain to the restricted code and to the local meanings which it constructs (i.e. the everyday nature of tacit exchanges or horizontal discourse such as it is defined by Bernstein). Horizontal discourse is a local discourse rooted in practical procedures; it is oral and wholly contextualized, and treats knowledge segmentally (i.e. *in situ*). It is invariably contextualized and connected with a specific task:

> The segmental organization of the "knowledges" of *Horizontal Discourse* leads to segmentally structured acquisitions.... Segmental pedagogy is usually carried out in face to face relations with a strong affective loading ... The pedagogy is exhausted in the context of its enactment, or is repeated until the particular competence is acquired ... In general the emphasis of the segmental pedagogy of *Horizontal Discourse* is directed towards acquiring a common competence rather than a graded performance.
>
> (Bernstein 2000, p. 159)

The extract above describes ordinary situations noted in the classroom observations on which my research draws. Note that this kind of pedagogy is illustrated in Bernstein's work by learning situations drawn from everyday life. Its application in a specific educational setting is likened to a process of adapting teaching to the targeted audience: "As part of the move to make specialized knowledge more accessible to the young, segments of *Horizontal Discourse* are recontextualized and inserted in the contents of school subjects" (Bernstein, 2000, p. 169). Bernstein then underlines the difficulties encountered by pupils who are allowed to produce "spontex" for the purposes of recontextualization: "A segmental competence, or segmental literacy acquired through *Horizontal Discourse*, may not be activated in its official recontextualizing as part of a *Vertical Discourse*" (Bernstein, 2000, p. 169). For Bernstein, the use of horizontal discourse within the terms of everyday life may admittedly help make specialized knowledge more accessible to pupils, but it may also amount to a form of pedagogical populism.

Several factors underpin the emergence of the production of horizontal discourse as the dominant school discourse. I referred to some at the beginning of this chapter, especially the emphasis on the need to establish a work group based on conviviality and participatory exchange in which everyone can (allow themselves to) contribute and intervene. Other factors contribute to the production of this form of discourse by both teachers and pupils, even if school discourse remains heterogeneous. For example, the individualization of tasks through the use of worksheets to be completed by individuals or through work in small groups tends to favour a teacher discourse that is closely tied to the provision of support and connected with the moment of execution (see Bautier 2006). The use of deictic words therefore replaces more formal or elaborated language and removes the need to resort to the words of knowledge and the words that serve to define the precise orientation of tasks and have no perceptible referent in the world. The words and expressions serving to situate knowledge objects in time and space, and which are precisely those which young pupils are required to learn in order to understand the cognitive work to be done ("over", "under", "above", etc.), are replaced in the restricted code by "here", "there", etc.

It has also become common in ordinary classroom practices and ministerial recommendations to assume that pupils (inasmuch as they are identified with and by their words, experiences and interests) will be all the more respected and motivated and their meanings will be all the easier to construct if objects and knowledge are connected with an everyday world of reference that values and acknowledges them and if the syllabus in working-class environments is based on the experiences and objects of everyday life familiar to working-class pupils. However, these experiences and objects largely contribute to the production of an everyday language, a tacit language and largely implicit form of communication also representative of the restricted code.

Despite these assumptions, if the recontextualization of segmented knowledge, or experiences, and the transformation of horizontal discourse into vertical discourse and the discourse of knowledge, which is more general and generic, are not put into practice through "close" school support aimed at the acquisition of this type of language use and aptitude for knowledge acquisition, pupils are unlikely to be able to achieve this on their own, unlike the social logic of competence.[5]

Horizontal discourse and the construction of inequalities

The co-construction of inequalities is situated within the logic of these processes. The notion of socialization – specifically the notion of cognitive and language socialization – is crucial here. The concept corresponds to the notion of cognitive orientation constructed through linguistic habits, a notion developed in Bernstein's early work. What kind of socialization and what work habits and uses of language does education construct for pupils? We may submit the hypothesis that if the situations constructed in class do not contribute to new cognitive and language socializations enabling the aptitudes presupposed by schools, pupils from working-class backgrounds may "fall into the trap" of horizontal discourse and remain unaware of the rapid and largely implicit shifts (where these exist) between horizontal discourse and vertical discourse. By virtue of its affective and communitarian dimensions, and in accordance with spontaneous language (i.e. the language of ordinary everyday life), horizontal discourse conveys the impression of the potential and equal participation of all pupils in school dialogue for the purposes of constructing the discourse of knowledge. However, there are several reasons why these oral exchanges, produced in restricted code, are in fact an illusion.

Highly differentiated enunciation and work registers for pupils

The linguistic interactions that occur in classrooms often have a conversational appearance: they involve non-educational everyday language (i.e. the words and discourse of knowledge are rarely used, explanatory discourse is rarely used) and rapid exchanges from person to person which do not lead to the construction of new knowledge (or, indeed, to the elaboration and "working-over" of language required for the construction of this new knowledge). As noted above, this convivial form of linguistic interaction conceals profound inequalities in pupils' register (i.e. situation-specific language varieties), which may be communicative and expressive for some and cognitive for others, as they participate in class. Furthermore, the pronounced localization and segmentation of knowledge corresponding to the horizontal discourse generally accompanying and regulating these interactions, procedural tasks and knowledge-building exercises mean that they are most often short-lived for pupils. This discourse conceals the hierarchical classification of forms and objects of knowledge and, as such, does not allow for the accumulation of knowledge. In accordance with the social logic of competence, it conceals the cognitive demands that are expected from all but effectively realized only by some pupils. It conceals the fact that these cannot be reduced to contextualized and segmented exchanges, but that knowledge that pertains to pupil initiative, reflexivity and reasoning as well as general and organized forms of knowledge that pertain to a vertical and disciplinary logic must be thus constructed. Pupils cannot recontextualize the knowledge acquired *in situ* and proceed to inscribe it within a vertical discourse if the linguistic characteristics and resources required to do so are not familiar to them.

A horizontal discourse that cannot construct the resources for interpreting and producing texts of knowledge

The aim and implementation of a more democratic and participative discourse which is more respectful of pupils' individual identities (in so far as everyone may contribute and intervene, and which, with Bernstein, we may celebrate) may therefore be inscribed in a linguistic situation that deprives pupils of any familiarization with the characteristics of vertical discourse: the resources of the written word, the words of knowledge. Horizontal discourse is not formal or literary; it pertains only to a very limited extent to the discursive universe of written language, and uses the syntax, vocabulary and the frequently incomplete linguistic forms of everyday life. In horizontal discourse, pupils cannot locate the resources required for the production of a text of knowledge (or, in Bernstein's terms, they will be unlikely to possess and understanding of the recognition and realization rules necessary for them to access "unthinkable" knowledge) and for the cognitive socialization that is expected today. When they are able to do so, they do so not by appropriating new forms of socialization so much as through a highly specific and procedural process (a point underlined by Bernstein).

A discourse of control on a moral and affective register

Horizontal discourse implies the introduction of another Bernsteinian concept – the concept of control. When exchanges are constructed from person to person through interactions that may retain the appearance of conversational everydayness, including when they pertain to knowledge, framing is weak and the relevant evaluation criteria appear chiefly moral, behavioural and social rather than cognitive (for example, for some pupils experiencing educational difficulties or from working-class backgrounds, the cleanliness of their work appears to them to be more important than its cognitive relevance).

The position of every actor – and their enunciative roles in particular – is constructed vaguely in relation to the legitimacy of the discourses of truth or knowledge. The choice of certain work themes (or knowledge themes?) can be based on a vote by the pupils or on their individual choices and motivations and thus no longer pertain to a learning progression or to the relevance of pupils' choices to a given learning objective. The teacher, speaking in the name of the classroom (or "us") may present himself as a participant in the work group rather than as someone with a specific legitimacy and authority (i.e. the legitimacy conferred upon her by the knowledge and expertise which she alone in the classroom is assumed to possess). The teacher may even claim not to know, thus encouraging a process of knowledge construction by the pupils. In primary education, pedagogic discourses produced in the name of "us" are common: "We will build a story"; "We will try to solve this problem." This classroom collectivity – to be distinguished from a learning collectivity – deliberately neutralizes the asymmetrical enunciative roles of the teacher and their pupils.

A horizontal discourse associated jointly with a discourse that is more regulative than instructional

In so far as horizontal discourse also reflects an evolution of learning and of teaching practices that value the implementation of pedagogical devices and the active involvement of pupils, it goes hand in hand with the seemingly near total disappearance, in certain schools and classrooms situated largely in working-class areas, of instructional discourse (the discourse of knowledge) in favour of regulative discourse, which serves to regulate activity and progress in the school.

Conclusion

Bernstein's model helps in constructing understandings of what underpins the paradoxical educational (and language) situations described above, particularly as they exist in France's priority education areas (ZEP). It is in schools and classrooms in these areas that, using Bernstein's concepts, the strong horizontal discourse, the strong regulative discourse, the weak framing and cognitive control characteristic of the current pedagogical model (including its objectives in terms of identity construction) are most evident. This would not be a cause of educational inequality if every pupil were equally able to recognize the knowledge issues and cognitive aptitudes behind discursive forms. Pupils with well-educated parents tend to identify the existence of vertical discourse "behind" horizontal discourse or in its brief and partial realizations during the rapid and largely implicit shifts between these discourses in classrooms, yet this research has tended to highlight radical differences between these and other pupils in this respect. As noted above, the linguistic modalities that solicit contributions and interventions from all tend to presuppose a self-founded, innately competent self-being which every pupil may draw upon according to their own resources. Education and the prevailing school discourse therefore ignore the specificity of cognitive and (more generally) cultural socialization processes that stretch the logic of educational action and discourse.

The current relativity of knowledge, like the need to construct a form of socialization more "social" than cognitive (at least in certain schools), implies that major differences between pupils' work registers should be tolerated; some pupils may offer responses and contributions such as, "It reminds me of such and such and I want to tell the class", while others tend to elaborate a new text of knowledge, an activity that serves to more completely transform and develop them.

The point is not to express nostalgia about an imposed, constraining and unequally appropriated vertical discourse. Yet if horizontal discourse is a means of respecting pupils and of enabling them to enter more easily into the universe of the knowledge and aptitudes valued by current literate societies, then it is necessary to train them for this purpose. This is not currently the case when schools in ZEPs may go so far as to impose forms of linguistic and cognitive socialization that devalue knowledge and critical thought, such as the learning of recontextualization, and when the recognition of every pupil is taken to be more important than what they need to know.

As a result, the exclusion of pupils is paradoxically encouraged: as Bernstein observes, pupils may "recognize" vertical discourse but may be unable to realize it, in so far as they are deprived by an omnipresent horizontal discourse of any access to the resources required for such a realization. Admittedly, as Claude Grignon underlines in this volume, the leeway is narrow between a point of view which hierarchizes knowledge and the language that constructs it through the imposition and recycling of dominant categories (what are in some instances arbitrary) and a relativism which ignores the instrumental and cognitive function of language and denies that the different uses of language make the same resources unavailable to all pupils. As Grignon remarks, and in contrast to what current practices may appear to suggest, horizontal discourse may serve to restrict pupils' capacity for expression and therefore their freedom if it is solely the echo of a restricted familiar and family code.

If a degree of caution is therefore in order, it is both a pedagogical and an ideological form of caution. What Bernstein's work and, indeed, my own research tend to demonstrate is the inseparability of language and the pedagogic measures that are effectively implemented in the classroom and which are themselves undergirded by specific conceptions that presuppose radical changes in the educational objectives of contemporary educational systems.

Notes

1 Note in this respect that some of the chief distinguishing features of the British educational system (the basis of Bernstein's constructions and analyses) – features that distinguish it from the French educational system, especially the greater focus in France on subject-specific academic knowledge – have recently begun to shape educational practices in France as well. I shall return in due course to the diffusion and significance of the notions of competence, communication, etc.

2 This trend has recently become dominant in France in conceptions of educational support for struggling pupils. The PPRE programme – designed to provide individual support aimed at ensuring educational success – is one of the most recent manifestations of this trend.

3 I.e. the ESCOL research group at the University of Paris VIII; and since 2005, the ESSI–ESCOL team, and for several years a network of pluridisciplinary researchers (RESEIDA) studying different educational levels (nursery, primary, secondary education).

4 The performance model can be likened to the "productive" model which Eric Plaisance uses to describe nursery school education before its transformation by the expressive mode. See Plaisance (1986).

5 It is worth emphasizing the similarities between Bernstein's HD/VD distinctions and the distinction drawn by Bakhtin between primary and secondary genre. In the production of a text of knowledge, the secondary genre entails a recontextualization of oral language productions as primary genre, as in Bernstein. See Bautier (2005).

8 Segmentalism

The problem of building knowledge and creating knowers

Karl Maton

A spectre is haunting education – the spectre of *segmentalism*, when knowledge is so strongly tied to its context that it is only meaningful within that context.[1] In intellectual fields, segmentalism occurs when a new approach or theory is produced that fails to integrate and subsume existing knowledge. The new approach typically announces the rebirth of the field but then goes on to tell the same fundamental story as previous approaches. In curriculum and pedagogy, segmentalism occurs when pupils learn a series of discrete ideas or skills as they move through a curriculum, rather than progressively building on what they previously learned. This *segmented learning* makes it difficult for students to apply their understanding to new contexts, such as later studies, everyday life or future work. Knowledge or understanding is thus locked within its contexts of production or learning.

The problem of segmentalism is more than an exclusively educational issue. It is central to contemporary social and economic changes. In his later work, Bernstein (2001) argued that we are entering a "Totally Pedagogized Society" where workers are expected to change skills at a moment's notice, constantly retraining and learning throughout their lives. Among policy-makers, the rhetoric of "lifelong learning" proclaims the need to continually build our knowledge, adding new skills and giving new meaning to our existing abilities, to meet the ever-changing demands of the contemporary economy (Field 2006). We are thus said to need knowledge we can build on, whatever the changing contexts we find ourselves in. That education is evolving to meet these needs finds prima facie support in changes to the traditional organization of educational practices. We are said to be moving towards a "post-" or "trans-disciplinary" landscape in which reflexive, heterogeneous and applied knowledge has come to the fore (e.g. Gibbons *et al.* 1994). The spirit of the age is fluidity, the belief that boundaries are dissolving, within education and between education and everyday life. From this perspective it appears segmentalism is being overcome.

In this chapter I develop the theoretical framework of Basil Bernstein to suggest this rhetoric does not always match reality. First, I briefly outline Bernstein's later work on "discourses" and "knowledge structures", and introduce concepts that develop this approach. Second, I use these concepts to analyse two contrasting examples of educational practices that are proclaimed by proponents as overcoming segmentalism, one from professional education at university, the other from the humanities in the school curriculum. Lastly, I discuss the social consequences of segmented learning and how they relate to contemporary economic changes.

Extending Bernstein: semantic gravity

Bernstein's later work can be understood as one of many attempts at understanding contemporary social change. Bernstein's contribution to this debate is unique in focus and in form. While many commentators have highlighted how workers are likely to more regularly change not only employers through their careers but also careers throughout their lives (e.g. Sennett 2006), Bernstein additionally focused on how this is making pedagogy a defining feature of social life: the "Totally Pedagogized Society" (2001). In terms of form, Bernstein was concerned less with offering a macro theory of social change and more with creating the conceptual tools necessary for making sense of those changes through empirical research.

One key set of ideas Bernstein developed concerns the forms taken by knowledge. He distinguishes, first, between "horizontal discourse" and "vertical discourse". *Horizontal discourse* refers to everyday or "commonsense" knowledge and "entails a set of strategies which are local, segmentally organized, context specific and dependent" (2000, p. 157). The knowledges constituting this discourse "are related not by integration of their meanings by some coordinating principle, but ... through the functional relations of segments or contexts to the everyday life" (2000, pp. 158–9). In other words, meaning is highly dependent on its social context. In contrast, *vertical discourse* refers to "specialized symbolic structures of explicit knowledge" (2000, p. 160) or scholarly, professional and educational knowledge and "takes the form of a coherent, explicit, and systematically principled structure" (2000, p. 157). Here meanings are less dependent on their contexts and instead related to other meanings hierarchically.

Bernstein then distinguishes between two forms of vertical discourse: "hierarchical" and "horizontal knowledge structures". A *hierarchical knowledge structure*, illustrated by the sciences, is "a coherent, explicit and systematically principled structure, hierarchically organized" which "attempts to create very general propositions and theories, which integrate knowledge at lower levels, and in this way shows underlying uniformities across an expanding range of apparently different phenomena" (2000, pp. 160–1). In contrast, a *horizontal knowledge structure*, illustrated by the humanities and social sciences, is "a series of specialized languages with specialized modes of interrogation and criteria for the construction and circulation of texts" (2000, p. 161). One issue these concepts highlight is that of *building* knowledge. Hierarchical knowledge structures develop through new knowledge integrating and subsuming previous knowledge, whereas horizontal knowledge structures develop through adding on another approach or topic area. We thus have *integration and subsumption* of knowledges in one form, and *accumulation and segmentation* of knowledges in the other.

With "knowledge structures", Bernstein was primarily concerned with theorizing the production of *new* knowledge. However, one can extend these concepts to explore curriculum and pedagogy by distinguishing between educational practices where pupils build on their previously learned knowledge and take that understanding forward into their future learning and living, and educational practices where learned knowledge is strongly bounded from other knowledges and contexts. This is to distinguish between what can be termed:

- *cumulative learning*, where knowledge is transferred across contexts and integratively builds over time; and
- *segmented learning*, where each set of learned ideas or skills is closely tied to its curricular or pedagogic context, problematizing transfer.

These concepts give us a means of taking the insights of Bernstein's later work forward into the analysis of learning. However, a more significant limitation of Bernstein's model is that his concepts are dichotomous ideal types. Though providing insights, they offer a series of distinctions that raise questions of where, for example, particular disciplines fit within the model, or whether the distinctions are too strongly drawn and too rigid. Further, the concepts highlight what *kind* of discourse or knowledge structure one might discover in research, but not what makes a discourse "horizontal" or "vertical" and what makes a knowledge structure "hierarchical" or "horizontal". This is not to dismiss the existing framework but rather to highlight the need to develop the theorization further to address the question of what underlies these different forms of discourse, knowledge structure and learning: what are their underlying generative principles?

Bernstein's model provides a clue as to how to answer these questions. A key feature of his definitions of discourses and knowledge structures is the different relations between knowledge and its social and cultural contexts they characterize. To overcome the dichotomies in Bernstein's framework one can thereby think in terms of *semantic gravity* or the degree to which meaning is dependent on its context (Maton 2009, 2010). Semantic gravity may be relatively stronger or weaker. Where semantic gravity is stronger, meaning is more strongly tied to its social or symbolic context of acquisition or use; where semantic gravity is weaker, meaning is less dependent on its context. Using this concept one can recast relations between different forms of discourse, knowledge structure or learning in a less dichotomous fashion and begin to excavate their underlying principles. One can understand these conceptual distinctions as representing points on a continuum of strengths of semantic gravity: vertical discourse has weaker semantic gravity than horizontal discourse; and within vertical discourse, hierarchical knowledge structures exhibit weaker semantic gravity than horizontal knowledge structures. Finally, cumulative learning depends on weaker semantic gravity, and segmented learning is characterized by stronger semantic gravity that constrains the transfer of meaning across contexts. Thus, one necessary condition for building knowledge and understanding over time may be weaker semantic gravity.

If semantic gravity underlies these different forms of learning, knowledge structures and discourses, this still leaves the question: what affects semantic gravity? To address this issue one can turn to *Legitimation Code Theory* (or LCT), an approach rapidly being taken up in educational research that builds on and extends the insights of Bernstein, among others.[2] LCT views the practices and beliefs of actors as embodying competing claims to legitimacy or measures of achievement. Their underlying structuring principles are analysed in terms of "legitimation codes", which conceptualize the "rules of the game" of social fields of practice. One dimension is "Specialization" or what makes someone or something different, special and worthy of distinction. Put briefly, discursive practices are analysed according to whether they emphasize as the basis of legitimate insight: the possession of explicit principles, skills and procedures (knowledge code); characteristics of the subject or actor, such as attitudes, aptitudes, dispositions or social background (knower code); both specialist knowledge and knower dispositions equally (elite code); or neither (relativist code).[3] These codes help excavate the underlying principles generating forms of knowledge; for example, hierarchical knowledge structures are often underpinned by knowledge codes, and horizontal knowledge structures are often generated by knower codes (Maton 2007; Moore 2009).

The rest of the chapter uses this framework of *semantic gravity* and *legitimation codes of specialization* to explore how the structuring of educational knowledge may constrain cumulative learning and enable segmentalism. To do so, and in a manner consistent with the focus on overcoming the semantic gravity of specific contexts, it uses the same concepts to analyse two different examples of educational practices that are said to enable cumulative learning: professional education at university and English at secondary school.

Professional education and "authentic learning"

In recent years professional education has been increasingly influenced by instrumentalist ideas that emphasize learning that has practical relevance for the future world of work. "Authentic" or "situated learning" has been widely promoted as the means of achieving this end. Proponents claim that to enable students to transfer their knowledge to contexts outside education, they require learning tasks that reflect the realities of practices in everyday contexts and which allow them access to the knowledge of experts with experience of real-world practices. From this perspective, for example, students of design should be encouraged to imagine they are employees in a design studio. Authentic learning is thus often associated with problem-based, case-based and project-based pedagogies offering students real-life examples of what, for example, designers do. Such "authentic learning environments" are said to create experiences that help students to think and act like practitioners in working contexts. In Bernstein's terms, they argue that vertical discourse should be reconstructed in the image of horizontal discourse in order to enable knowledge to move between educational and everyday contexts.

To analyse this approach, I shall draw on a major study conducted by Bennett (2002) at the University of Wollongong, Australia. Bennett investigated a postgraduate master's degree course for training instructional designers, professionals who design learning resources. One aspect of this study explores a task using "case-based learning" and designed according to principles of authentic learning. The task required students to analyse two case studies of real-life instructional design projects, each comprising approximately 15,000 words of unedited transcripts of interviews with three people who had worked on each project. A series of questions was designed to encourage students to think beyond the context of the two cases (Table 8.1).

Three features of this task are of interest here. First, the questions progressively ask for more generalization and abstraction: they begin by asking students to describe key issues in the cases and end by focusing on general issues about what they have learned. Second, the questions ask students to bring in knowledge from beyond the cases; for example, question 2 asks students to relate the cases to other literature they have read or their own

Table 8.1 Task questions

---

1   Describe the major stages and decision points in the process of developing the product. What are the major issues at each stage?

2   How do the experiences of the designers in this case relate to:
   a   other *literature you have read* about multimedia design and development or
   b   *your own experiences as a designer* (for example in your work or for EDGI913 [an earlier subject in the course])?

3   Choose a particular feature of the product which is discussed in the case.
   a   Describe *how you think* it relates to the original concept and goals of the project.
   b   From the information in the case *what do you think* were the major design issues in developing this feature?
   c   *Do you think* the feature is effective? Explain your reasoning.

4   What are the major project management issues in developing a multimedia CD-ROM that are highlighted by this case? (Use example situations from the case to support your ideas.)

5   What are the main things that *you think you learnt* from studying this case?

Source: Bennett (2002, pp. 75–6); emphases added.

experiences (Table 8.1). Third, the task is based on being a knower rather than imparting knowledge. It expects students to put themselves "into the shoes" of the interviewed professionals – emphasizing the dispositions of knowers. There is little guidance as to what procedures to use, and questions focus on eliciting students' perceptions and beliefs (see emphases in Table 8.1) rather than principles of instructional design. In summary, the task aims to weaken semantic gravity – encouraging students to make meanings that go beyond the learning context – and uses a *knower code* to do so.

Analysis of responses

Student responses were coded using what Bernstein (2000) terms a *language of description* (a means of translating between theoretical concepts and empirical data) for exploring the degrees of semantic gravity characterizing their answers. Figure 8.1 provides a brief summary (space precludes including the full language; see Maton 2009, p. 49). "Reproductive description" describes where students quote directly from the case materials. "Summarizing description" refers to when students put case materials into their own words. Further up Figure 8.1, the coding schema captures statements which move beyond description and introduce "interpretation", and then where students bring in value "judgements" of their own. "Generalization" describes where students draw out principles which remain limited to the case; and "abstraction" is where they derive principles that apply to a range of wider or possible future contexts. In the schema, "reproductive description" embodies the strongest semantic gravity – meanings are locked into the context of the case from which the quote is taken; and "abstraction" represents the weakest semantic gravity – meanings are decontextualized from the cases to create principles for use in other potential contexts.

Student answers were broken down into individual "units of meaning" and each unit was coded using the schema. The study comprised twelve students whose responses totalled 1,700 units of meaning. Overall results show that students managed to rise above "reproductive description" (see Figure 8.2). This is, however, what one would expect from postgraduate students and the unedited interview transcripts did not lend easily themselves to extensive quotation. However, around one-third of the responses remain

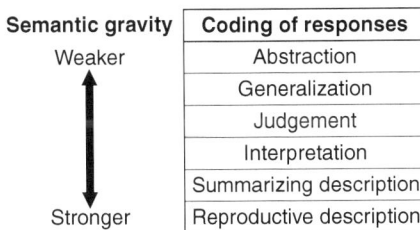

Semantic gravity	Coding of responses
Weaker	Abstraction
	Generalization
	Judgement
	Interpretation
	Summarizing description
Stronger	Reproductive description

Figure 8.1 Summary of coding schema for semantic gravity.

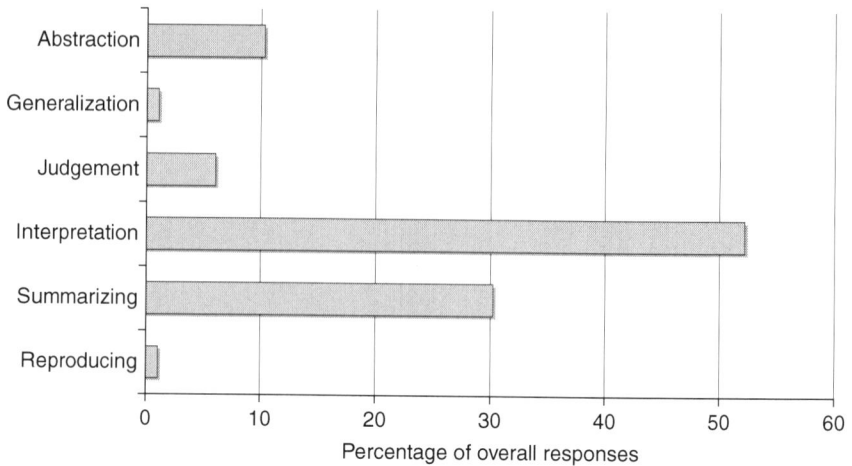

Figure 8.2 Total student responses (units of meaning).

descriptive and just over half are "interpretation". Relatively fewer proportions of the responses reach the levels of "judgement", "generalization" or
"abstraction". So, most of the responses exhibit relatively higher semantic
gravity. Meanings are mostly dependent on the context of the cases, *despite*
the questions asking students to think beyond the cases being studied.

One might not expect a high percentage of students' responses to be
"abstractions", because otherwise answers would be disconnected from the
learning materials. However, if we compare the responses of individual students, it becomes clear that some appear to be more capable of offering
responses that overcome semantic gravity than others. Figure 8.3 compares
the responses of two students. Overall, Joanne's answers are grouped further
down and exhibit stronger semantic gravity; they are more dependent on the
context of the cases than those of Steve. This difference is also shown by
instances where students' responses did rise above description, for example,
if we compare two further students, Liz and Ian. When Liz draws conclusions in her answers they remain grounded within the context of the cases;
for example:

> Tasks and responsibilities often remain unclarified in this "design" phase
> (Phillips & Jenkins 1998). The reflections of Rob Wright ... seem to
> reflect on a type of "juggling act" between responsibilities with instruc-
> tional design issues and scheduling a project of this magnitude.
>
> (Bennett 2002, p. 129)

Here Liz uses other literature to generalize about the design phase of the
project, but her conclusions are focused on the case (the experiences of one of
the designers) rather than developing principles for application to other

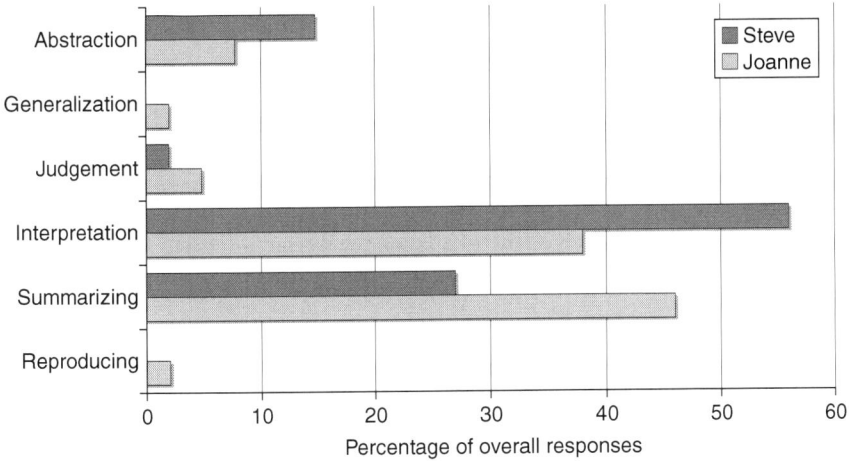

Figure 8.3 Responses of two individual students.

projects. This contrasts strongly with Ian's answers. He also draws conclusions about the cases but goes further to offer principles, including:

- A list of ideas that one might keep in mind when designing and producing a multimedia project. The issues examined in the two case studies sparked these ideas...
- Set priorities in your product development. Know what you must have and what aspects of the project are not vital.
- At some point, you must become precise in what features and content you want in your design. Working in generalities does not allow you to proceed effectively in the final stages of the project.

(Bennett 2002, p. 147)

Ian thus uses the cases as a launch pad from which to offer ideas to take forward into other contexts. Thus, some students could achieve "abstraction" but most remain immersed in the context of the cases.

Despite claims made by proponents of "authentic learning", Bennett's study showed it can create segmented learning: students' understanding remains rooted in the context (stronger semantic gravity). One reason for this, I argue, lies in its knower code. In authentic learning students receive little instruction about what procedures to use or what principles of knowledge they are learning. Instead, it emphasizes students imagining being in the case they are studying and drawing on personal experiences. This knower code tends to work *against* the integration of meanings. As Bernstein argues, to acquire educational knowledge, students need to be able to integrate meanings so that those meanings are not consumed at the point of their contextual delivery (2000, p. 160). To enable students' understanding to overcome the gravity well of a particular context and allow the conscious transfer of meanings to new contexts, they need the principles underlying knowledge and the principles for recontextualizing knowledge – i.e. for selecting meaning, relating it to other meanings, and relocating it within new contexts. Authentic learning environments render these principles invisible and instead ground knowledge within a context, expecting students to "pick up" the knowledge by "being there". By trying to reconstruct the vertical discourse of education in the image of the horizontal discourse of everyday life, authentic environments may make it *less* easy for students to take educational knowledge into their everyday lives. Just as importantly, it also sets up many students to fail because it is the ability to generalize and abstract that is rewarded in such tasks; the aim is for students to be able to derive higher-order principles and students will only succeed if they already possess that ability.

School English and *The Journey*

A second example is from a different kind of subject and level of education: English at school. Ongoing collaborative research is examining secondary school English, specifically a unit of work entitled *The Journey* which is compulsory for all students taking the Higher School Certificate in New South Wales, Australia.[4] In this unit students are required to explore the concept of "the journey", which can be "physical", "imaginative" or "inner" journeys. Here I focus on "Imaginative Journeys", which involves texts that "take us into worlds of imagination, speculation and inspiration" (Board of Studies NSW – BoS 2006a, p. 10). In 2005, students were set the question:

> To what extent has studying the concept of imaginative journeys expanded your understanding of yourself, of individuals and of the world?
>
> In your answer, refer to your prescribed text, ONE text from the prescribed stimulus booklet, *Journeys*, and at least ONE other related text of your own choosing.
>
> (BoS 2006b, p. 11)

The stimulus booklet comprises two poems, short extracts from three books, and a bookcover; the prescribed list includes: a work of fiction, a selection of poems, Shakespeare's *The Tempest*, a history of science, and the film *Contact*.

At first glance, this example appears to be very different to that previously discussed. However, using the conceptual framework we can see beyond these surface differences. In terms of aims, the syllabus claims that students will learn how to "explore and examine *relationships* between language and text, and *interrelationships* among texts" and how to "*synthesize* ideas to clarify meaning and *develop new meanings*" (BoS 2006a, p. 9; emphases added). In other words, *The Journey* aims to cultivate the ability to move beyond the context of any one text. The idea of *The Journey* suggests transformation, development and change. The aim is thereby to overcome semantic gravity, enabling students to learn knowledge they can take into encounters with new texts.

Three features of the task intended to achieve those aims are particularly relevant here. First, the task asks students to apply their knowledge beyond the curriculum by choosing text(s) of their own. Second, it expects a relatively high level of abstraction centred on the idea of *The Journey*. Third, it focuses on students as knowers: it asks about "your understanding of yourself, of individuals and of the world" and expects students to empathize with texts (see Christie and Humphrey 2008). There is also little guidance in curriculum documents as to how to select or integrate texts around the idea of *The Journey*, or indeed what this idea means. The syllabus includes a book of *Student Answers* (BoS 2006b) which provides examples of essays rated as achieving medium and high grades with comments by examiners. However, these are vague. For example, highly rated essays are described as a "sophisticated discussion", "insightful" and "a very sophisticated and purposeful response" (BoS 2006b, p. 114), or "complex" with a "judicious selection of texts", and "tightly written and strongly focused" (BoS 2006b, p. 101). Examiners' comments on mid-grade essays offer a little more guidance but are confined to stating, for example, that less description and more "analysis and evaluation" are required (p. 127), without explaining what this might constitute. In summary, the task aims at weaker semantic gravity, and uses a knower code to achieve that end.

One aspect of the research into this unit of study comprises analysis of texts produced by students, of which I shall briefly discuss two contrasting examples. The first is a low-achieving essay.[5] This essay has a segmented form – it discusses one text at a time, with each text strongly bounded from the others. Even when bringing texts together, the student keeps them apart; for example, the essay concludes: "I took three wonderful journeys." Discussion of each text is very concrete and related to real life. For example, when discussing the novel *Ender's Game*, the student proclaims:

> I found I could relate to Ender in many ways and I didn't stop to think that this story wasn't actually real, because when reading, I was so involved that I truly thought that what was happening around Ender and I was reality.

This highlights a further feature: it is a highly personal and subjective response. It is the student's personal experiences that serve as the basis for selecting, recontextualizing and evaluating texts; for example: "I felt very empathetic towards the character Ender. I found myself involved in the novel, travelling my Imaginative journey alongside Ender. I felt that Ender was a friend of my own." In short, the essay exhibits relatively stronger semantic gravity (meanings are strongly related to their contexts) and is based on a knower code – the student as knower is central rather than any specifically literary knowledge.

A second essay, offered in official syllabus documents as an example of success (BoS 2006b, pp. 102–14), represents a striking contrast. This essay begins and ends by bringing its chosen texts together in relation to an abstract principle; for example: "The journey, especially in the imaginative sense, is a process by which the traveller encounters a series of challenges, tangents and serendipitous discoveries to arrive finally, at a destination and/or transformation" (BoS 2006b, p. 102). The student then discusses each text in turn but by moving between concrete examples and abstract ideas; for example, when discussing *On Giants' Shoulders* by Melvyn Bragg: "In portraying their [scientists'] separate profiles as one story in a chronological line up, Bragg delineates the concept of a cumulative and ongoing journey, reflected in his thesis that science is 'an extended kind of continuous investigation'" (BoS 2006b, p. 103). Rather than relating the texts solely to empirical reality, meanings are constructed in a less subjective and personal manner, so that even when discussing him/herself, the student relates their experiences to abstracted principles; for example: "I personally have learned the importance of individuals interlinking with others to achieve a greater end, and influencing or inspiring others, as inherent in the concept of scientists standing on 'giants' shoulders'" (BoS 2006b, p. 103). In summary, it is as if the first student's ideas are weighed down by the gravity of each text they discuss: they address only one text at a time, usually in direct relation to their own experiences, feelings and beliefs. This is a highly segmental form of writing, where the basis of selection, recontextualization and evaluation is the student as knower. In contrast, it is as if the second student's expressed ideas enjoys lighter gravity: they are able to leap up further from the concrete base of each text or their own experiences to reach more abstract principles with which they can relate different texts together, and when the student brings their own understandings and experiences into the essay they are objectified and abstracted.

This is only part of the wider research, but it highlights how many students may be unable to recognize or put into practice what they need to succeed at in this compulsory unit of work. It is easy to read the essay question as requiring a subjective description of one's personal preferences and little guidance is offered in curriculum documents as to what the abstract concept of "The Imaginative Journey" means or how it should be used to analyse texts. However, it is clear from high-grade essays that achievement depends on the ability to overcome semantic gravity, i.e. using abstract principles to integrate meanings from different texts. Thus, many students may not only experience segmented learning, they also may also fail to gain high grades. They do so, I suggest, because the knower code leaves them weighed down by semantic gravity – they are not told the principles underlying knowledge but instead are expected to know them already. The task may thereby set up many students to fail.

Conclusion

This chapter extended Bernstein's ideas to explore segmented learning and argued that to understand this problem we must focus on how meaning relates to its context or "semantic gravity". I now consider the value of these concepts and how segmented learning relates to wider social, political and economic change.

The problem of segmentalism is, of course, not new for educators. However, the way of thinking outlined here provides a fresh way of seeing this problem. By developing Bernstein's framework we can explore how different forms of education share fundamental similarities. Though different forms of education (professional education and the humanities) in different contexts (universities and schools), both examples aim to overcome segmented learning and both put in place conditions enabling its existence. One reason is that both examples keep the principles of knowledge hidden from students and focus instead on students as knowers. Yet achievement depends on students' ability to generalize and abstract from what they are studying. So they reward what they do not teach. The result for many students is that anything they learn stays embedded in these learning contexts. In other words, not all students can overcome semantic gravity on their own, as these forms of teaching expect. The theoretical approach thereby enables us to see beyond the claims made for forms of curriculum and pedagogy to explore their effects.

The concept of semantic gravity also overcomes dichotomies in Bernstein's model of discourses and knowledge structures and enables the integration of curriculum and pedagogy into his later framework. Forms of discourse, knowledge structure and learning can be redescribed as points on a continuum of semantic gravity rather than as dichotomous ideal types. It also explores the underlying principles generating these different forms. A key property of these forms is their strength of semantic gravity – different strengths give rise to different forms. I have argued that weaker semantic gravity may be a necessary (though not by itself sufficient) condition for enabling transfer and building cumulative knowledge. So, if we wish to understand segmentalism, we need to explore semantic gravity.

The question remains: is segmented learning a problem, and if it is, how does it relate to wider issues in society? One of Bernstein's key arguments is that when the basis of achievement is kept hidden from students, only those who already know how to succeed will succeed, i.e. students who already have the ability to recognize and realize what is required, thanks to their family upbringing or prior education. In both the examples this background is likely to be from the cultural middle class. For example, to succeed at *The Journey* students require the ability to objectify themselves, abstract and generalize. There is a considerable body of work, using Bernstein and other thinkers like Pierre Bourdieu, showing how such abilities are found more often in students from cultural middle-class homes than from working-class families. Segmented learning is likely to be experienced more by socially disadvantaged groups – they are the students set up to fail. With segmented learning if you do not already have the principles of knowledge, then you are not going to learn them. So, segmented learning is not transformative. Instead, it is the academic classification of social backgrounds; it is classifying people according to where they started in society. Ironically, far from being a journey, it leaves students exactly where they began.

Segmented learning also matters in relation to current economic and social change. This returns us to Bernstein's critique of "lifelong learning" (2000). Policy-makers in industrialized countries argue that workers need to retrain continually, change jobs many times during a lifetime and be flexible. The rhetoric of "lifelong learning" suggests we need to learn knowledge to carry through our lives, building on our knowledge with new skills and giving it new meanings, as demands on us change. In other words, we need *cumulative learning*. The reality, as Bernstein argued, is somewhat different. He described contemporary forms of work and life as "short-termism": "where a skill, task, area of work, undergoes continuous development, disappearance and replacement ... Under these circumstances it is considered that a vital new ability must be developed: 'trainability'" (Bernstein 2000, p. 59). Trainability is "the ability to profit from continuous pedagogic reformations and so cope with the new requirement of 'work' and 'life'" (Bernstein 2001, p. 365). Rather than building our knowledge, we are expected to become almost like computer hardware – empty, devoid of commitments, waiting to receive the latest software, ready to reprogramme ourselves whenever needed. As Richard Sennett argued: "the emerging social order militates against the ideal of craftsmanship, that is, learning to do just one thing really well" (2006, p. 4).

In his studies, Sennett (1998) shows how psychologically and socially damaging this is for individuals and communities. Segmented learning matches this new social order: it models the movement from context to context where new knowledge fails to build on previous knowledge, and it projects identities that are oriented to the short term, focused on potential ability rather than existing knowledge, and willing to abandon past experience. In other words, segmented learning provides a basis for segmented identities and segmented lives.

Segmented learning matters: it withholds powerful knowledge from many people and is socially and psychologically damaging. One foundation of segmented learning is the knower code and its lack of explicit guidance about the principles underlying knowledge. This lack of guidance is a betrayal of students and a desertion of the role of the teacher. One thing I learnt from Bernstein is that we are in the business of teaching people, and so we should teach them something, something that will shape their ways of thinking, seeing and being, so that it stays with them and finds use throughout their lives. That is *true* lifelong learning, and that is what building on Bernstein's way of thinking still offers us today.

Notes

1 This chapter was originally a paper presented at the University of Lyon (2007). A substantially revised version was published as Maton 2009.
2 For examples of how LCT is being used in a wide range of educational studies, see Carvalho *et al.* (2009), Lamont and Maton (2008), Luckett (2009) and Shay (2008).
3 These concepts of LCT (Specialization) are more fully discussed in Maton (2000, 2007, 2009b) and Moore and Maton (2001).
4 See also Christie and Macken-Horarik (2007) and Christie and Humphrey (2008).
5 This essay was collected as part of a study published as Christie and Derewianka (2008).

Part IV

Classification and framing

The revision and permanence of curricula

9 Reviewing recontextualization of knowledge at university

From Bernstein's theory to empirical research

Sophia Stavrou

The current time is one of the most crucial periods in the history of higher education: universities are in a process of change. Furthermore, prescribed institutional changes such as curricular restructuring (often termed course "renewal") have effects on the academic content offered. This chapter addresses curricular transformations taking place within French universities over the last two decades, particularly since the implementation of the "European higher education area" policy, initiated in the late 1990s and of the "LMD" ("licence" (i.e. bachelor's), master's, doctorate) French Reform of 2002. I discuss the contribution of Bernstein's concept of the *recontextualization of knowledge* in investigating change in pedagogic models and in pedagogic content at the university level. I consider recontextualization as a concept which enables the examination of changes in the process most fundamental to education: the transmission of knowledge. The object of this empirical research is to examine transformations of knowledge within curricula in the human and social sciences at the university level and, particularly, their shift towards an alternative model of professionalizing courses based on the regionalization of knowledge.[1]

Recontextualization refers to the process of the selection and organization of knowledge within curricula. It serves as a principle that selectively appropriates, relocates, refocuses and relates discourses to constitute its own order of pedagogic discourse (Bernstein 1996, p. 33). Importantly, it relates to the structuring of transmission systems, of forms of knowledge, and of power and control relations concerning knowledge, generated by the recontextualizing principles. This Bernsteinian concept is anthropological, penetrating time and space, and aimed at investigating the selection of what is to be transmitted to learners and of how it is to be transmitted to them. The principles change according to sociohistorical contexts and to the "thinkable" within each society: Which knowledge? What ways of transmission? For whom (which individuals/learners)? Answering these questions involves a consideration of social order. Recontextualization enables an examination of the transmission of knowledge, in its material and pragmatic dimension, as a social phenomenon.

At the same time, recontextualization is a concept of a great significance in the current context of reform in higher education. We are now witnessing the emergence of a phenomenon that, 20 years ago, Bernstein named the *regionalization of knowledge* (Bernstein 1990). This involves the transformation of singular disciplinary discourses into larger regionalized pedagogic discourses, such as urbanism, communication and management. New fields of study are developed and established, which associate various disciplines with a transversal object of study and which are constituted through the selection of theoretical, methodological or other knowledge, abstracted from its field of origin and reorganized within transversal curricula. This phenomenon emerged particularly during the second half of the twentieth century, becoming progressively more extensive at the national, European and international levels. While many national higher education systems have experienced this phenomenon, the French case enables the observation of change in progress. In French universities, attached until recently to a traditional disciplinary division of academic structures, inherited from the Middle Ages, the regionalization of knowledge was introduced in the context of the implementation of the Bologna process, the definition in the *Attali Report* (1998) of the principles of "innovation", "pluridisciplinarity" and "professionalization" within courses, as a condition for the creation of a "European higher education area", and the reform that followed (LMD Reform, Decree no. 2002-482). The abrupt emergence of this type of transversal courses in French universities, especially at the master's level, reveals a significant change in the pedagogic model and not only an institutional prescription.

It is important to examine not the pluridisciplinarization of scientific production – this has existed for a long time in some scientific fields, especially in the positivist sciences – but rather the change that takes place as a result of the process of recontextualization of knowledge and its official institutionalization; a change that impacts all courses and, in particular, those in the humanities and social sciences. This is why it is necessary, at present, to question this new model in its own right – not to compare it to the former model of the division of academic disciplines – for the structuring principles it suggests, for its effects on knowledge and for what it enables individuals to acquire in terms of cultural and cognitive resources.[2] Analysing recontextualization shifts the focus from opposing categories to the process of the production of categories. If we consider Bernstein's conceptualization of the transition from the disciplinary model to the "regional" model as something that has many possible and different realizations, then we have to examine "regions of knowledge" as the product of a specific recontextualization of knowledge: as "one of the possibles" realized. The aim, then, is to understand what is happening within the pedagogic device. Why and how does the selection of this specific form of transversality occur? What are the transformations this pedagogic model supposes within the process of the selection and organization of knowledge?

First, I shall briefly present the institutional context from which the phenomenon of the regionalization of knowledge is generated. I will then discuss the recontextualizing logics of the different agents who contribute, through continuous negotiation, to the stabilization of its meanings and to the realization of this process within curricula. Lastly, I focus upon a socio-morphological analysis of the curriculum of a "region of knowledge", that of urbanism, aimed at revealing the internal relations of its pedagogic text:[3] the relations between and within contents, the principles that command them and the stakes they imply.

Official prescription: the emerging principle of the "regionalization of knowledge"

It is difficult to assign a date to the emergence of transversality of disciplines. This depends on how we define "transversality". The encyclopaedic culture ("Egkykios Paideia") in ancient Greece or even the German model of the "Studium Generale" in the Middle Ages can be considered as forms of transversality of disciplines. However, its establishment as an academic pedagogical model becomes most evident since the 1960s, initially in American and then in European universities.

Since then, scientists have made many attempts to elaborate on scientific projects of transversality. These projects are expressed in a plurality of terms. Transversality has been called inter-disciplinarity or pluri-disciplinarity or even trans-, poly- and multi-disciplinarity. In English, it also figures as super-disciplinarity or cross-disciplinarity. Each of these concepts expresses a different approach towards associating the disciplines. They can refer to a simple aggregation of disciplines, to relations of interaction between them, or to a transversality which is generated by a consensus on an object of study, a method or a theory. Without addressing the epistemological debates involved here, it is necessary to note that the disagreements over the establishment of transversality within the field of knowledge production reflect the struggle over its definition and realization as well as the stakes of structuring transversality as a realized project.

As mentioned, the form of transversality institutionalized within the European system of higher education is only one of its possible realizations: a form of "regionalization of knowledge" elaborated in the current sociopolitical context, operating on (and within) curricula. Thus, it is important to understand how the institution offers conditions for the possibility of change in the pedagogic model. In other words, it is important to understand how the institution structures the specific realization of transversality through the evolution of the official discourse it projects.

The principle of the "regionalization of knowledge" has been developed at a political moment where there is a rupture between the old functions of university as proclaimed by the Loi Faure[4] in 1968 and its new missions as defined in the Act of the Loi Savary[5] in 1984. The first were based on the humanist idea of forming the spirit through the acquisition of knowledge whereas, since 1984, universities are to "contribute to regional and national development, in the context of planning, towards economic growth and towards realization of an employment policy, foreseeing the current needs of the society and their predictable evolution" (Act no. 84-52). In this sense, the university acquires new functions that can be considered as "instrumental"; the social and economic contributions of universities are becoming more pronounced than the intellectual ones. The first explicit connections between education and professional fields – as evidenced by the possibility for professional representatives to participate in the definition of programmes and to contribute to teaching as practitioners, as well as the introduction of training programmes for students in private or public companies, etc. – can be noted within this same Reform Act. Furthermore, there is a specific reference to human and social sciences where the knowledge produced by these fields acquires a new value: that of their contribution to social policy, to employment or to territorial development.

Thus, the association of disciplines within new objects of study appears for the first time through the perspective of the reinforcement of links between higher education and the private or public sectors of the field of economic production. Accordingly, curricular construction increasingly becomes a matter of concern within the official recontextualizing field. Evidence of the official recontextualizing field's growing involvement here includes the possibility of contracts, concerning educational offerings, between the state and universities. Moreover, the reforms which followed confirm the tendency towards the establishment of a new idea of higher education; towards, in Bernstein's terms, a new pedagogic model of "projection" rather than "introjection" (Bernstein 1996, p. 56).[6] The Loi Jospin,[7] in 1989, called for "adaptability, creativity and the swift evolution of contents" (Act no. 89-486) in the university. It prescribed the constant revision of transmitted knowledge where the value of knowledge to be transmitted is henceforth viewed by the official field according to its contribution in fields external to education and to its transversal character as a competence.

Notably, transformations of the official discourse of recontextualization should be contextualized in relation to three developments which have taken place in French higher education since the 1980s: territorialization, contractualization and professionalization. At that time, decentralizing processes began to take effect in the French institutional context; territorial authorities and regional councils began making investments in universities, setting their sights on the contribution of the universities to the economic development of regions. Meanwhile, new forms of relations were established between the state and universities, in terms of the autonomy of universities and of the constitution of local policies. Finally, the aim of professionalizing higher education, clearly declared in the Bayrou Reform Act of 1997, tends towards the creation of "diplomas of vocational profile", a form of specialization for the traditional courses in the human and social sciences, and the introduction within these courses of modules supposed to improve employment prospects for graduates.[8]

These processes prepared the field for the reform of French higher education. The Bologna Declaration[9] of 1999 confirmed these trends and aimed at their implementation across all European countries so as to harmonize national educational systems. In France, the implementation of the LMD Reform in 2002 stands as the result of this movement and includes the ECTS credits system, the abolition of the "Deug" diploma (a two-year undergraduate University Diploma of General Studies) and of the "Maîtrise" diploma (a one-year postgraduate degree), the creation of two-year master's degrees separated into research and professional degrees and calls for the creation of new transdisciplinary courses of study. This reform, then, has led to important restructuring in French universities.

Curriculum change has been accompanied by a new mode of "steering" universities by the state. The state increases university autonomy over financing and course planning but, concurrently, it increases central control over pedagogic content and over evaluation procedures for accreditation, which become more and more systematic. The involvement of the state in curricular restructuring is revealed in the annual reports presented by different agencies of the Ministry of National Education.[10]

Tracing the evolution of the official discourse on higher education enables an understanding of the emergence of the regionalization of knowledge as a fundamental principle for the recontextualization of university knowledge, its definition and its institutional context. The new criteria for programme design and evaluation, the state's new role in "steering" universities, and the introduction of new actors in the process of course construction each contribute to the institutionalization of a pedagogic model promoting pluridisciplinarity and the professionalization of curricula within French official documents.

A struggle of logics within the recontextualizing field

Thus far, this chapter has addressed most specifically official prescriptions for the model of higher education in France. Next, and perhaps most interestingly, it is important to explore how the model has been realized. A Bernsteinian approach here rests upon a relational conceptualization of principles, individuals, knowledge, texts and practices. The concept of a "recontextualizing field" enables the consideration of the process of recontextualization from a dynamic perspective, as an ongoing process, implying relations of power and control between and within groups in the struggle for its appropriation. The reform space is plural and agents are plural, with differential normative frames of action. The regionalization of knowledge is accomplished through negotiations and compromises within the recontextualizing field. As Bernstein explains: "we move from a recontextualizing principle to a recontextualizing field with agents with practicing ideologies" (Bernstein 1996, p. 33).

In the current national context, recontextualizers are separated into the "official" and the "pedagogic" fields. The present research is focused on the ministry and its associated evaluation agencies, the vice-presidents and members of university councils, and the academics implicated in the development and teaching of such courses.[11] As discussed in the previous section, central control by the state's politico-administrative agencies, particularly over curriculum design, is intensifying. Relations within the recontextualizing field are hierarchical, based on the evaluation of each other's activity. Nevertheless, we can observe that there is no unique recontextualizing logic among these agencies, but rather many different logics entering into struggle. This is evidenced by the opportunity that all agencies have to participate in the definition of meanings.

The Ministry's agencies, especially the agents of the General Direction of Higher Education, are the main actors in this process, having the power to decide on the authorization of the courses. These agencies issue guidelines as to which indicators should be present in the four-year contracts signed between the state and universities. They also follow and control the work of the National Agency for Evaluation of Higher Education and Research[12] (AERES) and of the Universities' Councils of Studies and University Life[13] (CEVU) on accreditation procedures for the courses.

Academics designated by the Ministry of the National Agency for Evaluation of Higher Education and Research are responsible for the assessment of courses, measuring, to a "lower or higher degree", the professionalization and pluridisciplinarity of the programmes through standardized criteria. The professionalizing character refers explicitly to job prospects for graduates of the course, the connections made between the course and the professional field, the partnership with the profession's community and the monitoring of the employment of former students. Pluridisciplinarity refers to the pedagogic connections between departments and schools within the course (Expertise framework for master's degrees, AERES). In the absence of a reply to the evaluation reports they produce, these agents also adopt personal, professional logics – based on their academic background – for the accreditation of courses. Interviews carried out with these agents reveal that some of them look more specifically at the "contribution of each discipline to the thematic object of study" and at the "coherence of the pedagogic project", rather than at the professionalizing outcomes of course contents.

In order to optimize the chances for authorization of their courses and funding of their universities, the universities' councils are attentive to the ministry's discourse. For the members and the Vice-Presidents of the Councils of Studies and University Life, pluridisciplinarity and professionalization are fundamentals which need to exist within new courses; on one hand to "improve employment prospects for graduates" and on the other hand to "reinforce the attractiveness of French (and European) universities, in the context of international competition". From this perspective, the recontextualizing logic adopted appears as follows: disciplinary transversality means the creation of a "new object of research, of production", based on the interaction between disciplines, towards the development of new knowledge fields with potential in the economic field, so as to "open the university's qualifications to another labour market than to that of public service". However, they also introduce local logics of recontextualization, with a view to establish innovative courses in accordance with the region's needs, and scientific logics for the evaluation of the courses, insisting on "qualitative indicators", rather than quantitative ones. They also insist on "taking into consideration the diversity of disciplines", whereas for the ministry all courses are subject to common evaluation frameworks. For local agents, curricular restructuring "has to come from the inside" of the university.

Correspondingly, there is a dominant recontextualizing discourse of "resistance" within the pedagogic field, which is the main producer of "pedagogic texts". Academics claim to realize professionalization through a "generalist education" and through the creation of projects of epistemological transversality between disciplines. This discourse becomes critical towards the effects of the ministry's role in programme construction, such as the reduction of time dedicated to the teaching of general theoretical content and the adaptation of course contents to the current needs of companies, which "does not serve to consider the educational program as long-term training for students". However, as discussed in the next section of the chapter, this "resistance" discourse does not exclude the recontextualization of knowledge. This reveals the distinction between the conception of a scientific project and its realization in classrooms.

Finally, the influence of public and private organizations, and particularly of professional associations, becomes important in the development of courses. These associations consider pluridisciplinarity as a condition for the reinforcement and improvement of specialized competences for graduates.

The tensions, observed in interviews with recontextualizers point towards a compromise between two poles: on one hand, the objective necessity of knowledge and, on the other hand, the instrumental and arbitrary interest of pedagogic content. The effects of Bernstein's "introjected/projected model" on what Jürgen Habermas conceives as the "interest of knowledge" (1973) are evident here. The first model attributes to knowledge an interest in the emancipation of consciousness from natural constraint; the second model substitutes, for reflexive, emancipatory activity, the classification and dissection of knowledge, according to social practices and to the social division of labour, which are not universals.

The empirical comprehension of the concept of recontextualization allows this dichotomy to be overcome. The plurality of recontextualizing logics prevents collapse into a deterministic vision of the educational process which would consider the imposition of the regionalization of knowledge by a social group, in a linear way, without the possibility for the transformation of the symbolic device. Plurality in the contexts of the origins and interests of recontextualizers leads also to plurality in the construction of pedagogic discourse – specifically in comparing the "project to be realized" to the one "realized". Between the different recontextualizing fields and between the different levels for the construction of pedagogic discourse, the "pedagogic text" is subject to transformations, in one sense or in another. For this reason, it is necessary to go beyond politics of recontextualization, beyond what recontextualization aims at, in order to question the process in its material form:[14] as a "pedagogic text" which is transmitted to students.

Recontextualizing knowledge: a case study of a "regionalized" curriculum in urbanism

Here, the recontextualization of knowledge in the pedagogic text of "regions" is examined through the case study of a master's degree programme in "Urbanism and Development". "Pedagogic texts" bear the material trace of curriculum change within universities. As final and formalized products, they enable the analysis of the process to which they have been subjected to.

This recontextualization is examined in reference to indicators of the "stratification", "segmentation" and "hierarchization" of contents in the official programme of study[15] of the curriculum in addition to data from interviews, centred on teaching, with academics and students. The aim was to grasp the strength of classification and framing relations which characterize this curriculum as well as the principles structuring these relations. It is worth recalling that in Bernstein's theory, *classification* and *framing* are indices of the recontextualization of knowledge, of the relations between discourses, knowledge and practices and of the control which is exerted within each category. In other words, they are indices revealing the principles of social selection operating at the level of knowledge.

The thematic master's degree in urbanism has as its main object the study of urban planning. It is a hybrid curriculum characterized by a plurality of disciplinary pedagogic contents including geography, economics, sociology, law and architecture. Their coexistence in a common programme of study signifies the "openness" between disciplines.

However, disciplinary knowledge is presented in serial form in the curriculum: each discipline makes a specialized contribution towards the study of the specific transversal object. In the case of urban development, classical theories in each discipline are not taught as such, but as specialized theories for the object of study. Concepts are often taught independently of the theoretical model from which they are derived. In this sense, it can be argued that disciplinary knowledge undergoes a "de-contextualization" from the internal logic of its discipline of origin and then a "re-contextualization" within a new subject.[16] In reference to sociology, social scientific knowledge is addressed in terms of social problems related to urban development. Hence, despite the "openness" produced by transversality, the serialization of disciplinary knowledge persists. Transversality refers to the definition of the object of study as a set of problems which have to be addressed separately by each discipline, according to its own logic. This has implications for the internal logic of each discipline. In sociology for example, it is possible to observe a displacement of its object, from a sociological problem to a social problem or, more specifically, a displacement from the analysis of social action and of social relations to the resolution of problems produced by them. This specific recontextualization of sociology entails a difference between questioning the creation of a social categorization and having to deal with existing categories. The analysis of pedagogic content reveals that the teaching of sociology within "regions" does not answer to internal questions of sociology but rather to questions addressed with the thematic object of the master's degree.

Disciplinary transversality is, thus, more a collection of various disciplinary contents within a curriculum (serialization) than it is a pedagogic articulation of disciplines within teaching (integration): a sort of juxtaposition of different disciplines. For this reason, an absence of classification between disciplines can be observed. This is the opening suggested by the new pedagogic model: the abolition of classification and, thus, of power relations between disciplinary pedagogic discourses.

Nonetheless, classification does not disappear completely from the curriculum. The analysis of pedagogic contents reveals, as a theme that exists across contents, a strong framing of the selection of disciplinary knowledge and of their associations within and between it, with the aim of developing an action plan. In recontextualizing, the logic of action according to a professional activity dominates over the scientific logic. Consequently, articulation does not take place at the level of teaching but rather at the level of the application of knowledge in a professional context: a knowledge projected to practice, elaborated within transversal professional contents. This is evident, for example, in the case of the "Atelier of urbanism project"[17] unit. The transversal contents become more significant through the sequencing of the programme: the curriculum tends towards a transversal specialization of autonomous disciplinary knowledge. The course's legitimacy is justified by this type of content. The importance placed on this content, as opposed to disciplinary content, is evident in terms of the teaching hours and credits devoted to it. To review, the classification of knowledge between disciplines is fading, while the classification between disciplinary and transversal professional contents becomes rigid. This means that there is a power relation which prevails within contents, but which is expressed in a different way than in traditional disciplinary curricula.

According to the interviews with academics and master's students, the transversal professional contents closest to professional activity take "privileged places" in the expression of pluridisciplinarity. In the face of this type of content, academics abandon their disciplinary identities for transversal or plural pedagogic identities, where educational aims are not discipline-centred, but transversal, aiming at the development of action plans. However, it is worth highlighting that control within this specific communication context is rigid. The different stages of the procedures and the role of each member of the group are clearly defined, and final products are predetermined by the commands of organizations external to university (such as local territorial authorities).[18]

Another characteristic of this "region of knowledge" is the weakening framing of the relation between transmitter and acquirer, which enables the space to produce a potential change in the "pedagogic text". For the moment, I shall contend that this confirms the necessity of a condition of disciplinary heterogeneity: that is a pedagogy based not upon the individual (and individual performance) but upon group work and its dynamic as a group.

To continue, this "region of knowledge" is elaborated and realized through a pair of rules: "recognition" and "realization" rules (Bernstein 1996, p. 105). The recognition rule refers to the principle which defines the knowledge considered as valid and to be transmitted and acquired within a "region" and, thus, which orients the members of the context to its specialization. This rule is reflected through the equivalent place of all types of knowledge (technical operations, theoretical knowledge, disciplinary knowledge, practical competences, etc.), at the benefit of transversal contents, where clearly defined professional objectives take precedence. Disciplinary knowledge can be detached from its disciplinary field of origin, but it is never dissociated from the thematic object on which the various disciplines share focus. Disciplinary contents take the form of an introduction to a "region", whereas transversal contents reveal the specialization of the transmission context: the construction of an operational knowledge for professional practice. These contents demonstrate the value the course could potentially have in the labour market.

The "realization" rule refers to the way knowledge, already selected as valid, can be associated with other knowledge; the logic of articulation of knowledge. As observed, "regional" knowledge centres on themes. Disciplinary knowledge does not acquire its legitimacy until it is organized in relation to other types of knowledge in order to produce knowledge valid for the field of practice. In this sense, the framing of the communication context becomes rigid, since there is a reinforcement of the hierarchy between the "region of knowledge" (as a pedagogic system) and the field of practice. Consequently, there is a weakening of framing at the level of the pedagogic relation and, more generally, of the local social basis of the region, between transmitters and acquirers, and between disciplinary pedagogic identities and knowledge. However, the structuring of the "region" tends towards greater external control. In the case of urbanism, the "Urbanism Chart", established by professionals in this field, is an important reference for the development of the program of study, of the pedagogic contents and orientations of the projects to be undertaken. Cabinets of urbanism (i.e. private offices) and territorial authorities are highly invested in the pedagogic process, contributing to the recontextualization of knowledge to be acquired. Furthermore, the introduction of specific contents and specialized knowledge in the programme attests to the connection between the structure of the curriculum and the current context of the urbanist's profession.[19] Thus, while there are openings, there is also a new closure operating within contents. Framing (in)forms the classification of knowledge. The rigid control exerted by the field of practice eliminates the classification between disciplines and enables their association.

The pedagogic discourse in the curriculum of urbanism abolishes its opposition to "horizontal discourse".[20] It is embedded in the context of a specific professional practice; it is local and distinct from other discourses generated by other contexts of practice. This discourse is situated within the social division of labour. It is embodied by the latency of the segmentation of horizontal discourses, as opposed to a vertical scientific discourse. Therefore, the pedagogic model of the French universities is no longer criticized as "too abstract". However, the issue of the connection between theory and practice within transmission is always in suspense: terms are often reversed, but the power relation between these two poles persists.

In official texts, the connection between the regionalization of knowledge and professionalization refers to a closer relation between higher education and the economic field. On the other hand, within curricula, this connection is expressed through a mode of organization of knowledge which enables the recognition that the structuring of the curriculum tends to be determined by the needs of the professional activity. This recontextualizing principle implies some transformations at the level of the selection of knowledge and of its mode of transmission. At this point, the fundamental interest of Bernstein's approach – that what is interesting for analysis is not the presence of a specific type of knowledge in the programme, but rather the relations between knowledge and the way social selection operates within contents – should be stressed. This is one reason why Bernstein's theory extends beyond scientific relativism. The main proposition is less to question the value of transversal professional knowledge within university courses than it is to demonstrate how the field of practice orients the principles commanding curriculum construction. As Maton suggests (2005), the "relational autonomy" of the pedagogic recontextualizing field is weakening.[21] Heteronomous principles (external to the field of education) tend to dominate autonomous principles (internal to the field of education), such as its ways of working, practices, aims and markers of achievement. This tendency effects content and the recontextualization of knowledge, towards a higher level of contextualization and segmentation of knowledge. Furthermore, it effects the structuring of the relations between the individual and knowledge and, thus, between individuals.

Towards a Bernsteinian approach to curriculum change

This (ongoing) empirical research on "regions of knowledge" testifies to the heuristic character of the Bernstein's concepts for curriculum analysis. This is especially true as they allow for connection between macro and micro levels: from the analysis of struggles between discourses and of the stakes in these struggles at macro level to analysis of the constitution of pedagogic discourses within curricula. Classification and framing concepts enable the observation of the embedding of an *instructional discourse* (of knowledge, of competences, of the transversality of disciplines) in a *regulative discourse* of social order, through the control by external fields over communication (deemed legitimate according to the economic and social relevance of the knowledge to be transmitted). The specific form of transversality between disciplines, realized within transversal professional master's degree programmes, relates to specific recontextualizing principles. Therefore, the change to be considered is not the transition from a model of "disciplines" to a model of "regions of knowledge", but rather the transformation of boundaries between knowledge and within learning (Stavrou 2009). Bernstein's most interesting concept is not that of "regionalization", then, but that of the "recontextualization" of knowledge. The first is situated sociohistorically, contributing to a critical sociology; the second is universal, contributing to a sociology of description and enabling the understanding of generative processes.

A question arising from this research is: how do the relations of the classification and framing of knowledge observed in this "pedagogic text" operate at the level of acquisition? The effects can certainly be anticipated. For the sociologist, the classification and framing characterizing a pedagogic model produce specific forms of identity and influence the shaping of consciousness. However, in reading Bernstein, the shift from the process of the transmission of knowledge to the process of the acquisition of knowledge appears to occur automatically. This is why, in continuing to develop and expand Bernstein's work, we should focus more closely on the process of the acquisition of knowledge: how classification and framing relations are integrated by individuals, how these relations influence the way individuals perceive and act on the social world, and how they contribute to the construction of identity. For example, this research demonstrates that knowledge is "de-contextualized" from its field of origin and "re-contextualized" in new discourses and action plans, projected to relate to professional practice. This process is not visible for students, since they only acquire the recontextualized knowledge. Consequently, we could question the way that students appropriate this knowledge and the ways they can transfer it to other situations. This is work that remains to be done. Likewise, in his work to understand the mechanisms generating power and control relations within educational transmission, and to define and explain the stakes of this transmission process, Bernstein paved the way for work by other researchers.

The curriculum analysis initiated by Bernstein stands as an extensive contribution to scientific thought on education. For this reason, I would like to highlight the fecundity of his model of description and of his concept of recontextualization. On one hand, it enables symbolic control over curriculum development to be revealed through the content of "pedagogic texts".

On the other hand, it constitutes a socio-morphological approach which enables analysis to move beyond the determinism of the sociology of reproduction. The focus is not on inequalities between social groups but on relations within the "pedagogic text", structured by macro-social stakes, of which social inequalities are potentially (and often) the end result.

The originality of Bernstein's conceptualization of the "regionalization of knowledge" is evident as it reveals the construction of an autonomous cognitive category, considering the internal constitution of "regions of knowledge" as a relay of symbolic control and as a device where control is materialized. This implies the risks inherent in the segmentation (based on a social division of labour which is historically precarious and in contradiction with the vision of "flexibility" and "adaptability" for individuals as displayed in official national and European documents) of pedagogic discourse and, thus, of knowledge. Finally, it is worth highlighting the potential of change evident in Bernstein's sociology, as we can consider, for example, the grounds for the possible transformation of the relay. The dynamic perspective of the concept of recontextualization enables this, if we can reveal the closures of the process and where and how they operate. This is why I suggest a reconsideration of current curricular change within universities, the interrogation of the professionalization and regionalization of knowledge, and the recognition of other possible realizations.

Notes

1 This research is being conducted towards a PhD and has been funded by a doctoral studentship from the French Regional Council of Provence-Alpes-Côte d'Azur and supported by the Rectorate of the Academy of Aix-Marseille. This chapter is based on data collected between 2005 and 2006. Research was carried out on professional multidisciplinary master's degree programmes in the human and social sciences, created after the implementation of the LMD Reform (four-year contract 2004–7). The case study of the master's in urbanism rests upon qualitative data, official documents (directive documents, programme of study, teaching planning, course syllabi) and 17 interviews with policy interviewees (university's and ministry's agents contributing to curricular restructuring), academics (contributing to the development and implementation of the master's degree) and students of the course.

2 Bernstein himself was critical regarding singulars (disciplinary discourses): these discourses are characterized by strong narcissistic identities, producing discourses only about themselves and oriented to their own development, maintaining strong boundaries and hierarchies, protecting them from other singulars.

3 For Bernstein, the "pedagogic text" is a "privileged text". It refers to the legitimate curriculum and pedagogy, to any legitimate oral, visual, spatial, postural attitude or position.

4 Orientation Law no. 68-978 12-11-1968 (Loi Faure) in Higher Education.

5 Law no. 84-52 26-01-1984 (Loi Savary) on Higher Education, Title I, article 2.

6 For Bernstein, the "introjected" pedagogic model is more oriented towards symbolic control shaping consciousness for individuals. In contrary, the projected

model is rather oriented towards the value of the product in fields external to education.

7 Orientation Law on education, no. 89-486 10-07-1989, annexed report.

8 Ministerial order 9-04-1997 on Higher Education degrees.

9 Common Declaration of European Ministers of Education, 19 June 1999, Bologna.

10 The Ministry of Education's evaluation agencies contribute to the establishment of the "regionalization of knowledge" by adopting a critical discourse towards the former model of disciplines. We can refer here to the General Inspections of Administration of National Education and Research (IGAENR) report: "the struggle of disciplines to preserve their status in the program model and of academics to maintain their DESS degrees pollutes even more the courses of study" (IGAENR 2005, p. 25). "Courses which have a specific public and prospects shouldn't lose their advantages (practical courses open to professional fields) and be dissolved within general and not specified specialised courses" (IGAENR 2005, p. 29).

11 This chapter refers to national and local agencies involved at the micro level of the process of the recontextualization of university knowledge. However, it is necessary to take into consideration the presence of agencies at the European or international levels, which have assumed an increasing role within this process, especially since the Bologna Declaration (they often appear as implicit actors). These agencies include the European Commission and its experts, the European University Association, the European Association of Institutions of Higher Education, the European Association for Quality-Assurance in Higher Education, the European Students' Union, "Business Europe", "Education International", UNESCO, the OECD, etc.

12 Expertise functions for curricular assessment, at the national level, are held by the AERES agency. Created in 2007, this agency succeeds the former "Scientific, Technical and Pedagogic Mission" of the Ministry of Higher Education and Research. The Agency of Evaluation of Research and of Higher Education is declared as an independent administrative authority with three evaluation missions: (1) evaluation of higher education and research establishments; (2) evaluation of research units; (3) evaluation of higher education courses and diplomas.

13 At the internal (university) level, agents responsible for curricular expertise are academics (elected members) having administrative roles within university councils, especially the Council of Studies and University Life. This council's function is to make propositions to the university's Administration Council regarding orientations and contents of courses of study, evaluation modalities for students and planning of the university's degrees.

14 I refer here to the materiality of the educational institution which Emile Durkheim brought to light during his lectures at the beginning of the twentieth century, collected by Halbwachs in *L'évolution pédagogique en France* (1938). As Ramognino argues (2002), in sociology of education, one needs to analyse the trace of the cognitive and symbolic forms of what can be observed: programmes of study, oral language of institutional actors, physical spaces, walls, interactions. Thus, the Bernsteinian theory of description and the socio-morphological approach to curricula enables the examination of the recontextualization process in its materiality, of the material relations between knowledge, discourses and individuals defined by the curriculum.

15 Stratification refers to the logic of the distribution and assembly of contents in the programme or within each content area. The hierarchization of contents is measured by the volume, in teaching hours and credits of each content and its importance within teaching units. Finally, the segmentation indicator enables the measurement of the degree of integration or separation between contents and the definition of the principles to which they are oriented.

16 Sociology appears in the first year programme of the master's degree, within a "regionalized" teaching unit, entitled "Economic development and social logics". Besides a brief introduction to the history of the discipline, sociology is addressed in terms of targeted issues in which knowledge is (re)contextualized in the urbanism's prism such as the "resorption of shantytowns, functioning of social housing, inhabitants' investigations and neighbourhood planning, city contracts, urban management of proximity, involvement of inhabitants" (Master of Urbanism, Detailed presentation of contents, 2005–6).

17 This teaching unit (which represents 96 out of 336 teaching hours for the whole programme) consists in grouping students in pluridisciplinary teams of diagnostic-scenario-planning, in order to respond to real commands by project managers. As presented in the master's brochure, this content aims at developing competences and skills including "elaboration, project conducting, articulation of urbanistic instruments and methods, professional positioning within work relationships, pluridisciplinary team working". Contents of this atelier (workshop) are defined by external regulation and conditions set by the professional field. For example, elaborating projects is considered a major new direction for the professional activity of urbanism, induced by the Loi de Solidarité et de Renouvellement urbain (Law of Urban Solidarity and Renewing).

18 These elements call into question the connection between the requirements of professional activity and the principles of elaboration of the "regionalization of knowledge". What determines the placement of specialists from different disciplinary fields within urbanism? Is it the specificity of the field of practice? Or rather the educational-academic object which needs to associate disciplines for its study? It is worth highlighting that within this curriculum, the only pluridisciplinary course's contents are those which explicitly refer to the profession's practice.

19 In the transition from the DESS degree of urbanism to the development of the master's degree (following the implementation of the LMD Reform), the volume of teaching hours for disciplinary contents has considerably decreased (economy: from 48 to 18 hours; architecture: from 27 to 18 hours; sociology: from 30 to 18 hours). On the other hand, new contents, which are essentially focused on knowledge and competences connected to the profession's requirements and their evolution in the labour market, are introduced into the programme and include "Territorial diagnostic", "Communication, negotiation and mediating", "Communal planning" and "Land ownership policies and authorizations".

20 I refer here to Bernstein's typology of knowledge categories and the distinction he made between two types of discourses existing within the educational field: a "vertical discourse" consisting of assimilated school or academic knowledge described as coherent, explicit and systematically structured, in which the circulation of knowledge is accomplished through explicit, official or pedagogic distribution rules, and a "horizontal discourse", characterized as oral, local, context-dependent, tacit, contradictory between contexts, but not within con-

tents, and segmented in its realization according to segmentation and special-ization of practices in the society, an "acquisition of a particular view of cultural realities, or rather of a way of realising these realities" (Bernstein 1996, p. 165).

21 By developing Bourdieu's concept of "autonomy", Maton (2005) brings to light the necessity to make a distinction between a "positional" and a "relational" dimension of autonomy, in order to address contemporary change within the field of higher education. The positional dimension refers to the origins (social position) of actors running higher education whereas the relational autonomy refers to the principles these actors are adopting in their activity.

10 Applying a sociological analysis of pedagogic discourse

Éric Mangez and Catherine Mangez

Schooling in Belgium has always been provided by both private and public agencies, which gradually formed networks to carry out their missions. At the lower secondary school level, the network of independent Catholic schools (a state-funded private agency) currently provides schooling to about 60 per cent of each student cohort, while the network of the French Community (a public agency) provides schooling to about 30 per cent of each cohort of students. The remaining students receive schooling in other networks organized by communes, provinces or other private actors.

This institutional configuration means that each network is subject to regulations imposed by law, while simultaneously enjoying some autonomy (especially with regard to the drafting of course programmes). They must therefore interpret the government's legal injunctions and apply them to their own practices and regulations. In theory, the law does not intervene in pedagogical matters. However, many actors within these agencies acknowledge that the Belgian education reform movement of the 1990s, and especially the "missions"[1] decree of 1997, significantly encroach on both teaching objectives and methods. This is believed to be the case even in the independent Catholic network, whose identity is associated with freedom in teaching methods. An opinion of the Council of State of 23 April 1997 also points out that, as a result of the reform movement and, in particular, the decree, "funded institutions, and particularly the independent network, have seen their freedom reduced in areas such as curricula, educational choices, level of education and choice of students".

This constitutes, then, a particularly interesting institutional configuration providing the opportunity to observe, within the same segment of time and space, the interpretive work carried out, as mandated, by different networks on the same collection of documents (the "missions" decree and the various directives associated with it). The present chapter is concerned only with the educational responses of the network of independent Catholic schools and of the network of the French Community. First, we seek to demonstrate that the work of these two networks has, in effect, been based on the same paradigm, as defined by law; then based on the same matrix of possibilities and constraints, they have adopted, though at the margin, two different orientations in terms of the pedagogical model employed; and finally that it is possible to relate these pedagogical orientations and models to the values expressed by the networks, as well as to the positions and trajectories taken by pedagogical coordinators within the division of labour of each network.

The sociology of educational discourses

Visible pedagogy, invisible pedagogy; performance and competence

The work of Basil Bernstein (see especially 1975, 1997) provides tools for describing and analysing pedagogic discourse. While these may, in turn, generate successive subdimensions, three fundamental dimensions structure every pedagogical model in Bernstein's thinking: curricular classifications, the framing of teaching–learning relationships and evaluation criteria.

In analysing these dimensions, Bernstein created two pedagogical ideal-types:[2] the visible pedagogical model and the invisible pedagogical model. The visible/invisible distinction must be analysed from the standpoint of students: it is primarily in reference to them that the pedagogical model is either visible or invisible. In the invisible model, the tasks to be performed are global tasks; the sequencing of the tasks is loosely defined, or, implicit; the student may have difficulty understanding the aims of the task; only the teacher understands the specific objectives being pursued, and these objectives are highly integrated. A comprehensive theory of child development underlies invisible pedagogy. Conversely, visible pedagogy is characterized by an explicit division and sequencing (strong classification) of subject matter and learning; it places less emphasis on individual creativity, and the hierarchies in its teaching–learning relationships are more explicit, as are its evaluations. Frequently, though not always, it is based on behaviourist approaches to learning.

Bernstein's various descriptions of these pedagogical models are very fertile. For example, he points out that invisible pedagogies make certain student characteristics highly visible to the teacher, especially those associated with their personality and inner life. With regard to visible pedagogies, focusing on a child's standing in relation to predefined learning levels obscures each child's uniqueness, and instead creates classifications that make the relative standing of each student directly visible.

In his more recent work, Bernstein (2000) distinguishes between performance and competence models of pedagogy. In many ways, this conceptualization of performance pedagogy resembles Bernstein's earlier visible pedagogical model, while his concept of competence pedagogy may be compared to the invisible model. Thus, the distinction between performance and competence, which emerges in both the social world and the field of theory developed by Bernstein, constitutes a new way of perceiving the older visible/invisible distinction. However, the concept of competence is equivocal, and in practice has sometimes been interpreted inconsistently. In its humanistic and open version, it refers to the objective of creatively developing each student's potentialities within an integrated curriculum. Elsewhere (especially as promoted under the rhetoric of the "new managerialism" and associated techniques such as the development of and accountability for meeting – as measured by standardized external evaluations – content standards), it has served to redirect pedagogical practices towards performance defined in a narrower sense (i.e. performance-based curricula) (Broadfoot and Pollard 2006).

While traditional classifications have been highly structured around disciplines, recent works identify new forms of classification. At the level of higher education, especially in Anglo-Saxon countries, some authors have demonstrated a shift from a discipline-centred, theoretical curriculum that the scientific community evaluates for its "intrinsic value", towards an interdisciplinary, applied curriculum (oriented towards the resolution of problems) that is evaluated for its performativity and exchange value on the labour market (Naidoo and Jamieson 2003). By convention, the literature (Ensor 2001) refers to these two models, respectively, as the Mode 1 Curriculum and the Mode 2 Curriculum. This may be compared to the recent work of Bernstein (2000), in which he identifies a process of curricular "regionalization". This process, which is applied primarily in higher education, involves shifting from curricular classification based on distinct disciplines to a region-centred or problem-centred curriculum, incorporating various disciplinary approaches, with both cognitive and instrumental aims. This type of curriculum depends more on the problems that need to be resolved and on the individuals that define these problems (i.e. social and economic actors), than on the disciplines and on the individuals (who present themselves as) responsible for these disciplines (i.e. academic actors).

The social uses of pedagogic discourse

Bernstein's model of invisible pedagogy, which has been associated since the 1970s with kindergartens and private schools in particular (but which we may assume is today being employed in certain areas of public schooling and in university education), emerged because it led many (especially, perhaps, proponents of "progressive" education) to believe that it constituted a way to combat the reproduction of social inequality (a process in which education, particularly "traditional" models of visible pedagogy, had been increasingly implicated). In contrast to this view, which sees the invisible pedagogical model as a force for social emancipation, Bernstein suggests that the shift from visible to invisible pedagogy is part of a transformation in methods that gives rise to further educational inequality. The new methods are receiving their impetus from and working for the benefit of a new section of the middle class.

This new middle class is the product of the increasingly complex world of work requiring, among other things, greater flexibility, versatility, imagination and creativity. This class also euphemizes power relationships. Its members become symbolic agents of control and its orientation differs from that of the old middle class, which belonged to a world involved in the production and circulation of material (rather than symbolic) goods. Whereas in the old middle class, social control was achieved through impersonal rules, in the new middle class it is achieved primarily through interpersonal communication processes emphasizing mutual respect, persuasion, listening and the recognition of each person's individuality. Consequently, the invisible model supported by the new middle class leads to new control methods based on self-evaluation and peer evaluation, leading to implicit competition and imposing additional responsibilities on each student within a logic of "contract" or personal project.

The pedagogical norm and its reinterpretations

The spirit of the reform

The concept of competence, which is of special interest to us since it is central to the pedagogical component of the reform movement we are examining, originated in the social sciences. Although the concept is vague and polysemous, or perhaps due to these qualities, it has become a core category in thinking revolving around the skills expected of workers and the definition and evaluation of these skills. The concept of competence started to be deployed in educational systems when enterprises, and their managers, incorporated it as a principle guiding task definition, individual assessment and career regulation (Rope and Tanguy 2000).

While in the world of business, the concept of competence is linked primarily with post-Fordist type questions of managerial efficiency (Brown 1995), this does not imply that once it is incorporated into the world of education, it will be understood through the same prism. Competence, in conjunction with the educational reform movement associated with it, has been linked to a series of explanatory principles raised by educational, political and administrative elites in an exercise designed as a way of formulating a critique of existing pedagogical practices and as a desirable pedagogical prospect.

Referring to Boltanski and Thévenot (1991), one might say that these explanations belong primarily to (1) the world of civic-mindedness (we need to promote "the success of the greatest number" by way of "schools favouring success for all" and by defining objectives in terms of "core" minimal competences that everyone should attain) and (2) the world of inspiration (the importance attributed to the fulfilment of the child, which must have a central place in learning, and the critique of the psycho-emotional effects of repeating a year and of relegating students to lower educational streams).

These two worlds respectively constitute central reference points for the "the social left" and the "cultural left" (Liénard and Capron 2000) or, as Boltanski and Chiapello (1999) put it, for a "social critique" and an "artistic critique". To this, we can add the world of industriousness based on the efficiency achieved, for the most part, as children who are fulfilled in school will take pleasure in learning; this ensures that the educational endeavour will be effective.

On a pedagogical level, we can select from the "missions" decree, and from the various documents with which it is associated, key elements that have been analysed according to Bernstein's theoretical concepts. In particular, the texts make fluid pedagogical time and space, notably by employing the concepts of "cycle", "differentiated pedagogy", the "pedagogical continuum" and the "elimination of repeating a year". They also emphasize the need to acquire cross-curricular competence, the belief that segmented learning cannot be justified and the need to give increased status to horizontal teacher–student relationships. Thus, they weaken classification and promote teaching–learning relationships that aim at greater horizontality. On the other hand, these texts also make provision for the eventual creation of batteries of standardized external evaluation. While the networks have not yet incorporated this measure, there could of course be significant developments here in the future.

The power of the current pedagogical movement is indicated, notably, by the development of legislative documents that have declared certain lessons taught in class to be illegal. For example, as indicated by the government of the French community in its comments on and statement regarding the purposes of the "missions' decree", from now on straightforward completion of conjugation tables is against the law: "Concretely, a lesson designed to get students to complete conjugation tables, but lacking a direct connection with reading or listening comprehension, with writing or with improving verbal competence, categorically contradicts the present decree" (Government of the French Community, Exposé des motifs et commentaires, 6 May 1997). It is somewhat surprising to see a government take a position on the legitimacy of an activity (henceforth, having inextricable legal and pedagogical dimensions) that consists of completing conjugation tables. As far as we know, no other country has gone so far in its legal requirements regarding educational practices.

Course programmes

Thus far, we have briefly described a range of pedagogical orientations and content resulting from the publication of the "missions' decree" and its related documents. The decree and its related documents were themselves intended to influence the preparation of the programmes by the networks. We have since witnessed the creation of a new cohort of course programmes. The objective of the present section is to reveal the structure of the

pedagogic discourse expressed by these texts. To identify historical variations in pedagogy within and between the networks, we have created a
corpus (of about 1,000 pages) using the following texts: the programmes of
the French Community (FC) in 1985, the programmes of the FC in 2000,
the programmes of the independent Catholic network (IN) in 1985 and the
IN programmes in 2000.

We have decided to examine these texts in terms of the relative occur-
rence of the various keywords they contain. Our analysis thus places great
store in naming processes. According to Bourdieu, sociology must:

> examine what can be expressed in words when it constructs "social
> facts", as well as what is contributed by the battle over classification – a
> dimension in every class struggle – in the formation of classes, be they
> social classes, age classes, sexual classes, as well as clans, tribes, ethnic
> groups or nations.
>
> (Bourdieu 2001, p. 155)

Thus, sociological interest in ways of naming reality is based on the claim that
social relationships penetrate and permeate language, which then serves to
reveal social phenomena. Our effort to select words likely to indicate pedagogical trends was based on Bernstein's theoretical framework. The database formed
includes 18 statistical units (referring to course programmes) and 75 variables
(referring to keywords). In total, about 13,000 observations were made.

Factor analysis of the database reveals two principal components of pedagogic discourse. The variables listed below provide the essence of the pedagogical language's principal component (20 per cent of the total variance)
and its second component (16 per cent). They are presented in their order of
importance as factors. The only variables listed here are those whose saturation coefficient is greater than 0.5 (in absolute value).

The first component is easy to understand: it is negatively correlated to
the variable "construct/" (−0.673) (which refers to a constructivist perspective on education) as well as to the variable "situation" (−0.524) (which
refers to the simulation of real-life situations for students). However, to a
large extent this component is largely circumscribed by variables such as
"effort" (0.874), "exercise" (0.743), "lesson" (0.860), "subject" (0.778),
"schoolmaster" (0.709) and "teacher" (0.843). A series of terms forming the
core of a traditional pedagogy are also highly correlated with the first factor:
"aptitude" (0.753), "attitude" (0.581), "observation" (0.555) and "objectives" (0.598). This model, developed by child psychologists influenced by
behaviourism, emphasizes the need for teachers to clearly define their "objectives". In addition, it advocates meticulous and methodical "observation" by
teachers of student "aptitude" and "behaviour". Following convention, we
will call the first factor the "behaviour" factor.

The second factor does not create interpretation problems inasmuch as it
is greatly influenced by terms that are central to the reform movement we

Table 10.1 Grouping of the two principal components

Variables	Saturation coefficients for factor 1	Variables	Saturation coefficients for factor 2
Effort (effort)	0.874	Information (information)	0.849
Leçon (lesson)	0.860	Formatif (formative)	0.844
Professeur (teacher)	0.843	Projet (project)	0.789
Cahier (notebook)	0.813	Apprentissage (learning)	0.724
Matière (subject)	0.778	Consigne (instructions)	0.716
Persévérer (perseverance)	0.769	Certificatif (attestation)	0.705
Aptitude (aptitude or ability)	0.753	Élève (student)	0.698
Exercice (exercise)	0.743	Actif (active)	0.659
Adolescent (adolescent)	0.733	Structuration (structuring)	0.652
Esprit critique (critical spirit)	0.710	Autonomie (autonomy)	0.633
Maître (schoolmaster)	0.709	Plaisir (pleasure)	0.622
Construit/(construct/)	−0.673	Tâche (task)	0.606
Erreur (error)	0.654	Compétence (competence)	0.606
Enfant (child)	0.649	Situation (situation)	0.594
De base (basic)	0.628	Performance (performance)	0.591
Objectif (objective)	0.598	Savoir (knowledge)	0.591
Désir (desire)	0.598	S'approprier (appropriation)	0.575
Transversal (transverse)	0.582	Découvrir (discovery)	−0.564
Attitude (attitude)	0.581	Assimiler (assimilate)	−0.545
Réussite (success)	0.575		
Observation (observation)	0.555		
Correction (correction)	0.536		
Progrès (progress)	0.524		
Situation (situation)	−0.524		

are examining. Of course, there is "competence" (0.606), but there are also "situation(s)" (real-life simulations) (0.594) for the "student" (0.698), who must be "active" (0.659), the advantages of pedagogy centred on a "project" (0.789) and "formative" evaluation (0.844), which enhances the status of "autonomy" (0.633). The second factor is negatively correlated with the variables "assimilate" (−0.545) and "discover" (−0.564), which symbolically refer to the idea of moving the student towards knowledge that is "already there". Following convention, we will call the second factor the "competence" factor.

Based on Bernstein's language, we see that the first factor, on its positive side (to the right of the *x*-axis in the factorial design below) corresponds to a pedagogical orientation more visible than the second, which, on its positive side (the upper *y*-axis), moves in the direction of the invisible pole. The first factor is in fact positively correlated, at once, with terms symbolizing strong classifications and framing and a clear division between and sequencing of the educational activities and objectives pursued (exercise, objective, observation, lesson) and an explicit and hierarchical teaching–learning relationship (schoolmaster, teacher, child and effort). The second factor is positively correlated with terms symbolizing a loose classification of learning (situation, project, competence) and weaker framing in the form of a less explicit teaching–learning hierarchy (the "student" is "active" and displays "autonomy", the evaluation must be "formative").

The coordinates of each variable are defined by the strength of its correlations (saturation coefficients) with each of the two factors forming the axes of the figure.

When we examine various course programme scores for the two factors in Figure 10.2, we see, first, that the old programmes tend to scatter horizontally, that is, along the "behaviour" axis, while the new programmes scatter vertically, along the "competence" axis. This indicates that there has been a shift in the debates and differences of opinion. In 1985, these were based on the model represented by the "behaviour" factor. In 2000, they dealt with the language of reform as represented by the "competence" axis, though some programmes were more closely linked to this language (especially literature programmes and programmes in the independent network) than others (especially the more "scientific" programmes and those in the Community network).

How to read the graph: the *x*-axis represents the "behaviour" factor; the *y*-axis is the "competence" axis; the programmes are identified by a code referring, first, to the period (1985 or 2000), then to the network (Independent or French Community) and, lastly, to the discipline.

In Figure 10.2, arrows were drawn to indicate, discipline by discipline, historical shifts in pedagogic discourse. Notably, most of the shifts in the graph occurred concurrently from right to left; that is, moving away from the language of the "behaviour" axis (indicated by a lower score on this axis), and from the bottom toward the top, that is, moving towards the language of "competence" (indicated by a higher score on this axis).

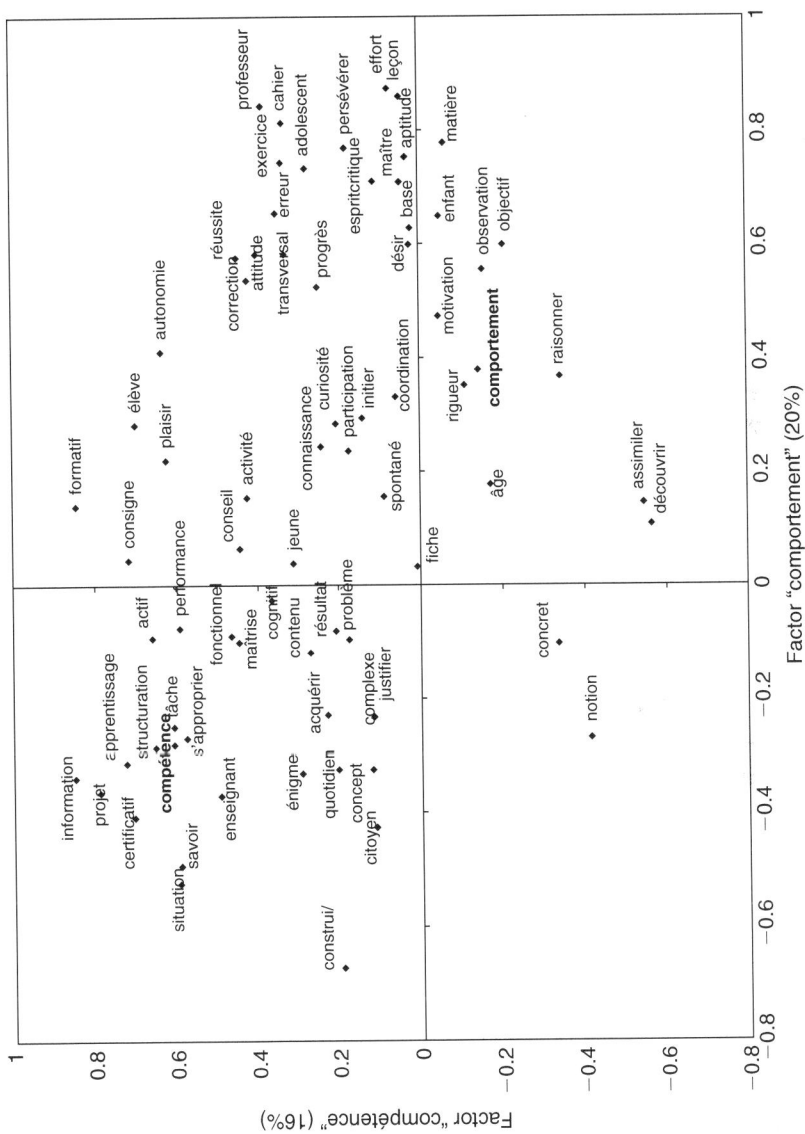

Figure 10.1 Saturation coefficients for 75 variables (2 factors selected).

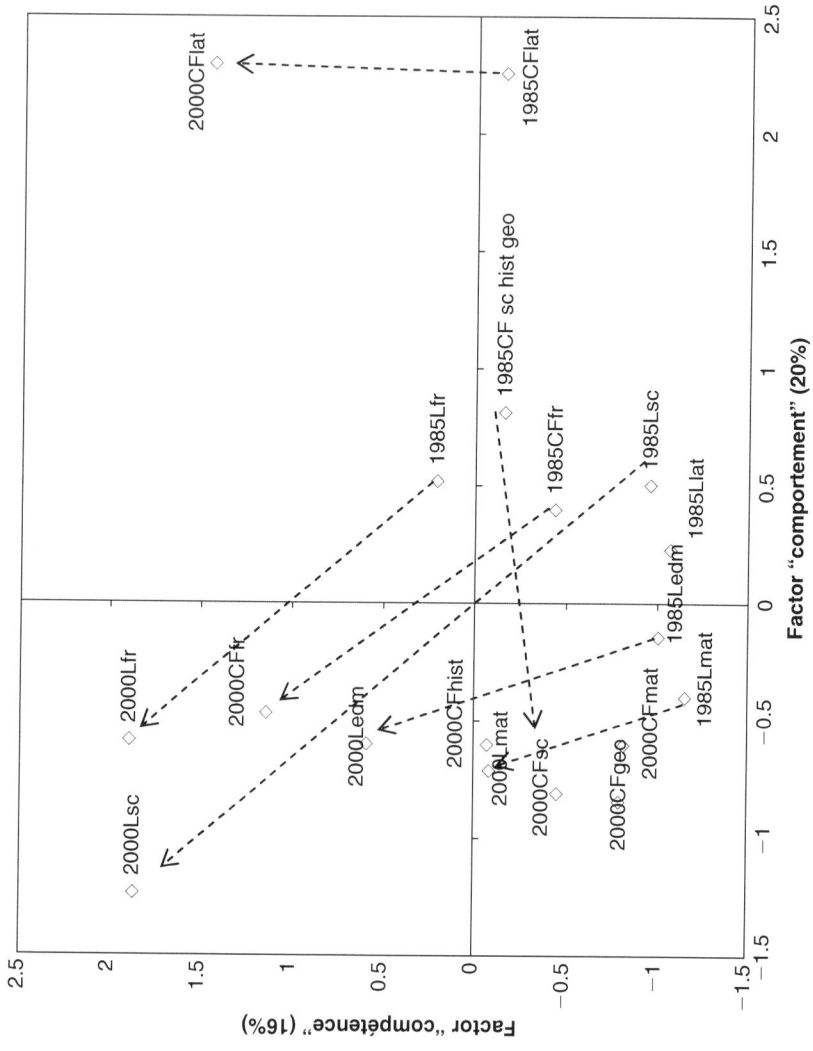

Figure 10.2 Factor scores for course programmes.

In addition, the analysis reveals that in 1985 it was primarily authors of course programmes for the French Community who mobilized the legitimate pedagogical narrative. In 2000, the legitimate narrative was transformed to give increased legitimacy to the principle of "construction of knowledge", to "projects", to the simulation of real-life "situations" and to the concept of "competence". This time it was the independent network programmes that seemed to be the most replete with occurrences of its language. A more detailed analysis of the programmes in certain disciplines confirmed this different positioning of networks along the visible–invisible continuum (Mangez 2004). Interpreting the same documents, the pedagogical coordinators of the two networks took slightly different directions: in the independent network the pedagogies became less visible, while in the Community network the pedagogical model became more explicit.

In each of the two networks, the actors who mediated the reform by expressing it as course programmes revealed strong convictions regarding the point of view they were defending. The representatives of the independent network willingly acknowledged that their conception of the term "ability" was broader and more open than that of the Community network representatives. They were proud of this and felt that their position was legitimate, more audacious, more innovative and less conventional, etc. By contrast, the Community network representatives said that their position was more precise, clearer to teachers, more operational, more realistic and less vague, etc. Our objective in the remainder of the chapter is to determine the relationship between, on the one hand, the positions held within the pedagogical field and, on the other hand, the structure of the relative positions held by the mediating agents in question, the trajectories they followed, the institutional configuration in which they evolved and the values they mobilized.

The conditions in which course programmes were created

In each of the two networks, the heads of programmes were former teachers whose trajectory was differentiated from that of their colleagues (regular teachers "in the field"): they were educational advisors or area supervisors in the independent network (EA-AS) or inspectors in the Community network (IC). These two groups differed in a number of ways including: their professional trajectories; the types and volume of resources available to them; and their standing (status and mission) in relation to regular teachers in the field (Draelants *et al.* 2004). An examination[3] of these characteristics allows us to understand how these two groups were formed, and thus give meaning to the pedagogical options they defended. However, our intention here is to describe, rather than explain, their comprehensive stance; it is not to establish causal relationships between their status and the positions they took.

Educational advisors in the independent Catholic network

The organizational morphology of the independent network, which provides schooling for about 60 per cent of the population, is unique. Since 1957, the network has been organized into a federation of local organizational authorities (consisting of several similar institutions). Each local organizational authority has the right to dissociate itself from the federation and operate independently (though this has been made much more difficult following the "missions" decree). Consequently, it is not possible to provide an organizational chart that defines unequivocally the positions of power and power relationships within the network. The network is "held together" through a form of membership in which interpersonal relations and communication play a central role. Freedom (in the sense of political liberalism), personal development and celebrating differences (the uniqueness of each person) are all important values to the network and may be understood as renewed forms of Catholic values. Beyond its Catholic denomination, the network's identity relates strongly to its attachment to its independence (Charlier 2000).

The most basic characteristic of the career trajectory for an EA-AS and, more generally, that followed by mediating agents working in the area of independent (private) education, is that it is not very bureaucratic and somewhat vague. The twists and turns and ordeals punctuating this trajectory tend to vary from individual to individual, depending on the opportunities and circumstances in which they find themselves. Nonetheless, it is possible to discern certain recurring features. They all began their careers as teachers, mostly in institutions low down in the status hierarchy. Early in their careers, they proved to be very active in their institution by getting involved in one of its projects or getting deeply involved in a team activity. They all quickly joined work networks beyond the confines of the institution to which they belonged. In this way, they were able to make contact with, among others, individuals already occupying posts as mediating agents. They provided this extra work on a volunteer basis, going above and beyond the hours normally worked by teachers. They did not count the hours they put in, and they were enthusiastic, positive and spontaneous in this endeavour.

Accordingly, they were eventually noticed and solicited by a network director or by a mediating agent already working in the field. Frequently, they themselves did not know exactly why they had been chosen. In any case, it was not a mastery of their discipline that distinguished them. What set them apart from the majority of their colleagues were their character traits, the way they conducted themselves in these groups, an expressed interest in spontaneous pedagogical practices, and an ability to stand back and take stock. Even though the recruitment process was vague, they all realized that they owed their position primarily to their commitment to atypical pedagogical practices setting them apart from standard teachers "in the field".

The mission of an EA-AS is essentially one of teacher support/coaching and training, but for which there is no form of legal authority. Statutorily, the EA-AS remain teachers; they have been assigned tasks as mediating agents. This assignment, which differentiates them from their original occupational group, comes with no institutional guarantees: officially, there is nothing to guarantee that, at the end of their mandate, they will not return full time to their work "as a (normal) teacher in the field". Thus, the only recognition they receive is from their peers (the other mediating agents) and superiors, and is strictly symbolic. They are often critical in their portrayal of regular teachers in the field. They certainly have an objective interest in describing these teachers as "resistant to change", since their mission as mediating agents in the independent network is precisely to serve as agents of change.

Most of them have continued teaching, on a part-time basis, in their institution. They thereby have maintained a link with regular teaching, in an effort to boost their legitimacy in the eyes of teachers. However, this relationship with the "field" is very specific: the EA-AS work in their own classes with their own students, as part of their own institution, all of which are more likely to reinforce their efforts to implement their own practices than to portray them as observers of diverse practices and student populations. As we will demonstrate later, and contrary to what they often maintain, the EA-AS, objectively speaking, directly observe this diversity less frequently than do Community network inspectors.

Inspectors in the French Community network (IC)

The French Community network provides schooling for about 30 per cent of the primary school population. The organizational morphology of this network is very different from that of the independent network. It takes the form of a state hierarchical structure. The power relationships are formalized in an organizational chart. The network is "held together" bureaucratically and upholds the concept of "public service". Likewise, values such as equality and neutrality constitute an important point of reference (Charlier 2000). Historically, these values were formed as part of a plan, supported by both socialists and radical liberals, to deliver the masses from Catholic, clerical obscurantism.

In the education provided by the Community network, the heads of programmes are inspectors (IC). In contrast to the EA-AS of the independent network, IC often come from institutions located higher up in the educational status hierarchy. They form a group in which the average age is greater than that of mediating agents in the independent network. In addition, a much lower proportion of heads of programmes in the Community network are women.

Their trajectory differs from that of independent network agents in that it is established on the basis of exams under bureaucratic control. The age required for taking these exams is 35; in addition, it is necessary to have obtained positive inspection reports as a teacher and to have accumulated at least ten years of service. The exams deal with different topics, including didactics and knowledge of legal provisions (reforms, decrees, etc.). Candidates must also provide a critique of a lesson in front of a jury. Attaining the status of inspector requires holding a completed university degree (long-course higher education). This is unlike the position of educational advisor, which requires only a teaching degree for lower secondary classes (short-course higher education). Passing these exams gives access to a definitive status, namely, a career appointment when a position becomes available. Owing to these stable institutional resources, the "danger" of again becoming a full-time regular teacher is, at this point, almost nil.

The mission of an IC is primarily one of management and secondarily one of support, which is frequently also described as a mission of "guidance" in the discipline's "didactics". This differs from the perspective of the independent network agents, who speak of "support or coaching" on the "pedagogical" level. To explain their function, the IC automatically refers to various legal provisions regulating them; they use this legal legitimacy to define their management mission. Management can extend beyond monitoring conformity with programmes; it may also comprise managing grants or safety conditions, as well as conducting specific fact-finding missions at the request of the minister. While there are exceptions, the management mission of an IC generally takes precedence over their "guidance" mission.

Conclusion

Compared to pedagogical preferences of educational advisers in the Independent network, those of inspectors (IC) in the Community network are closer to the visible model. Inspectors clearly form part of a division of labour subject to bureaucratic and hierarchical control, that is, a structure in which the boundaries between tasks, missions and hierarchical levels are visible and regulated. As such, we have demonstrated that the professional trajectory employed by Community inspectors is characterized by explicit tests, which also constitute a visible model. Similarly, the social relationships between inspectors and regular teachers "in the field" manifest the characteristics of a visible relationship (explicit hierarchy: management (or control) takes precedence over guidance, and the hierarchical pre-eminence of inspectors is legal).

In addition, the trajectory followed by inspectors has conferred on them a status that clearly distinguishes them from teachers. Thus, in their course programmes they tend to detail what teachers must perform more than EA-AS do. In addition, the work performed by teachers constitutes a resource for them inasmuch as it provides them with a sphere of control: the controllable nature (characteristic of the visible pedagogical model) of teachers' work legitimates the position of inspectors in the division of labour. Thus, the greater accent placed on segmented exercises, which they justify in pedagogical terms, is for inspectors an expression of their position of superiority and control vis-à-vis teachers.

Conversely, we may characterize the tests associated with the trajectory of EA-AS in the independent network as containing certain features of an invisible pedagogical model: the individuals being evaluated (prospective EA-AS) are neither aware of the criteria employed to evaluate them, nor when (and, indeed, if) they are being evaluated. The tests rely on interpersonal communication processes. Similarly, the relationship linking educational advisors and teachers is closer to the invisible model (euphemized hierarchy, with no formal hierarchical superiority).

To illustrate in greater detail, in the French programme of the private (nonstate) sector, the link of subordination between structuring activities and functional activities appears equivalent, in the symbolic pedagogical order, to the social relationship between teachers and the EA-AS. Functional activities have the highest standing; they require initiative, dynamism and innovation and are the only activities that can be evaluated. They are the symbolic embodiment of the position and trajectory adopted by the EA-AS, and especially of the latter's principle of differentiation (having shown themselves to be different from most teachers – more dynamic, more reflective). Structuring activities have lesser value in the programmes of the independent network, which refers to them as easy-to-implement "recipes" that cannot be evaluated. They are there as the symbolic embodiment of the position and trajectory adopted by teachers with regard to the EA-AS. The work performed by teachers is only a resource for the EA-AS if the latter need "advice". The non-prescriptive aspect (characteristic of the invisible model) of the independent network programme implies that the path to be covered between the programme and the implementation of learning sequences is longer and more complex that of the Community network programme, which places greater store in the detailed descriptions of learning sequences. However, it is precisely the support/coaching provided to teachers along this path that constitutes the principal mission of the EA-AS. Here, too, one sees the emergence of a link between the characteristics of the programme and the position of the EA-AS in the division of labour: the path to be covered legitimates their position in the division of labour.

If one is to believe not only the mediating agents in each network but also consultations with teachers (Van Campenhoudt *et al.* 2004), the expectations of a significant proportion of teachers regarding programmes involve practical directives, series of exercises with answer books, and lesson models on which they can draw directly. We thus end up with a seeming paradox: as directors of programme configurations draw closer to teachers statutorily, the more the configurations they produce move away from and become more critical of teacher concerns and expectations. Stated differently: those from the two networks for whom the objective "danger" of once again becoming a regular teacher "in the field" is highest, especially as a result of a lack of stable institutional resources, are also those who create the pedagogical configurations furthest removed from the supposed expectations of teachers;

also, in creating these configurations they symbolically differentiate themselves from them and thereby restore the principle that, following the thread of past trajectories, was initially the cause of their differentiation from the aforementioned regular teachers "in the field".

The hypothesis we have developed, which aims to establish links between, on the one hand, pedagogical preferences and, on the other hand, the relative positions and trajectories of creators in the field, by no means contradicts the hypothesis according a particular pedagogical culture to each network. Rather, it seeks to demonstrate how a culture persists and becomes part of the social and organizational conditions that made it possible. However, it should not overshadow other types of explanations, especially those based on differences in values between the networks.

As we have pointed out, albeit briefly, the two networks examined here convey different values. The Community network – as a state network – and its agents set great store by the concept of "public service" (Charlier 2000) and by values such as equality, neutrality and compliance with legal standards. Historically, this network was formed to combat religious obscurantism: it viewed access to knowledge as a way to liberate the masses in the face of the ascendancy of religion. The visible pedagogical model, given that it accepts the standard yardstick by which we measure student performance, and because its approach is based on a fragmentation of knowledge (rather than on an integration of knowledge that relates to a student's experiences) is probably more in keeping with values such as neutrality and equality. Today, the independent network sets great store by values such as opening up, personal development and the uniqueness of each individual. By accentuating a student's activities and giving greater value to meaningful practices, the invisible pedagogical model actualizes these values.

Notes

1 This refers to the decree of 24 July 1997 defining the mission priorities in *Enseignement fondamental* (basic education) and *Enseignement secondaire* (secondary education), and coordinating appropriate structures.
2 Bernstein himself always refused to view these models as ideal-types. However, his justifications for this refusal were unconvincing. In our view, all the models in question have attributes of an ideal-type in the sense that they involve theoretical constructions accentuating the dimensions along which they are formed and remove any aspects that might eventually pollute the pure logic of each model. In any case, we use these models as ideal-types inasmuch as they serve as "pure" theoretical reference points, from which we examine certain empirical realities so as to identify how the latter either resemble each other or move away from the models in question.
3 The prerequisites for access to the position of intermediate officer in the various networks will soon undergo reform. We have presented the characteristics of the old system since it is the one that concerned most agents holding positions today, and in all cases those responsible for drafting programmes

11 The recontextualization of scientific knowledge and learning activities

Translating the French-language curriculum into the writing of a tale in a *classe de 6e*

Nadège Pandraud

Reading *Pedagogy, Symbolic Control and Identity* stands as a crucial moment as I work to complete my doctoral dissertation, which focuses on French language learning within *classes de 6e*[1] in Marseilles. Developing and conducting a thorough and adequate sociological analysis of the learning activities involved in such settings is a challenge. In this chapter, I shall underline two principal difficulties I have had to struggle with in this process. First, in writing a monograph focused on the classroom, I face the risk of overlooking institutional and more "macro" components of school learning in my analysis. A second problem, associated with the first, is how to integrate in the analysis dimensions of learning that are most often perceived as separate. Learning, as it takes place in the classroom, results from the coordination between a transmission activity, a reception activity and some aspect of knowledge. Synthesizing data collected in the classroom, a largely "collective" entity, is not always easy since observations conducted within them are most capable of capturing empirically the individual – and not always connected – behaviours of teachers and pupils. Moreover, research on pedagogical practices in school has been conducted predominantly in fields such as didactics, psycho-sociology and sociolinguistics, not sociology. The challenge, then, is to integrate from a sociological viewpoint the output of the research from these different fields.

In working to address these concerns, my reading of Bernstein has proved invaluable, as he provides a sociological theoretical framework that, more than most, allows for an articulation between the micro and macro levels of observation and an analysis of learning activities which takes into account the collective aspects of learning.

My study centres on pupils' appropriation of knowledge. Thus, pupils' learning activities and the cognitive effects of those activities constitute a central focus of my observation. Pupils' learning activities are considered to be the result of collective work led by the school institution and, subsequently, reappropriated by individuals within it. My purpose is to analyse the work of transmission that takes place within schools. Therefore the guiding question of my study is: What pedagogic activities promote – or what is it about these pedagogic activities that promote – the acquisition of knowledge and cognitive tools that allow pupils to extend and enhance their potential?

The descriptive language developed by Bernstein, especially his concepts of classification and framing and the distinction he draws between instructional and regulative discourse, provide the lens through which I analyse the effects of the school institution on learning activities. However, a description of learning activities requires an extended theoretical frame that also considers anthropological aspects of the activities observed in the case study presented in this chapter.

In this chapter, I first present my reading of the Bernsteinian concepts employed in my study. Then, I describe the framing modalities observed in the study, detailing how they generate limitations and possibilities, constraints upon and freedom for invention by teachers and pupils as they conduct their activities in the classroom. In doing so, I rely here on a particular case study of the writing of a tale in a *classe de 6ᵉ*.

A selective reading of Bernstein

As mentioned, Bernstein's theory aims to describe and capture the social process of learning in its entirety: from the "macro" level to the "micro" level of pedagogic practice in the classroom. The school is described as an institution encompassing a collection of heterogeneous activities.[2] Every activity is specific – even if, at different levels, each shapes the pedagogic action taking place in the classroom – and Bernstein adjusts the use of his concepts according to the specific activity at hand.

The observation of learning activities: classification and framing

In regard to my own work, I find Bernstein's theory especially valuable, first, in making possible a description of the genesis of each activity involved in the construction of pedagogic discourse (conceptualized as a collection of discourses, knowledge, practices or activities). Bernstein provides principles of description – the concepts of classification and framing – that demonstrate how activities occur both as the result of previous activities and also serve to generate further ones.

The theory enables an observation of how external social relations are translated within the school, how "a more global" is translated into "a more local". Thus, the learning activity achieved in the classroom can be described as the result of the modalities to which teacher and pupils adhere within an institutional framework. This framework precedes them and shapes their activity. Pedagogic action is inscribed in a *collective* work wider than the individual work of teachers and pupils. Importantly, carrying out a pedagogic action necessitates that rationalization – the development of curricula, a determination of the appropriate pacing of instruction, the distribution of individuals inside learning spaces – occurs prior to it. While there are various ways for teachers and pupils to build this framework, the point to emphasize is how this pre-existing framework shapes possibilities for action and the degree of freedom of invention allowed to individuals.

This framework can be described in terms of classification and framing modalities. I focus here on the framing that shapes pedagogic action. Bringing to light "the different forms of legitimate communication realized in any pedagogic practice" (Bernstein 2000, p. 12), the concept of "framing" describes control as it is applied to pedagogic action, i.e. it describes: "The selection of communication; its sequencing (what comes first, what comes second); its pacing (the rate of expected acquisition); the criteria; and the control over the social base which makes this transmission possible" (Bernstein 2000, pp. 12–13). Thus, the concept drives the analysis towards a focus on the selection of knowledge and the way knowledge is recontextualized into teaching forms. It also drives it towards a focus on control as it produces social relations, conceived here as the type of pedagogic relation between teacher and pupils, and even the social structuring of learning tasks. In this chapter, I focus on the learning actions achieved by pupils and the type of regulation, or control, the pedagogic discourse has over them. Therefore, I will also describe the teacher's framing of the task and its effects on the pupils' learning activities.

According to Bernstein, framing is the possible realization of classification operations achieved previously. The concept of classification describes the "translation of power, of power relations" whereas the concept of framing describes the "translation of control relations". In particular, Bernstein employs the concept of classification to analyse how pedagogic discourse is constructed in the field of knowledge production and in the recontextualizing field. Classification describes how external power relations translate into categories within pedagogic discourse as well as the relations between and within categories (of individuals, of discourses, of practices); for instance by the hierarchical distribution of knowledge into disciplines, or by the development of different and opposing types of pedagogies (visible or invisible) and the differential promotion of these educational models by social groups according to their position within the division of labour (and, even more specifically, according to their position within the middle class). Thus, the possibilities of framing appear limited by previous operations of classification. Yet, in accordance with the focus of my study, I will attempt to describe how framing can reproduce classification rather than how classification generates framing. Indeed, I seek to demonstrate that pedagogic action can either repeat or transform existing classifications.

Furthermore, classification not only specializes knowledge (by classifying it into disciplines, for example), it also gives rise to interruptions in social space: "We can see that classification constructs the nature of social space: stratifications, distributions and locations" (Bernstein 2000, p. 12). Here, this means particularly that classification affixes social labels to spaces and assigns places (such as "good" or "bad", "incompetent" or "skilled" pupil...). Consequently, at the level of pedagogic action within the classroom, classification can be retranslated by individuals (teachers and pupils) into perceptions. Thus, it can be assumed that classification is concretely retranslated into forms of self-confidence or insecurity, impacting on the extent to which pupils direct their attention and efforts towards classroom activities or shaping what they come to expect from the learning situation. I wish to emphasize also the reciprocal relation between classification and framing that takes place at the level of pedagogic action: framing can reproduce or transform the previous classification. Moreover, classification, in so far as it can be retranslated into the perceptions held by teachers and pupils, may guide the selection of framing in the classroom.

Pedagogic discourse: a hybrid of instructional discourse and regulative discourse

A second valuable aspect of Bernstein's approach can be found in the concepts of instructional and regulative discourse. With these concepts, it seems possible to reach beyond the cultural approach in sociology which contrasts school culture with family cultures. Bernstein defines pedagogic discourse as a principle which recontextualizes several heterogeneous discourses; pedagogic discourse is in fact an entanglement of two principal and distinguishable discourses: "a discourse of skills of various kinds and their relations to each other, and a discourse of social order" (Bernstein 2000, pp. 31–2). This distinction allows for the argument that schools effectively transmit specialized knowledge which should expand and enhance pupils' knowledge and skills. School culture itself is not a cultural arbitrary. Neither is it a pure translation of scientific knowledge, however, since school culture results from a choice, from the selection of a few elements from scientific discourse, and also since scientific knowledge is recontextualized from a theory of instruction – which, as presented here, is made up of a theory of the pupil (i.e. a theory of the individual and of his or her development) as well as a theory of knowledge and of its construction. Therefore, school knowledge is to be considered as a combination, a reciprocal entanglement of two heterogeneous discourses. According to Bernstein, "the instructional discourse is always embedded in the regulative discourse and the regulative discourse is the dominant discourse" (Bernstein 2000, p. 13). The second proposal of this quotation might be questioned, but I hold that the instructional discourse – that aims at enhancing the pupils' potential – contains a regulative discourse – that produces a social regulation. However, the instructional discourse does not melt into the regulative discourse. Modifications and possible distortions of the instructional discourse may occur and be observed. For instance, the instructional discourse may contain not only cognitive norms but also social norms. It will be useful to present and examine those norms.

The French-language curriculum in collèges

In addressing the French-language curriculum, my focus here is not specifically on its development in the recontextualizing field. Rather, I seek to examine its role in guiding learning activities in the context of French-language classes as they are undertaken in collèges.

Historically, the teaching of French has been structured around the objective of mastering the French language and was based on the learning of vocabulary, grammar and texts. However, Minister François Bayrou's 1995 curricular reform served to usher in what has now been more than a decade of important changes in the teaching of French. Under this reform, curricular recontextualizers developed a curriculum structured around the mastery of discourses, introducing a distinction between language and discourse.[3] My study aims at analysing the effects of this new type of transmission on the learning of French.

First of all, it should be stressed that learning the French language is no longer central to the teaching of French. On a political level, the knowledge selected by pedagogic authorities for inclusion in the curriculum may be examined in respect to the three rights proposed by Bernstein: "the right to individual enhancement", "the right to be included" and "the right to participate" (2000, p. xx). As Bernstein states, these three rights determine the possibilities for achieving an effective democracy. At an analytical level, comparing the new curricula with the criteria of these three rights enables a measurement of the balance between the regulative component and the instructional component of pedagogic discourse as it is enacted within schools.

In returning to the teaching of French, linguists can be credited with making those operating in the official recontextualizing field aware that learning discursive forms has become a necessity in today's society, especially in fostering and enabling political participation, as such knowledge is necessary in the expansion of critical skills and the deconstruction of the discourses shaping social life. The curriculum, then, privileges discourse both because of a political and an epistemic turn. It should also be stressed, however, that learning the norms of the written language remains a necessity for younger generations as it provides them with powerful cognitive tools (Goody 1994). To return in more practical terms to the position of language in the teaching of French, I have observed in the fieldwork underpinning my doctoral dissertation that, in some classes more than in others, little time is dedicated to the teaching of grammar and spelling even though many pupils have not acquired a sufficient mastery of the language and its norms. Since learning sequences are governed by and structured according to discursive genres, the selection of linguistic contents is not strictly linked to the inner logic of the language and its functions. Rather, language is dealt with as an attribute of a certain type of text. For example, the present and the present perfect tenses may be studied during a sequence about autobiography. The focus on discourse creates difficulties for the teacher in terms of sequencing and makes it difficult for pupils to build a cumulative knowledge of the language.

In terms of the writing process, it is important to note that texts are no longer read as the objects of an emotional and/or aesthetic investment on the part of the pupil. They are considered, rather, as objects of discourse (i.e. the aim of reading a text now seems to be the recognition of discursive forms). This creates a separation between reading and writing. It must be recognized, however, that writing is rooted in reading and involves a constant intertextuality; a text's meaning is shaped by other texts from which it references or borrows.

The writing of tales constitutes an interesting point from which to observe the type of transmission based on discourse. The category of "tale", in the teaching of French, emerges from two classifications:

- On the one hand, tales can be classified based on textual and discursive typologies: the tale is categorized as a narrative (as opposed to a descriptive, explanatory or argumentative) discourse. In a *classe de 6ᵉ*, the teaching of French focuses on narrative and descriptive discourses.
- On the other hand, tales can be classified based on literary genres: sometimes the object of study is the novel, sometimes the short story, sometimes the tale itself, and sometimes all are considered together as, for example, the narrative genre in opposition to the poetic genre.

Narrative is to be learnt as a genre (the literary genre and the discursive genre) rather than as a symbolic activity. For instance, the study of tales is focused upon the formal characteristics of the genre as well as the narrative discourse; that is, textual knowledge of the narrative pattern. Narratologic knowledge, the formal techniques linked with genres which have been introduced in the teaching of French since the 1970s, theoretically provides valuable tools for reading and writing.

With this new teaching and type of transmission based on discourse, the place and status of the written production in the learning of French becomes uncertain compared to its place and status in previous periods. Formerly, pupils wrote stories at school with the clear objective of writing "in a correct and elegant Language" (Daunay and Denizot 2007). Literary works were to be imitated. Pupils were told to write according to the patterns of literary texts which served as models for them. The aim of training was to acquire the common language and the national culture. Today, the status of the written production in the teaching of French has become uncertain, as have the purposes assigned to the teaching of French and, more generally, to schooling.

If the purpose is the recognition of discursive items, the main objective of reading is to locate discursive traces; as such, writing tasks can be considered as a sort of school exercise aimed at applying rules or formal knowledge rather than at the authentic production of written texts. On the other hand, if the production of texts by pupils is considered important, could the purpose then be not only the mastery of discourses, but also the building of a common culture and a common language? Is the implicit object to train children to become creators? The debate whether or not comprehensive schools should be maintained and the fast pace at which curricular reforms follow one another are examples among many of the uncertainty noted above.

Thus far I have attempted to suggest that a common cognitive value is no longer attributed to school. This may be why, in the curriculum, the instructional discourse has become more abstruse than ever before. I hypothesize that the uncertainty concerning the purpose of teaching and, likewise, the knowledge to be transmitted, may cause insecurity among both teachers and pupils in terms of their pedagogic and learning actions. Problems which have not been resolved and uncertainties that remain at the level of the pedagogic authority may reappear in the classroom at the moment when the teacher has to shape the activity of transmission. For example, in the teaching of French, how can the transmission of knowledge about language and of knowledge about discourse be brought together? This is a problem that one teacher in the study, who discussed his difficulties in organizing the sequencing of the teaching of grammar, encountered. Moreover, what place and status is given to written production in the learning of French? How should the task of writing a tale in a "sixth form" class be addressed?

In following this examination of the potential framing outlined in the curriculum, I next examine the framing achieved in the classroom and its effects on learning activities by presenting a case study of the writing of a tale. The case study draws on observations collected in a *classe de 6ᵉ* of a collège, characterized by a socially mixed population of pupils, in Marseilles. While Basil Bernstein's concepts will be useful here, accounting for the activities carried out in the classroom will require an expanded theory.

Writing a tale in a *classe de 6ᵉ*

Integrating Bernstein's approach into an anthropological approach

Following Bernstein, I hypothesize that pupils' achievements, the choices they make (in this example, the stories they wrote and their choices concerning plot and style) and those choices made by the teacher (the way he or she configures and coordinates the writing task) are shaped by an instructional discourse (ID) and a regulative discourse (RD). To grasp how the tension between ID and RD relates to and impacts on learning activities, it is first advisable to examine the tales that the pupils have composed and to observe, "in action", the process by which they compose them. Such observation requires a break from existing social classifications of the tale, including the school's, and the framing generated by these classifications. It requires also a break from our ordinary readings of children's stories, for these readings may entail a double separation: between "reality and fiction" and between "literary and non literary stories" (Molino 2003). Towards this end, I will suggest a more anthropological hypothesis, whereby pupil's stories are considered as part of an extended set of stories: I assume that these children's stories contribute to the development of the "fictional function", i.e. of a narrative activity that is universally shared (Molino 2003).

It must be kept in mind, throughout these observations, that the activity of writing a tale shares some of the aesthetic characteristics of literary writing. For this reason, and following François (2004), my observations will take into account the intelligibility of the story in terms of its adherence to the norms of language and text as well as "the rest"; that is, "all that makes a text not only comprehensible but also worthy of being told" and received and which also explains why, "when different people tell the very 'same' story, there will not be, however, two exactly similar texts" (François 2004). The stories produced can deviate from the expected, well-known, model of the tale.

My approach, then, involves a description of the narrative techniques and procedures employed within the stories and also their possible aesthetic effects on the reader. These techniques encompass a large set of tools and procedures that correspond to all the possibilities of the "fictional function", as described by Molino (2003), that writers may use. These include the plots, patterns and themes that shape the represented world, and all of the rhetorical and stylistic procedures implemented by authors: the tools with which the writer constructs the plot, puts into words his or her perceptions and sensibilities and, in brief, develops his or her own writing.

Such a description works to reconstruct the choices, such as the topic of the story and the style of writing and storytelling (François 2004), pupils make as they write. It also serves to detail some of the ways in which pupils invest themselves in their writing.

The tales: traces of the pupils' investment in their own writing

I should first remark that all of the tales I read for this study were, from a reader's standpoint, comprehensible. Moreover, every text possessed characteristics that would qualify them as "stories" rather than simply as accumulations of unconnected facts.[4] However, different tales had different, and unequal, narrative qualities which produced, as a result, greater or more limited effects on the reader.

The tales with more limited effects tended to be rather short; their plots were not very gripping for they presented little that was unexpected and largely lacked the element of suspense. The reader could not enter "another world", identify with the characters or construct their own visualizations of different scenes. These texts contained the framework of a story (the narrative pattern); they presented the scenario of the story. In these tales, traces of a mixture of genres could be found (in the themes they introduce, for instance), but there were few traces of an aesthetic work on the materiality of language. These stories confirmed pupils' ability to write a coherent text, but it was evident that these pupils still had to learn how to develop patterns and themes, or, the rhetorical art of storytelling (see Appendix 11.1 for an example of the identical patterns developed within two pupils' stories). Thus, two difficulties facing pupils were identifiable: the ability of the writer to take into account the reader of his or her text and the need for the form of their texts to be improved.

Other stories, containing not only a framework but also a singular way of storytelling, proved more gripping for the reader. These stories produced a variety of aesthetic effects including, in particular, a sense of realism, elements of the unexpected, or characters with whom the reader could identify. These effects resulted from aesthetic work on the materiality of language, from the *mise-en-scène* of a particular pathos, atmosphere, setting and situation, from the author's ability and willingness to "play with" language, from creative combinations of what is usually kept separate (the world of ordinary reality and the marvellous world of tales),[5] and from pupils' imitations of the styles of sentences they had read previously, as they borrowed forms, patterns and figures from other tales or stories and reorganized them into a new or original synthesis. In these stories, various manners of writing and storytelling were observed that could not be organized hierarchically according to a single and predefined value scale. In any case, the effects on the reader were produced by what, if deleted, would not decrease the reader's understanding of the story but which, when included, turn reading into a pleasure. In other words, the depth of a story seemed to be linked to language which not only provides the reader with facts or events but also produces a particular manner of shaping them.

In attempting to analyse the quality of the pupils' tales, I have discovered that writing results from a complex investment. Writing can be invested in by pupils as a space of liberty and as a pleasure: the pleasure of entering the playing space that language becomes for the storyteller and the writer and the pleasure of reinvesting their sensibilities and their own imaginativeness. In this case, pupils begin making aesthetic judgements while developing their stories. In the interactions between pupils who were writing together, the effects each wished to produce and the narrative procedures and writing style each intended to employ were discussed. For example, the use of a particular language register in capturing a character's speech, or whether or not to represent and integrate the characters' thoughts in the story (the choice of the narrative point of view) was topics of such discussions. My observations also demonstrate that pupils had some narrative knowledge. Moreover, the presence of free associations between what the pupils were writing and linguistic or iconic forms they had read, heard or seen elsewhere seemed to be linked to the pleasure of writing. Pupils developed heterogeneous forms belonging to cultural memories which provided a creative basis for their writing. Then, pupils produced a singular combination of these forms as they brought them into the specific universe of the marvellous tale. Lastly, it should be noted that the narrative activity did not exactly involve self-expression but, rather, it led to a narrative exchange. Pupils' investment in writing was certainly personal, peculiar to each individual, but the possibility of its being connected with others through language was also considered. The writer was incorporated into a cultural time and space allowing him or her to reappropriate various cultural memories[6] (Halbwachs 1997). Consequently, reading cannot be separated from writing. Writing results from a social relation between, at least, a writer and a reader (Ramognino 2006), and the narrative exchange can be either facilitated or limited by the framing of the task. For this reason, one objective of this study is to discern whether pupils are provided with the possibility of reappropriating and expanding their understanding and appreciation of their own place in this relation and exchange.

Framing modalities and writing acts

In the case study presented here, five class sessions were devoted to the writing of a tale. Pupils worked in pairs to achieve this task. They were told to write a "marvellous tale". They had previously read fairy tales (Grimm, Perrault and traditional Russian tales). A summary activity followed these readings. In order to carry out their task, pupils were provided a sheet detailing the genre of the "marvellous tale" and summarizing its characteristics (the type of characters and the components of "the marvellous", etc.). In writing their own tales, pupils were instructed, first, to develop a "plot pattern" and a "narrative pattern". They could rely on two additional sheets outlining the structure of the narrative pattern (initial situation, disrupting factor, twists and turns, resolving factor and final situation). The analysis that follows considers the possibilities that this type of framing provides to the pupils in carrying out their writing task.

A framing based on the literary genre

In the case study, the framing of the lesson is evident in the teacher's selection of the genre of the tale. The literary genre of the "fairy tale" provides pupils with symbolic forms (such as stereotypical figures and patterns of fairy tales or the aesthetic and discursive forms commonly employed in writing them). However, pupils were observed to include in their writing not only elements which were distinctive of the classical fairy tale, but also different semiotic and aesthetic forms drawn from their own cultural lives.

In this way, they wrote stories which, at various levels, combined different genres.[7] Furthermore, current literature and films contributed at times to the production of hybrid tales. The teacher allowed the pupils, to a certain degree, their own rendering of the genre of the "marvellous tale". However, pupils' renderings were restricted to what the teacher identified as the limits of the genre.[8] Such framing restricted pupils' writing possibilities and did not allow them to completely develop their own rendition of the tale. Real discursive practices always comprise a mixture of forms and the linguists themselves assert that the limits between genres are temporary and not entirely inflexible. In the field of literary production, the genre is a formal and temporary synthesis of all the literary and discursive forms that exist at a time. When genres are recontexualized in school, they are converted into a (limiting) writing norm. In this type of recontextualization, the aesthetic component of literary procedures (their effects on the reader) disappears. I wish to stress that, according to the task and to the learning action taking place, the same discourse about knowledge can be either instructional or regulative. In the recontextualization detailed above, the instructional discourse turns into a regulative discourse and the social relation that is built is dogmatic or conformist.

In the case study presented here, the "narrative pattern" and the "plot pattern" through which the pupils had to develop their tales constituted the formal discursive and textual knowledge which currently structures reading and writing activities at school. The "narrative pattern", however, may prove a source of difficulty, rather than a benefit, for pupils as it is a highly abstract formalization and can be difficult to acquire and to recontextualize for them. Moreover, the relevance of the classical occidental marvellous tale (of which the "narrative pattern" is a sort of reduced model), as the specific discursive form highlighted by Propp, does not stem from the form itself, but from its effects (i.e. from the symbolic features of the tale, the obstacles (constraints) confronted and the solutions (opportunities) offered (Molino 2003)); symbolic features that allow the potentialities of human action to be tested and examined.

In regard to framing as it relates to the difficulties, mentioned above, that pupils might face while writing a story, it should be recognized that there are other ways of composing a story. My observations reveal that, rather than the "narrative pattern", what helped pupils understand how they could improve their texts were the teacher's attempts to recreate the interaction between writer and reader. As they reread their tale with the teacher, pupils listened to the teacher read their texts aloud. Together, they managed to pinpoint sections that needed to be rewritten or revised to make the text more intelligible and its style more fluent for the reader. Through these rereading phases with the teacher, pupils learnt above all to adhere to writing conventions (conventions of language and text). The art of developing patterns was also addressed by the teacher, who suggested to pupils that they imitate stories they had read, that they replicate the style of a particular sentence or section of a story they had read previously. This art, however, was not listed among the items targeting the transmission of knowledge in the curricula.

The present framing can be contrasted with the teaching of rhetoric in the past. Then, themes to be developed and their textual organization were given. Thus, pupils did not have to invent the topic of their compositions by themselves. Rhetorical procedures were taught and pupils could learn how to develop topics or patterns (Douay-Soublin 2005). The current modality of transmission presupposes, in a sense, that pupils are spontaneously creative, that they immediately know "what is worthy of being told" and that they already have at their disposal a sufficient set of literary and rhetorical forms. Consequently, this modality of transmission is likely to generate social differentiations; this type of framing tends to reproduce the classification between social groups.

Though the focus of this chapter is on the effects of framing on pupils' learning, I wish to insist that the development of framing entails a series of complicated choices on the part of the teacher. On the one hand, even if the teacher wishes to introduce his or her pupils to the pleasures of writing and to make them aware that writing consists of rereading and revision, he or she cannot ignore the curricula (i.e. the injunction to transmit discursive items). On the other hand, there is no permanent knowledge about the genre of the tale, nor is there a theory of narratology that adequately incorporates the tale and its discourse. Consequently, when working on the revision of the form of the pupils' stories, the teacher has no substantial tools, other than referring them to the "narrative pattern", with which to provide guidance to the pupils. In commenting on the stories of pupils which were deemed as needing improvement and which, consequently, received low marks, the feedback of the teacher in this case study most often referred back to the "narrative pattern". For instance, the teacher commented on one story that: "[The] twists and turns part is to be expanded." In addition, the difficulty for the teachers in devising appropriate guidance for their pupils remains to "help telling without preventing from telling" (François 2004). Due to the different or contradictory aims he or she has to combine and due to the limited knowledge he or she has for coordinating writing activities, the teacher has a narrow range of options with which to carry out his or her pedagogic actions.

The generation and adjustment of framing through action

Classroom observations also sought to reveal the conditions under which, throughout the course of the several lessons dedicated to the writing of tales which served as the basis of this case study, the teacher maintained or revised, adjusted and readjusted the initial framing of the topic according to his perceptions of pupils' experiences with the writing activity. Importantly, writing in pairs promotes a cultural exchange between pupils and also, depending on the teacher's focus and his or her ability to listen, an "openness" on the part of the teacher towards his or her pupils and their cultural knowledge.

In fact, in the case study presented here, the teacher revised framing on "a case by case basis" according to his interactions with different groups of pupils. In particular, it was observed that the teacher decided whether to maintain or revise the framing of the genre of the tale depending on pupils' explanations to him about what they were doing and why they were doing it. An example of the aesthetic arguments provided by a pupil in an interaction with their teacher is included in Appendix 11.2. This practice implies yet another condition, however: that pupils dared to allow themselves to discuss their work with the teacher. More generally, I want to emphasize that knowledge appropriation results from cognitive work required to acquire specialized knowledge, but also from a social relation. The pedagogic relation must be examined, then. Regarding the process of recontexualization, the point is also to examine how the recontextualization of knowledge, at the level of pedagogic action (of framing), generates different levels of attention to the task among pupils and also how it generates different types of expectations, in the sense of the "expecting views" developed by Koselleck (1990), among them in terms of the learning situation and schooling more generally. These get translated into their sense of freedom for invention in their learning activities and into varying levels of confidence within the learning space. In the case study, pupils receiving the best framing in carrying on with the task and improving their stories and "writing skills" could very well be those who had already been successful throughout the task – successful enough to be able to argue their point – and those who were not entangled in a "dogmatic relation" to knowledge and/or in a "conformist relation" to the teacher (Charlot 1999) in the framing of the genre of the tale; that is, the most successful pupils are those who are in a position to reinvest knowledge into their writing task and to derive pleasure from it.

These observations emphasize a type of framing and a "relation to knowledge" produced by it that renders the pupils' written activities in the classroom and the knowledge acquired there – in particular the pupils' cultural knowledge – relatively invisible. Likewise, they highlight a relative uncertainty regarding learning aims that serve to make expectations for the text that is to be assessed unclear. In such a context, for pupils, verbalizing and discussing what they have done and why they have done it might prove to be as important as actually doing the task.

Conclusion

The new curricula based on discourse generate difficulties for the pupils in building a cumulative knowledge of the French language. Framing based on discursive genres is hardly likely to help children in addressing the specific problems they encounter while developing their tales. Rather, it tends to limit the narrative exchange of reading and writing and to reduce the pleasure pupils take in it. Further observation of pupils' learning activities and of the effects of the framing operating on them is to be encouraged if a better understanding, especially of pupils' relations to knowledge as generated by pedagogic discourse – relations that either encourage or limit the enhancement of their own potentials – is to be gained.

As to the issue of the social differentiation produced and maintained in the classroom, observations of how the pupils' tales are assessed by their teachers is particularly relevant. In the case study presented in this chapter, it is interesting to note that the highest marks were assigned to tales that were constructed and written according to the formal criteria of the classical "marvellous tale" genre, but also to those which included a mixture of various genres and forms. The assessment of the tales, then, is not in fact based on the literary genre, but on the aesthetic qualities of pupils' tales. As explained earlier, the assessment tends as a result to operate as an instrument of social selection.

In forthcoming work, I seek to compare different framing modalities. In another *classe de 6ᵉ*, located in a school with a "socially disadvantaged" student body,[9] it was observed that learning focused almost entirely on the recognition and location of discursive elements during the reading activity, while the time devoted to learning the French language was very limited. This choice is identified as a cause of deficits for pupils, particularly for those who experience great difficulty in learning the French language. Finally, another step in the analysis will involve an examination of the genesis of the framings shaped by teachers in different types of schools.

Appendix 11.1

An example of the identical patterns in the description of an encounter between opposing characters and of confinement as developed within two pupils' tales

> Tale 1: *An old man and his mouse live in a forest. The mouse regularly takes walks in the forest. One day, she meets a black cat and tells her master about it.*
> "On the following day *(the old man)* got up very early to go to the castle and fetch his wife. Just as the mouse had, he saw a black cat. This time, however, the cat was in the company of an old lady, who offered the old man a banana. Unsuspectingly, the old man accepted the offer, swallowed the banana and fell asleep straightaway.
> 'When he wakes up, she muttered to herself, he'll be sentenced to gaol'.
> As the old woman had said, he woke up in gaol, but he was not alone."

> Tale 2: *Two friendly princes go hunting wild boars once a week.*

"One day, half way to their hunting place, they heard a soft, captivating woman's voice asking them to follow. The two curious and courageous princes launched into the adventure. They instinctively followed the invisible woman's voice.

'Ha! Ha! I have caught you in my trap! All your life you will remain at my service and work for me! I am hardly partial to beauty! But I need strong people like you to build my castle that will be the widest and the most beautiful of all castles. You will be my life long prisoners! Only one thing can save you: if you manage to find a way out of the labyrinth, you will be free! But no one as yet has ever found it.' "

Appendix 11.2

An example of a teacher's revision of the framing of the genre of the tale during classroom interactions:

The teacher (P) goes from writing group to writing group. The following interactions between P and two pupils have been recorded:

P: Well ... concerning what Flavie had done, have you discussed what was to be kept and what was to be dropped?

CLAIRE: Well, yeah, but ... in fact she doesn't want to drop much of it.

P: Well, Flavie, why? This is the problem with you, you know. You must learn to do it. Your last composition, remember, you couldn't finish at the same time as the others, so you must get to become more synthetic, mustn't you? And only write what's

FLAVIE: but I do like ... I do like describing.

P: You like describing, right, but we'll have other occasions for it later. Here, in a tale, it's not the point. Or else descriptions are, er ... very fleeting, well, er, very short ... She was beautiful, you see, in general, her eye colour and how her dress looks, see? Except in ... maybe in Perrault's a little, but Perrault is something else altogether, a special language. We base ourselves more on what the Grimm brothers have done.

FLAVIE: But it's mostly when I describe feelings, for example when the king does ...

P: Yes?

FLAVIE: When the king does speak, well then afterwards he felt something like hatred, or ...

P: Well, listen, this is it, exactly. It's not describing. This can be useful; it's not a problem. You have to choose between what's useless, things we can do without. But if you keep it though, it's a little bit more for the reader, to identify himself with the characters. So this, feelings, well, you can keep it. So, then, you are still working on the ups and downs; is that it?

FLAVIE: Yes....

Notes

1 In France, this is the first year of comprehensive lower secondary school, with a population of 11–12 year-old pupils. Collèges are the equivalent of British comprehensive lower secondary schools.
2 At various points throughout his body of work, Bernstein focuses on different aspects of the social construction of pedagogic discourse: on its production in relation to matters, such as the division of labour and power relations, often presented as "external" to the school; on the recontextualization of knowledge as it occurs in the intellectual and pedagogical fields; or on the recontextualization of knowledge in the classroom.
3

> If the purposes of the former curricula – to express oneself, to acquire a culture, a method, and to become autonomous – remain relevant, from now on they are governed by the learning of discursive forms. This learning gives to acquisitions a general guideline, and a context: social life is formed by discourses, discourses transmit the culture, the language. For everyone, the language always appears as real discursive practices.
>
> (Enseigner au collège, Français, programmes et accompagnement, CNDP 2004)

4 Indeed, every story I read contained a conclusion, a narrator and an appropriately and sequentially organized series of events following at least a minimal plot.
5 See Petitat (2006), who develops the hypothesis of a "plurality of worlds" that shapes reality. We constantly intertwine the world of "practical achievement" with various fictional worlds.
6 In *La mémoire collective*, in particular with the parable of the passenger, Maurice Halbwachs argues that even a highly individual social activity such as walking around issues from a social relation. Whenever a visitor walks around in London, for example, he or she may borrow or draw from various cultural memories to shape his or her perception of the city.
7 Some of the pupils' tales included direct or indirect references to *Shrek* or to Myazaki cartoons, to books such as *Harry Potter* and also more distant borrowings from the tale and "the marvellous" (detective stories, cloak-and-dagger stories, etc.).
8 For example, the teacher accepted a parody which mixed references drawn from different tales and that redefined stereotypical "fairy tale" characters within the world of ordinary reality. But he refused to allow pupils to include extraterrestrial figures in their stories as he deemed them characteristic of another historical form of the fantastic, not "the marvellous", but rather "science fiction".
9 This collège has a community composed of 85 per cent working-class children.

12 Educational texts and contexts that work discussing the optimization of a model of pedagogic practice

Ana M. Morais and Isabel P. Neves

We have devoted more than 20 years of our research lives to finding out answers to the major problem of improving the learning of students, especially the disadvantaged, without decreasing the level of conceptual demand. The research has been focused on the contexts of learning in families and schools, teacher education, and the construction of syllabi and textbooks (e.g. Morais and Neves 2001, 2006; Morais *et al.* 2004; Morais, Neves and Afonso 2005; Neves and Morais 2001, 2005).

Students' learning has been studied across the whole educational system, from kindergarten to higher education, mostly in the subject of science education. We have constructed various models to direct the research and also models to analyse our results. As a result of this research, we have come to a model that conceptualizes a school pedagogic practice that seems to have the potential to lead children to success at school, narrowing the gap between children from differentiated social backgrounds.

Although we have incorporated research perspectives from the fields of epistemology and psychology, Bernstein's theory of pedagogic discourse (1990–2000) has provided the main theoretical framework for our studies. Its powers of description, explanation, diagnosis, prediction and transferability have supported more rigorous research on the production of new knowledge in education. The power of Bernstein's theory, then, has facilitated advancements in our own work.

This chapter intends to: (1) present the model introduced above and describe its characteristics; (2) present the model at work; (3) explain how this model can be extended to the contexts of teacher education and the construction of curricula and syllabuses; and (4) discuss the optimization of the model.

A model of school pedagogic practice

Figure 12.1 outlines diagrammatically the main characteristics of this model of pedagogic practice.

The main sociological characteristics of the modality of pedagogic practice that research has shown to be fundamental for students' scientific learning are the following:

- clear distinction between subjects with distinct statuses – strong classification of the teacher–student relation;
- teacher control of selection and sequencing of knowledge, competences and classroom activities – strong framing, namely at the macro level, of selection and sequencing;
- student control over the time of acquisition – weak framing at the level of pacing;
- clear explication of the legitimate text to be acquired in the context of the classroom – strong framing at the level of the evaluation criteria;
- personal relationships of communication between the teacher and the students and between the students themselves – weak framing at the level of the hierarchical rules;
- interrelation between the various kinds of knowledge of a discipline to be learned by students – weak classification at the level of intradisciplinarity;
- blurring of the boundaries between the teacher–student and student–student spaces – weak classification between spaces.

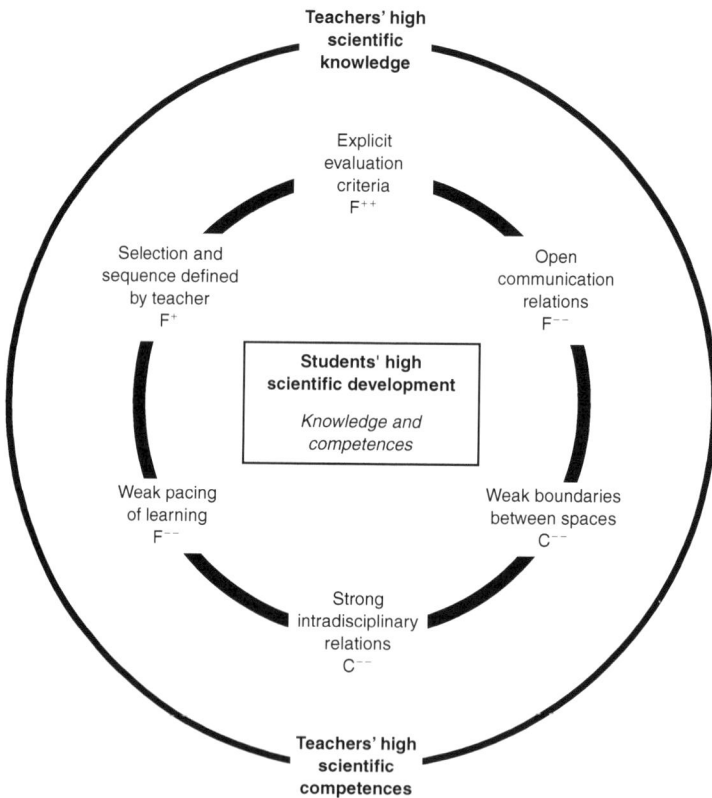

Figure 12.1 Model of a mixed pedagogic practice.

The studies we have carried out also suggest the importance for students' learning of the relation between students' knowledge and experiences and the knowledge to be acquired, with higher status for the latter; that is, a school–community relation characterized by strong classification and weak framing.

According to our research, these characteristics may lead students to successfully develop complex scientific knowledge and competences. However, this can only occur if teachers possess a high level of scientific knowledge and competences which means that no optimum methodologies can compensate for poor scientific proficiency.

Our initial study was designed to compare three pedagogic practices: two that corresponded broadly to the two extremes – the traditional teaching–learning process of generally strong classification and framing and the progressive teaching–learning process of generally weak classification and framing – and a third which was in the middle in terms of teacher and student power and control relations (e.g. Morais *et al.* 1992, 1993). Throughout this study we perceived that a pedagogic practice where both teacher and students have control according to specific characteristics of the practice but where power would stay with the teacher would successfully promote student learning. For example, it was already clear at the time that evaluation criteria should be explicit (strong framing) and that hierarchical rules should be regulated by weak framing; that is, characteristics of traditional and progressive schooling should be present together in the same practice. We started then to develop studies that worked with mixed pedagogic practices by experimenting with several combinations of the various characteristics of the organizational and interactional contexts of classrooms (e.g. Morais and Rocha 2000; Morais and Neves 2001; Morais *et al.* 2004). These were studies which were focused on various samples of students at various levels of schooling and which used a variety of methodologies that, on the whole, constituted a mixed methodological approach (Morais and Neves 2006). During this research process we came to develop a *mixed pedagogic practice* with the characteristics indicated in the model presented above.

The model at work

In this section of the chapter, we show how the model has worked in the studies we have carried out. We selected one study that was developed at the primary school level where two distinct pedagogic practices were implemented by two different teachers teaching science to a total sample of 26 children in two different schools (Silva *et al.* 2005; Morais, Neves, Silva and Deus 2005). A book of activities with a teacher's guide was produced and provided to the teachers to help them develop children's knowledge (regarding "the growth of living things") and investigative competences. Underlying these activities was the model of pedagogic practice derived from previous studies.

We constructed an instrument that was used to characterize teachers' pedagogic practices (Silva *et al.* 2003). The instrument includes indicators for the various characteristics of pedagogic practice, in the instructional and regulative contexts, through which teachers' practice can be characterized in reference to four degree scales of classification or framing. As an example, we show in the Appendix 12.1 and 12.2 the part of the instrument that refers to evaluation criteria and intradisciplinarity. By using the instrument we could analyse transcripts of audio and video recordings of the teaching–learning process that took place in the two school classes. The characterization of the two pedagogic practices is detailed in Table 12.1.

The data presented in the table make evident differences between the practices of the two teachers. If we concentrate on two selected characteristics, evaluation criteria and intradisciplinarity, it is clear that the teacher of Sunflower School develops a practice that is in accordance with our model by making evaluation criteria very explicit at both the macro and micro levels (very strong framing: F^{++}) and by establishing strong intradisciplinary relations between the various kinds of knowledge (very weak classification: C^{--}). On the contrary, the teacher of Daffodil School develops a practice that departs from our model by leaving evaluation criteria implicit at both levels (weak framing: F^-) and by establishing weak relations between the various types of knowledge (strong classification: C^+). Taking into account the table in its entirety demonstrates that this pattern of difference between the two teachers stands in general for all characteristics of pedagogic practice.

The following excerpts illustrate some values of classification and framing attributed to the pedagogic practices of the two teachers with regard to evaluation criteria and intradisciplinarity, when the indicator *constructing syntheses* is considered (see Appendix 12.1).

> Would chickens have grown if they had no food? [Discussion with the children] Do they [the living things] grow under any condition? [Discussion with the children] No. They don't grow. They need special conditions to grow; that is, plants need water, animals need food, so, they don't grow under any condition ...
>
> (Sunflower School's teacher)

The teacher reads aloud the sentences of the book of activities:

> ... throughout the year, we have observed changes in seeds, in the chicken, in the silk worms and also in your own body. We saw that they changed, right? ... they grew, they grew. So write down in the first space. Go on! Have you already written?
>
> We learned that when things grow they are ... alive, go on write this down, on your worksheet, they are alive ... finished?
>
> (Daffodil School's teacher)

Table 12.1 Characterization of two pedagogic practices in primary school

		Sunflower School		Daffodil School	
		Macro level	Micro level	Macro level	Micro level
Instructional context	*Discursive rules*				
	selection	F^{++}	F^{+}/F^{-}	F^{++}	F^{++}/F^{+}
	sequence	F^{++}	F^{+}/F^{-}	F^{++}	F^{++}/F^{+}
	pacing	F^{--}/F^{-}	F^{-}/F^{--}	F^{+}	F^{+}
	evaluation criteria	F^{++}	F^{++}	F^{-}	F^{-}
	Relation between discourses				
	intradisciplinary relations	C^{--}		C^{+}	
	interdisciplinary relations	C^{-}/C^{--}		C^{+}/C^{++}	
	School–community relation	$C^{++}F^{--}/F^{-}$		$C^{++}F^{+}/F^{-}$	
Regulative context	*Hierarchical rules*				
	teacher–student relation	F^{-}/F^{--}		F^{+}/F^{++}	
	student–student relation	F^{-}		F^{+}/F^{-}	
	Relations between spaces				
	teacher space–student space	C^{-}	C^{-}/C^{+}	C^{-}	C^{-}
	student–student spaces	C^{+}/C^{-}	C^{+}	C^{-}	C^{+}

The first excerpt evidences the existence of (a) very strong *intradisciplinary relations* (C^{--}), because distinct concepts of the theme under study (the growth of living things) are integrated, and (b) explicit *evaluation criteria* (F^{++}), because syntheses are clear and constructed with the children. The second excerpt evidences (a) weak *intradisciplinary relations* ($C+$), because distinct facts of the theme are interrelated and (b) implicit *evaluation criteria* (F^-), because the teacher tells the children what they should write without explaining its meaning.

In order to evaluate the results of the two practices in terms of children's learning, we used Bernstein's concept of code to appreciate children's specific coding orientation (SCO) in the specific context of concept understanding; that is, their possession of recognition and realization rules in that context. We conducted semi-structured interviews with the children before and after the learning process. Figure 12.2 shows the results of the interviews, when we consider three levels of children's performance and the social composition of the schools. The graphs highlight major differences between the two groups of children. As a consequence of the exposure of the working-class children in these two schools to differential pedagogic practices, the development of scientific knowledge and understanding among Sunflower School's children was greater than the development of scientific knowledge and understanding among Daffodil School's children. This is particularly relevant as other studies (e.g. Domingos 1989) have shown that working-class children are at a double disadvantage when they learn in working-class schools, as is the case at Sunflower School.

From the results it is clear that the teacher who developed a pedagogic practice closer to our model led their children to a higher degree of scientific literacy when compared to the teacher whose pedagogic practice departed

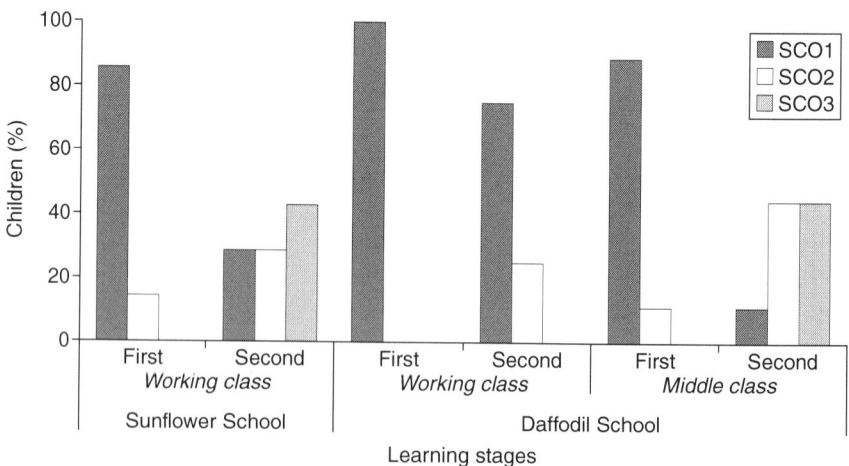

Figure 12.2 Evolution of children's specific coding orientation in the two schools.

from the model. And, most importantly, the results show that pedagogic practice can overcome the effect of social class.

The small size of the sample of this study might lead us to think that these conclusions are not valid. However, the fact that these results confirm results of previous studies conducted with distinct samples at different school levels increases the degree of validity of the studies as a whole. It should be noted that this kind of study requires depth and rigour at all levels of the research, something that cannot be attained with large samples.

Although the model of pedagogic practice has succeeded in raising the students' level of scientific knowledge and competences and in narrowing the gap between students of different social backgrounds, our research has also provided us with information that can allow us to go much further. We will deal with this in the last section of the chapter.

Extension of the model to other educational contexts

In this section of the chapter we will concentrate on two studies, one similar to the study described above but conducted at the level of higher education and the other focused on the context of curricula and syllabi. With the first we intend to show how the model can be applied to a different level of schooling and with the second to contexts other than those directly relating to teaching–learning situations.

The model in a context of higher education

The study developed in the higher education context focused on lessons on Science Teaching Methods for those pursuing a degree in Science Education (Santos 2007). We wished to examine whether or not the model of pedagogic practice we had developed through research in lower levels of schooling could be applied successfully to higher education in terms of enhancing university students' learning. We studied two distinct pedagogic practices implemented by two different teachers in two different classes and we analysed students' learning with regard to their specific coding orientation to selected knowledge of the discipline. We also constructed an instrument to characterize pedagogic practice similar to the instrument employed in the study described earlier (see Appendix 12.1 and 12.2) but adapted to the new context (Santos and Morais 2007).

The following are excerpts from the transcripts of the lessons which refer to the indicator *constructing syntheses* for the discursive rule *evaluation criteria*.

> F[++] ... to make a synthesis of all we have done in the past three lessons ... what is it that we have learned? [the teacher discusses with the students all relevant points and ends up with a structured conclusion written down on a slide]: "Science is an organized body of knowledge in permanent evolution that is the result of a dynamic process of problem

solving and that involves a non-linear set of inter-linked stages (problems, hypotheses, planning and experimenting, observation, interpretation of results) where laboratory work plays a crucial role".... this is the broadest idea ... there are other more restricted ideas that we have constructed along the process ...

(Clear syntheses constructed with the students and recorded)

F^+ ... as a synthesis of the past three lessons we can say that ... [the teacher presents the conclusion written down on a slide]: "The level of conceptual demand of the teaching–learning process is a consequence of the degree of complexity of the scientific and metascientific knowledge and of the cognitive competences and also of the degree of intradisciplinarity between distinct kinds of scientific knowledge".[... When we plan the teaching–learning process, on the basis of given knowledge and competences, we should be aware that this process can have a range of various degrees of complexity and that education should not be restricted to the lowest degrees.

(Clear syntheses constructed by the teacher and recorded)

F^- ... What is it that we want to teach to our students? ... [The students start collecting their own materials, without taking any notes of what the teacher was saying] It's the language of competences that I want you to learn here. It's those competences you have mentioned that we have to develop with our students. They have to do with reasoning, they have to do with attitudes, they have to do with mobilization of scientific knowledge, they have to do with the processes of science; it's all that.

(Syntheses not clearly constructed by the teacher and not recorded)

These excerpts also evidence distinct degrees of intradisciplinarity. The first and second excerpts can be classified as C^- because they are syntheses that indicate a relation between various concepts of a given theme under study. The third excerpt can be classified as C^{++} because it is a synthesis that presents factual knowledge of a given theme.

Given limitations of space, the results that refer to the characterization of the practice and to students' SCO are not presented in this chapter.

The model in a context of curricula and syllabuses

The next study was developed in the context of current Portuguese education reform (Ferreira 2007) and is part of broader research that intends to analyse the recontextualizing processes that occur within the official recontextualizing field and between this field and the pedagogic recontextualizing field. We will focus on the former by analysing the curricula and syllabuses produced in that field, particularly two main documents: the Essential Competences (EC – the general principles) and the Curriculum Guidelines (CG – the specific principles). The analyses were centred on the subject of Natural Sciences, on the theme of Earth Sustainability, and some specific aspects related to both *the what* and *the how* of educational processes were studied: science construction, conceptual demand, intradisciplinarity and evaluation criteria. For each one of these aspects we constructed instruments organized to account for the four main sections of the syllabi (knowledge, aims, methodological guidelines and evaluation) in terms of four degree scales of classification or framing and the respective descriptors for each case (e.g. Alves *et al.* 2006; Ferreira *et al.* 2006). The analysis required that the text of the syllabi be divided into units of analysis; that is, short sections of the text with a given semantic meaning.

Table 12.2 shows the *Aims* section as included in the instrument for *intradisciplinary relations*. The following are examples of units of analysis.

Intradisciplinarity

C^{++} It is recommended that, within this thematic, the students understand the existence of various types of water and the relation of these types with their distinct uses (CG).

C$^-$ Understanding that ecosystem dynamics result from the interdependence between living things, materials and processes (EC).

C^{--} Another aspect to be highlighted is the articulation of the themes. The suggested sequence intends that, after having gained understanding of the concepts related to the structure and functioning of the Earth system, the students are able to apply them in situations that relate to human intervention on the Earth ... taking into account the sustainability of the Earth (EC).

Table 12.3 shows the *Methodological Guidelines* section as included in the instrument for *evaluation criteria* related to knowledge of the "external sociological dimension of the construction of science". The following are examples of units of analysis.

Evaluation criteria

F$^-$ It is suggested the discussion of real problems, such as accidents at nuclear power plants, the addition of lead to petrol ... These problems can serve as opportunities to discuss social and ethical questions that lead students to reflect about the pros and cons of some scientific innovations for the individual, society and the environment [no additional explanations are given] (CG).

F^{--} The planning of field trips to industrial plants located in the school area and the corresponding analysis of costs, benefits and social and environmental risks associated with industrial activity is recommended [no additional explanations are given] (CG).

Table 12.2 Intradisciplinary relations in the Natural Sciences syllabuses – a section of the instrument

Sections	C^{++}	C^{+}	C^{-}	C^{--}
Aims	The aims are focused on the relation between knowledge of a simple order within the same theme. Or Scientific knowledge essential to the understanding of the relation between various content knowledge within the same theme is omitted.	The aims are focused on the relation between knowledge of a simple order of distinct themes. Or Scientific knowledge essential to the understanding of the relation between content knowledge of distinct themes is omitted.	The aims are focused on knowledge of a complex order or between this and knowledge of a simple order, within the same theme.	The aims are focused on knowledge of a complex order or between this and knowledge of a simple order of distinct themes.

Table 12.3 Evaluation criteria for knowledge of the "external sociological dimension of science" present in the Natural Sciences syllabuses – a section of the instrument

Sections	F^{++}	F^{+}	F^{-}	F^{--}
Methodological guidelines	Strategies/methodologies are provided for the transmission/acquisition of knowledge, related to the external sociological dimension of science, and of its relation to the development of competences associated with this dimension. The meaning of these strategies for the teaching/learning of meta-sciences is explained and the importance of metasciences in science education, according to the curriculum perspectives, is referred to.	Strategies/methodologies are provided for the transmission/acquisition of knowledge, related to the external sociological dimension of science, and of its relation to the development of competences associated with this dimension. The meaning of these strategies for the teaching/learning of meta-sciences is explained and the general importance of metasciences in science education, with no reference to the curriculum perspectives, is referred to.	Strategies/methodologies are provided for the transmission/acquisition of knowledge, related to the external sociological dimension of science, and of its relation to the development of competences associated with this dimension, but the meaning of these strategies/methodologies is not explained.	Strategies/methodologies are very generically provided for the transmission/acquisition of knowledge, related to the external sociological dimension of science, and of its relation to the development of competences associated with this dimension.

No values of F^{++} and F^{+} were present in the syllabi which means that the evaluation criteria were never made explicit.

The analysis of both curriculum documents – Essential Competences (EC) and Curriculum Guidelines (CG) – is presented graphically in Figures 12.3 and 12.4. Figure 12.3 (Intradisciplinarity) and Figure 12.4 (Evaluation criteria) refer to all the four sections of the documents and to the sections taken together.

Briefly, we can say that the relative value attributed to intradisciplinary relations within scientific knowledge decreased generally when passing from the *Essential Competences* text to the *Curriculum Guidelines* text which evi-

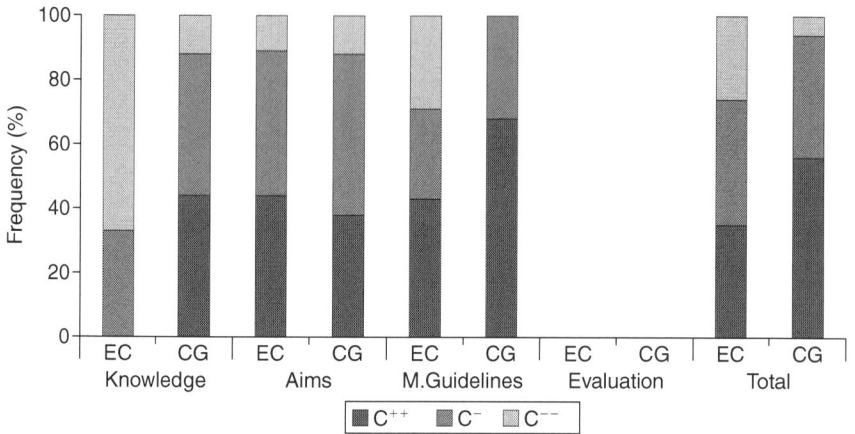

Figure 12.3 Intradisciplinary relations in the Natural Sciences syllabuses.

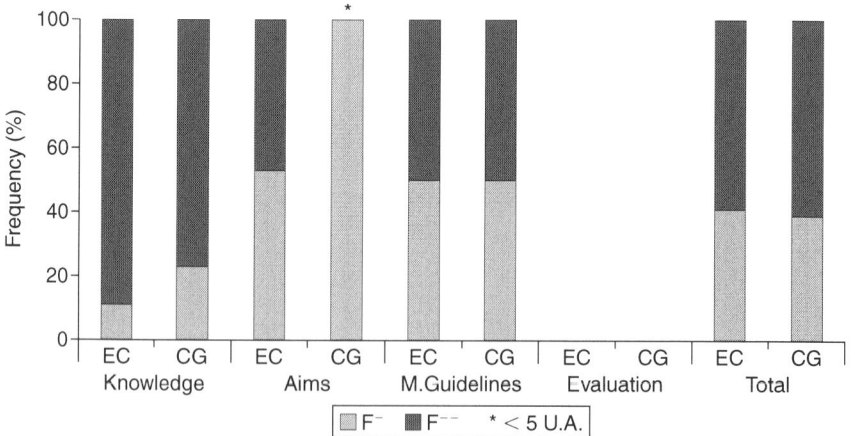

Figure 12.4 Evaluation criteria for knowledge of the "external sociological dimension of science" in the Natural Sciences syllabuses.

dences a recontextualization that took place within the official recontextual-izing field, of the message contained in the official pedagogic discourse. As a consequence, science teachers will receive two contradictory messages and, if they follow the specific guidelines, they may be led to devalue intradiscipli-narity in their pedagogic practices.

With regard to the evaluation criteria, we can say briefly that, even when the construction of science is present in the syllabuses, as it is in the case of the external sociological dimension of science, the message regarding the process of science construction is implicit and, in many cases, totally implicit (F^{--}) in both the EC and CG texts. As a consequence, teachers may disregard or be unable to introduce it in their pedagogic practices.

The research cases described above show how it is possible to study differ-entiated texts and contexts by using the same theoretical relations and con-cepts. This makes it possible to make comparisons along the educational system and may therefore increase the conceptual level of the conclusions.

Optimization of the model

As stated earlier, our model is the result of the many studies we have carried out and, for this reason, we have some confidence in the conclusions we have reached. However, we believe that we need to go much further in increasing the rigour of future research if our model is to reach a higher degree of preci-sion in terms of its transferability to curriculum development and classroom practice.

Thus, on the basis of the present model, we intend to construct a new theoretical model to be tested in future research. This model will contain hypotheses that, based either on theory or our previous results, will be focused on the main weaknesses of the previous model.

First, there are two characteristics of pedagogic practice, *school–community relations* and *interdisciplinary relations* that need to be studied in more depth. In the first case, we have always started from the assumption that classifica-tion between discourses, that is between school knowledge and everyday knowledge, should be very strong because, in the school, the former should have the highest status of the two. However, we believe that students' learn-ing may be enhanced by allowing their knowledge and experiences to enter into the school, signalling communication between school and community. Thus we propose to conceptualize a school–community relation character-ized by both classification and framing, although framing has an ambiguous meaning here because it does not refer to the relation between subjects. This clearly needs further development.

In the case of interdisciplinarity, we have always worked on the wide-spread assumption that the blurring of boundaries between disciplines is favourable to students' learning but, in practice, we have nearly always con-ducted our research either in contexts where a given discipline of science is institutionally isolated from other school subjects or in contexts where that isolation was created by us, as it is the case of kindergarten or primary school. The latter was the consequence of trying to encourage teachers in our samples to concentrate on the subject of science in contexts where little status is traditionally accorded to it. However, in some studies some relation was established with other disciplines, such as mathematics and Portuguese, which means that, when we characterized pedagogic practice on a four degree scale of classification between distinct school subjects, the value of C⁻ could be attributed to interdisplinarity. Thus far, there is no evidence in our studies that this blurring of boundaries is favourable to students' learning or, rather, we have not yet been able to single out this characteristic as favourable. Theoretically, the opposite could be defended as students socialized throughout their school lives with strong classifications between distinct school subjects may end up not learning anything if they are pushed to learn all subjects in a context of interrelation. Interdisciplinarity increases the level of abstraction and is easier to implement successfully when there is already some proficiency in separate areas of knowledge. Moreover, disadvantaged students may find particular difficulties in learning in interdisciplinary contexts. Thus, this aspect of the practice needs further attention.

The other area where the model requires further optimization involves the indicators selected for each characteristic of pedagogic practice. Indicators have varied according to the study that is being carried out. For example, the indicators for the discursive rule *selection* differ from the context of the kindergarten to the context of higher education. However, some indicators have been common to all contexts, as is the case of *Constructing syntheses*, because we have considered them important in the characterization of any pedagogic practice. We have tried to select a sample of indicators that are relevant and representative of the multitude of indicators that can be defined as characterizing pedagogic practice, but this selection needs to be more rigorous. On the other hand, we want to reduce the number of indicators by determining which are sufficiently powerful to represent the whole of a given characteristic of pedagogic practice and to make the descriptors of these most relevant indicators more precise and concise. This will be useful for future research and, most importantly, will increase the power of the transferability of research results to education in practice, by making their use by teachers and curriculum developers easier. It is also important to determine if both macro and micro levels should be kept in the analysis or if indicators of one of them can be representative of both levels. Another aspect that needs further development is the determination of which indicators can be common across all characteristics of pedagogic practice such as, for example, evaluation criteria and hierarchical rules. This is something we have already attempted but that, so far, we have had difficulty achieving.

Another important aspect to be considered in future studies is the study of one characteristic of the pedagogic practice at a time, controlling the values of all other characteristics. This is particularly relevant for characteristics which have been less studied. For instance, if we want to find out how important interdisciplinarity is for learning, we should analyse the influence of different values of this characteristic while keeping the values of other characteristics equal in all school classes of the sample. However, this procedure should not interfere with the wider procedure we have referred to before, where we construct a model and see how it works.

It is important to note that throughout our research it became clear that some characteristics of pedagogic practice are closely interlinked in such a way that the values of classification and/or framing of one characteristic may determine the values of some others. For example, explicit evaluation criteria (very strong framing) requires (a) student control over pacing (very weak framing), so that there is time to explicate the criteria, and (b) student control at the level of the hierarchical rules (very weak framing), so that students can freely raise questions and have their doubts discussed.

An important point of a different order that we wish to address in future research is related to teachers' scientific proficiency in terms of knowledge and competences. Our studies have shown that many teachers, particularly at the kindergarten and primary school levels, fail to have scientific knowledge and competences. In order to achieve a higher degree of rigour when studying the effect of given pedagogic practices, we need to include in our research controls for teachers' scientific proficiency.

Finally, we wish to emphasize that we are not looking for a model that works in all circumstances; that is, a model that works in all contexts, whatever the conditions, and with no need for any adaptations. For example, we can start with a very strong framing of selection and, later on in the year, when students have already acquired the recognition and realization rules for the specific context of that classroom, we can let them have some control over the selection of activities, materials, etc. However, if learning is to occur, selection should never be regulated by weak framing. We conclude by emphasizing that all of our research indicates that there are characteristics of pedagogic practice that are indispensable for successful learning and that we should work to optimize them.

Appendix 12.1

Appendix 12.1 Relations between discourses: intradisciplinary relations

	Indicators	C⁺⁺	C⁺	C⁻	C⁻⁻
Macrolevel	Exploring themes under study	Knowledge previously learned is never referred to when exploring a new theme. Relations between distinct kinds of knowledge are ignored.	Knowledge previously learned is only referred to if it constitutes a condition to the understanding of the new theme.	Knowledge previously learned is necessarily referred to when exploring a new theme.	Knowledge previously learned is the starting point for exploring the new theme. Relations between distinct kinds of knowledge are made and explained.
	Doing tasks	The tasks do not require the relation between distinct kinds of knowledge.	The tasks make only a brief reference to the knowledge already learned.	The tasks contain relations between various kinds of knowledge of a same theme.	The tasks integrate the knowledge of various themes studied.
	Applying learning to new situations	The situation of application requires only factual aspects of the theme under study.	The situation of application requires the relation between distinct facts of the theme under study.	The situation of application requires the relation between distinct concepts of the theme under study.	The situation of application integrates concepts of the distinct themes studied.
	Constructing syntheses	The syntheses contain only factual aspects of the theme under study.	The syntheses contain the relation between distinct facts of the theme under study.	The syntheses contain only conceptual aspects of the theme under study.	The syntheses integrate distinct concepts of the theme under study.
Microlevel	Students' questions	Questions related to other themes are ignored. The answers to students do not interrelate distinct kinds of knowledge.	Questions related to other themes are not ignored but distinct themes are not interrelated in the answers to students.	Questions that relate to various themes are accepted and used to make a brief relation between the distinct kinds of knowledge studied	Questions that relate to various themes are not only accepted but are used to emphasize the relations between the distinct kinds of knowledge studied

Appendix 12.2

Appendix 12.2 Relation between subjects – discursive rules (evaluation criteria): teacher–student relation

	Indicators	F++	F+	F-	F--
Macrolevel	Exploring themes/problems under study	Explanations are very detailed, illustrated and exemplified and the various aspects are recorded on children's worksheets.	Explanations are detailed and illustrated but only the main aspects are recorded on children's worksheets.	Explanations are slightly detailed and illustrated and only some key sentences or words are recorded on children's worksheets.	Explanations are not detailed nor illustrated and recordings are not made.
	Doing tasks	Children are informed of the task they are going to do and the respective procedures are explained.	Children are informed of the task they are going to do but the respective procedures are only explained in generic terms.	Children are informed of the task they are going to do but the respective procedures are not explained.	Children are not informed of the task they are going to do and respective procedures are not explained.
	Constructing syntheses	Syntheses are quite clear and constructed in interaction with the children. They are written down on the blackboard and on children's worksheets.	Syntheses are orally made by the teacher with no interaction with the children. The teacher checks that they have been written down by children on their worksheets.	The teacher tells the children what they should write on the blank spaces of the worksheet, without discussing/clarifying its meaning afterwards.	No syntheses are made.
Microlevel	Discussing the questions of the tasks	Children are told, in interaction with the teacher, what is incorrect and what is missing and the meaning of the correct answers explained.	Children are told, with no interaction, what is incorrect and what is missing and the meaning of the correct answer is explained.	Children are generically told the answers to the questions, and their meaning is not explained.	Some points are made about the questions but incorrections are not pointed out and answers are not given.
	Recording information on worksheets	All recordings are written on the blackboard in order that children write them on their worksheets with the help of the teacher who checks that they are correctly transcribed.	All recordings are written on the blackboard in order that children write them on their worksheets, but the teacher does not check if they are correctly transcribed.	Only some of the most important recordings are written on the blackboard in order that children write them on their worksheets, but the teacher does not check if they are correctly transcribed.	Children make the recordings they wish on their worksheets as the teacher does not require that any recordings are made.
	Incorrect students' statements	Children's statements are reformulated/corrected/completed in detail, in interaction with the children.	Children's statements are reformulated/corrected/completed with no interaction with the children.	Children are told that their statements are incorrect but no reformulation is made.	Children's statements are not corrected nor reformulated.

Part V

Epistemological perspectives

13 The essential tension

An essay on sociology as knowledge

Johan Muller

Essential tensions

It is a great pity that the work of perhaps the two most creative sociologists of education of the last 50 years, Basil Bernstein and Pierre Bourdieu, should have been marred by what seems to have been a professional animus, with references to and pot shots at one another running through their work. Beyond this shadow boxing, the work of each moved round that of the other, never resulting in the kind of engagement that might have led to a theoretical supersession that would have strengthened the common endeavour of sociology, a supersession of the kind that they both argued for in their late work, as I will show below.

Despite early fruitful relations – Bourdieu arranged for the French translation and publication of the 1971 "Social Class, Language and Socialization" paper in the series he edited for Editions de Minuit, *Le Sens Commun*, as Bernstein (2000, p. 177) reminds us – the sniping will be what most people will remember. Bourdieu (1991, p. 53) famously accused Bernstein of "fetishizing" "legitimate language" (the elaborated code) by not relating it to "the social conditions of its production and reproduction", a canard Bernstein is moved to deal with twice (2000, pp. 122 and 177). Bernstein returned the compliment by repeatedly characterizing Bourdieu's oeuvre (starting in Bernstein, 1990) as dealing only with "relations to" (meaning, the social relations between actors) and unable to deal with "relations within" (the social relations of symbolic forms), a lack Bernstein himself only addressed with respect to knowledge in his last work. For all that, they at times used remarkably similar theoretical terms: they both used the concept of "field" (though Bernstein later used the term "arena" without significant change of meaning); they both spoke of "recontextualizing"; and "code" and "habitus", in the end, do the same conceptual work.

There is also a deeper consilience in the careers of these two peerless neo-Durkheimians: they both began with the same problematique, attempting to account for the complicity between symbolic and social formations, and they both ended up with a deep concern for the malaise in sociology in general, and in sociology of education in particular. It is this joint late concern that is a major focus of this chapter. In order to understand the roots of this malaise, two key fault lines in science and culture will first be examined.

Two cultures?

The dislocation between the *Trivium* (grammar, logic and rhetoric – later to become the humanities) and the *Quadrivium* (arithmetic, astronomy, geometry and music – later to become the sciences), and the precedence of the *Trivium* over the *Quadrivium* in the medieval university, depended for Durkheim (1977) upon the attempt to fuse the power of abstract Greek thought with Christianity, the Word with the World. The *Trivium*, governed then by Christianity (Catholicism) and concerned with inner tutelage (carried by the Word), was to be the condition for understanding the World; Word before World, inner cultivation as a condition for outer appropriation, as a condition for mediating the inner/outer dislocation, as Bernstein went on to elaborate. This placed the theologians in control of the social distribution of knowledge, until the scientific revolution forced a reversal of precedence, and a gradual secularization[1] of the humanities, which crystallized into various kinds of philosophico-literary-artistic elites in different parts of Europe, and into a decidedly mandarin literary elite in the British universities of the early twentieth century.

It was at these secularized guardians of elite "traditional" culture that C.P. Snow aimed a broadside in his Rede Lecture, entitled *The Two Cultures and the Scientific Revolution*. Affecting membership of both literary culture and scientific culture, Snow characterized scientific culture as optimistic and forward-looking, though he knew it was regarded as shallow and philistine by the cultivated literary culture of the literary elite. He derided the mutual incomprehension of the two cultures: "The degree of incomprehension on both sides is the kind of joke which has gone sour" (Snow 1993, p. 11) and lamented the "sheer loss to us all" (p. 11). The fault he laid squarely at the door of the literary intellectuals, calling them "natural Luddites" who lacked the culture to grasp the second law of thermodynamics, which he characterized as equivalent to knowing something about Shakespeare. He compared Britain unfavourably to the then Soviet Union, who produced educated men and women with a grasp both of literary and scientific culture, and then went on to say that industrialization was the only hope for the poor and the Third World, and that the best the developed world could do was to produce as many engineers as it could and export them to where they were needed in the developing world.

The fallout was immediate, and has continued, the book version of *The Two Cultures* having been reprinted 31 times by 1993. Despite his oversimplifications, Snow had hit a nerve. The most extreme response came from F.R. Leavis, doyen of the literary elite. In a lecture first given also at Cambridge, then published in *The Spectator*, and republished in Leavis (1972), Leavis heaped derision on Snow's "embarrassing vulgarity of style", on his ignorance, and on his ineptitude as a novelist; he is, said Leavis, as "intellectually undistinguished as it is possible to be". Leavis' attack drew an avalanche of responses, which called it *inter alia* "bemused driveling" of "unexampled ferocity" (see Kimball 1994).

The ferocity of the response, reminiscent of the old antagonism between the *Trivium* and the *Quadrivium*, should not obscure its terms. Leavis is clearly turning the tables on Snow, trying to win back control over discernment for the literary intellectuals, and away from the "philistinism" of Snow and his plea for recognition of the "culture" of science. Leavis' principal argument is to deny that science has such a thing as a "culture", on the grounds that it has no intrinsic moral resource; it is a discourse of "means", and cannot deal with "ends" which is the province of "real culture", like literature. Snow from this point of view has thus an anti-cultural bias, which serves to mask the moral challenges of science by presenting them as capable of being dealt with by science on its own. In short, Leavis responds in Humboldtian spirit by reinvoking the necessary connection between inner and outer that formed the rationale for *Trivium* precedence. Snow, in Leavis' argument, is thus attenuating their dislocation.

As we will see, this argument receives some support from Bernstein, surprising as it might seem. Before we get there, however, it might be useful to examine briefly an approach to the "culture of science" that deals with a second fault line.

Tribes and territories

In 1973, Anthony Biglan (1973a, b) published a pair of papers that popularized a set of disciplinary distinctions that have been remarkably enduring. The first and most significant distinction was between disciplines that were "hard" or "soft".[2] Biglan meant to mark out a continuum between the disciplines in terms of the degree to which they operated within a "paradigm" or not. Biglan meant by "paradigm" what Thomas Khun had originally meant by a paradigm, that is, "the degree of consensus or sharing of beliefs within a scientific field about theory, methodology, techniques and problems" (Lohdal and Gordon 1972, p. 58). There is in other words a great measure of agreement in the discipline as to what is known, what constitutes a novel problem, and what constitutes a legitimate way to address it. Notable about this definition is its implications for solidarity: it designates the degree of "social connectedness among scholars". Where "paradigmicity" is high, as Durkheim had already spelt out in his analysis of increasing specialization, this permits greater functional differentiation and hence requires greater interdependence, the hallmarks of organic solidarity, making possible significant time economies. Where disciplines do not share a paradigm, we find low differentiation, low interdependence and hence low social connectedness. This has some specific entailments for the organization of teaching and learning as we will see below.

Biglan also distinguished between "pure" and "applied" disciplines. This distinction has not been given the same conceptual underpinning as the "hard/soft" distinction, but has also stuck. Taken together, they form a four-part continuum. Other distinctions, like that of Kolb, followed suit (see Table 13.1).

Biglan influenced a number of researchers, notably Tony Becher, who influenced in turn Ruth Neumann, Susan Parry and Jens-Christian Smeby, among others. I will briefly follow Becher, not least because he was influenced by Bernstein in his early work.

Becher (1989) expanded and filled in the purview of Biglan's quaternary. He started out by distinguishing four layers of what he called academic culture: a generic common layer pertaining to all academics everywhere, academic culture proper; a layer pertaining to Biglan's four disciplinary clusters, which Becher calls *tribes* and their different cultures; and two other sublayers pertaining to disciplines and subdisciplines. The tribes are the key layer: each tribe has its own intellectual values, its own cultural domain and its own cognitive territory. In this way Becher tries to make explicit the inescapable duality of the social and the cognitive in considering the worlds of knowledge work – the "relations to" and the "relations within" of Bernstein. This point will recur.

Becher sets out to characterize both the *cultural style* and *knowledge style* of each of Biglan's tribes, with qualified success. I summarize these in the Tables 13.2 and 13.3.

Table 13.1 A typology of the disciplines

Biglan (1973 a, b)	Hard pure	Soft pure	Hard applied	Soft applied
Kolb (1981)	Abstract reflective	Concrete reflective	Abstract active	Concrete active
Examples	Natural sciences	Social sciences	Science-based professions	Social professions

Table 13.2 Cultural style of the tribes

Hard pure	*Hard applied*	*Soft pure*	*Soft applied*
Competitive, gregarious, politically well organized, task-oriented, high publication rate	Entrepreneurial, cosmopolitan, role-oriented, patents rather than publications, contract work	Individualistic, loosely organized, person-oriented, low publication rate, funding less important	Status anxiety, prey to intellectual fashions, power-oriented, low publication rate, vulnerable to funding pressures

Table 13.3 Cognitive style of the tribes

Hard pure	Hard applied	Soft pure	Soft applied
Cumulative; pursuit of universals; discovery/ explanation	Purposive; mastery of environment; products/ techniques	Holistic; pursuit of particulars; understanding/ interpretation	Functional; enhancement of practice; protocols/ procedures

Much of this will be contentious, especially the designation of the social sciences as interested only in particulars, with which both Bourdieu and Bernstein would strenuously have disagreed. Nevertheless, this account does capture something essential going on between the tribes, especially if we recall Biglan's master trope of "paradigmaticity" and "social connectedness". The "hards" are higher in social connectedness, so they collaborate more in teaching, especially at the lower levels where far less is contentious. Consequently, they spend far less time than the "softs" in lesson preparation. Since their teaching, research and supervision is better integrated, and since they spend less time on supervision – less than a quarter of the time spent by "softs" (Smeby 1996) – they have far more time for research, which they see as their fundamental mission as academics. The "softs" by contrast spend far more time both on lesson preparation and on actual teaching; they spend far more time on undergraduate teaching than on supervising postgraduates, unlike the "hards"; and supervision is a far greater chore for the "softs" than it is for the "hards", because they invariably supervise outside their own specific research focus area (Neuman *et al.* 2002). Invariably then, they end up researching and publishing less. The implications for the "pures" and "applieds" could likewise be unpicked.

Crude as this kind of approach to knowledge work may be, what it does display is an attempt to understand the relations of variability between symbolic structures and social structures, and the way in which these might be connected. But this attempt is ultimately limited. The potentially fecund variable of "paradigmaticity", which refers if only schematically to differentiation in both the symbolic and the social, is in Becher's analysis only really elaborated in the social/cultural domain. The discussion of cultural style (relations "to") is more convincingly brought out than that of cognitive style (relations "within"), and their relation is assumed rather than demonstrated. Along with Becher we can grasp that higher differentiation might mean greater social connectedness and interdependence in the social domain; but what would higher differentiation in symbolic structure actually look like? How would it vary? Talk of universals versus particulars and "holistic" versus "cumulative" does not take us very far. It is here that Bernstein makes his great late contribution, as we shall see.

We see this gap in Becher's analysis most clearly when we look more closely at the "*hard/soft*" metaphorical couple, and ask the question: should all disciplines aspire to "paradigmaticity"? Is "hardness" a normative ideal for all disciplines to which "softness" is but a weak and premature approximation? Are the "softs" merely cognitive juveniles in the kingdom of knowledge? Ought and will they still grow up? Kuhn and Popper certainly thought so: the prefix "pre" in Kuhn's description of the social sciences as "pre-paradigmatic" is symptomatic. "Hardness" in this view is a quality that, though historically conditioned, can be delayed but not denied. It is a quality that defines science and scientificity. By this view, the social sciences, and the humanities too for that matter, are deficit natural sciences: all knowledge is seen through a law-like glass. With variations, this is the "mathematized" or "mechanical" world picture that the humanists have resisted ever since the dethronement of the *Trivium* during the Renaissance. "Positivism" is the current code word favoured by the postmoderns, the humanist heirs in our present long twentieth-century moment.

It was this view that Vico opposed on behalf of the disciplines of the inner – the humanities – in the sixteenth century (Berlin 2000, 2001). But before we get to the humanities, let us try to get clarity on the troublesome social sciences. How should these be regarded? With Kuhn and Popper, as deficit sciences? Although both Bourdieu and Bernstein followed the Kuhnian lead of conceiving the distinction in disciplinary culture through a "paradigm" lens they each drew different conclusions from it, as we shall see. Below, I will show that Bourdieu had, in the end, a qualified expectation that his beloved sociology would one day join the sciences in rigour and prestige; while Bernstein had a far more pathos-filled view of the possibilities for social scientific growth. Neither of them really dealt with the humanities within this debate in any substantive way, despite gestures to the contrary.

Towards a "realist rationalism"

How then should we conceive of the relative "hardness" or "softness" of the social sciences in general, and of the discipline of sociology in particular? Does viewing the world, and science within it, as social products not make sociology terminally historicist, and consequently place strict limits on the generalizability of any sociological propositions, and therefore on their possible hardness? Does an historical analysis of social conditions not preclude talk of "truth", science's preferred proxy for speaking about hardness? Can the idea of the necessity of logical truths survive a description of their social genesis? In one or other way, this question has dogged the sociology of knowledge since its inception. A view common in the field is that you can't have both, and that a social description of the generation of truth does indeed put the idea of "truth" in question – or at least a strong idea of it.

In his last publication, the record of his last course of lectures at the Collège de France, Bourdieu (2004) returned to this vexed question with the intention of showing that a robust idea of the truth (hardness) can indeed survive its historicization. Tracing the lineage of the subdiscipline from

Mertonian structural-functionalism, through the impact of Kuhn, the sociologists of the "strong programme", to contemporary "laboratory studies" as exemplified by Knorr-Cetina (1981) and Latour (1987) (all of them interestingly enough indebted in one way or another to Durkheim), Bourdieu shows how the field of science studies has shifted from Merton's realism to the contemporary constructivist disdain for "truth" which so infuriates the scientists. In this last work he sets out to rehabilitate a robust idea of truth within a sociological framework, to show both why and how sociology can be "hard".

For Bourdieu, the cardinal error of the contemporary laboratory studies approach is its interactionism, unleavened by any idea of objective structural social relations. He modestly credits himself with introducing the notion of "field", which he regards as a theoretical concept that breaks with treating social actors naturalistically as sole generators of meaning. The object of science studies is posited as the scientific field, or set of scientific fields, each with specific properties and each structured in terms of the possession of scientific capital. The two principal features of scientific fields are their degree of autonomy/social closure, and their degree of formalism (or mathematicization), which allows both for the formulation of increasingly precise relations among scientific objects and also marks a break with the everyday features of commonsense. He notes that theories weak in scientific "eminence" tend to display low powers of formalism and "to appeal to external powers to enhance their strength" (Bourdieu 2004, p. 58), also noting that fields low in autonomy, like the social sciences, have endlessly to "reckon with external forces which hold back their *take-off*" (Bourdieu 2004, p. 47). Nevertheless all scientific fields must have some degree of autonomy: because of this autonomy, says Bourdieu, scientific fields obey a different logic to that of political fields.

The higher the degree of autonomization, the steeper the price of entry, which is an increasingly specialized and formalized competence. In autonomous fields, where closure is more or less complete (Bourdieu 2004, p. 69), scientists, by virtue of their entry credentials, tacitly agree to the existence of objective reality. Scientific fields thus tend to generate closure, allowing the peer community to arbitrate competition among peers and also to arbitrate the real (p. 70). In this way, the particular logical necessity of science is generated by field properties and mediated by field dynamics. This is because "[s]cientific fields are universes within which symbolic power struggles and the struggles of interests that they favour help to give its force to the best argument" (p. 82). Truth is thus the product of the very particular properties and dynamics of scientific fields.

Bourdieu hopes with this analysis to have provided the lineaments of a sociology of truth. He brings into a broad consensus the seminal contributions of Durkheim and parts of Cassirer, Popper and Kuhn, Merton and the Mertonians, and some of the weak constructivists like Collins. In this way, he provides an account of how knowledge communities operate, and how this operation has a necessary connection to truth/hardness, here, the "best argument". Truth is the product of consecration by agreement, according to accepted rules, the "mechanisms of universalization". We can therefore historicize or sociologize the circumstances for producing truth, but not truth itself: "Science is a construction which brings out a discovery irreducible to the construction and to the social conditions that made it possible" (Bourdieu 2004, p. 77).

When talking in this manner, it is clear Bourdieu is thinking about the "hards": we can socialize the "hards", he implies, but we can't take away their truth. But what of the "softs", of sociology? Because of low closure and weak autonomy, the "order" of sociology is "contaminated" by "principles of the political order and of democracy" (Bourdieu 2004, p. 73). Consequently, at present, "truth is plural", "as the current phrase goes" (p. 73), he says parenthetically. Sociology has thus no one truth to take away. More formally, sociology is a field in which the sociocognitive conditions for the production of singular truth have not yet come about, so "that the 'force of the best argument' (as Habermas puts it) has a reasonable chance of winning" (p. 82). Sociology, we must conclude, is a "not yet hard" "soft".

This is a rather depressing conclusion. What is a "realist rationalist" to do in the meantime? It is quite clear that Bourdieu's own strategy for "consolidating" sociology is based on his field analysis, and can be described as organizing the field by bringing all viewpoints into view and constructing a supersessionary viewpoint. He is constantly constructing dialectical opposites and a desired synthesis: "one has to move beyond the acceptable choice between idealist constructivism and realist positivism, towards a realist rationalism" (2004, p. 77). Presumably when everyone agrees to adopt a "realist rationalism" sociology will be readier to effect closure, both socially and cognitively. But he is not optimistic: "social science will never come to the end of the effort to impose itself as a science" (p. 115), he concludes glumly. Is it perhaps because, as he hints towards the end of his analysis, the object of sociology is itself a subject of objectification? Are we condemned to weak closure because we are unable to expunge our own worldly commitments in our analyses? Is the sociologist's humanity sociology's fatal flaw, the enemy within? Or is it something about the kind of structure that sociology as a knowledge form takes? It was this path that Bernstein chose to explore.

Is "hard" vertical and "soft" horizontal?

Even Bertrand Russell, who coined the terms, thought that "hard" and "soft" as knowledge identifiers were "somewhat vague" (Russell 1929, p. 75). "Paradigmaticity", the criterion suggested by Biglan, has the merit of pointing to both social and cognitive conditions, to "relations to" and "relations within". But the elaboration and clarification it seems to demand has not been forthcoming, especially not of the cognitive conditions, the "relations within". As we saw above, Bourdieu makes a stab at clarifying things, but his analysis is in the end mainly about the "relations to", as Bernstein (1996) complained. What of the "relations within"? This section begins with a brief description of Bernstein's ideas on the differentiation of knowledge.

For Bernstein, knowledge structures differ in two ways. The first way is in terms of what may be called *verticality* (Muller 2006). Verticality has to do with how theory develops. In hierarchical knowledge structures, it develops through the integration of propositions, towards ever more general sets of propositions. It is this trajectory of development that lends hierarchical knowledge structures their unitary triangular shape. In contrast, horizontal knowledge structures are not unitary but plural; they consist of a series of parallel and incommensurable languages (or sets of concepts). Verticality in horizontal knowledge structures occurs not through integration but through the introduction of a new language (or set of concepts) which constructs a "fresh perspective, a new set of questions, a new set of connections, and an apparently new problematic, and most importantly a new set of speakers" (Muller 2006, p. 162). Because these "languages" are incommensurable, they defy incorporation into a more general theory. The level of integration, and the possibility for knowledge progress in the sense of greater generality and hence wider explanatory reach, is thus strictly limited in horizontal knowledge structures.

Verticality can also vary in horizontal knowledge structures. There is a continuum within horizontal knowledge structures between those whose internal coherence holds up against repeated challenges and are thus conceptually robust, as compared to those whose internal coherence breaks off relatively readily, at the first challenge so to speak. The key question then becomes, not so much what hinders progression in all horizontal knowledge structures, but rather what internal characteristics distinguish those horizontal knowledge structures such as sociology that *proliferate* languages from those like linguistics where language *proliferation is constrained*. It was in search of a sociological answer to this question and to provide an alternative to what he saw as Bourdieu's sociological reductionism (see Bernstein 1996) that Bernstein began, by setting out his distinction between vertical and horizontal knowledge structures.

Alongside verticality, there is a second form of knowledge variation, *grammaticality*. I have suggested that verticality has to do with how a theory develops internally (what Bernstein later referred to as its *internal* language of description). In contrast, grammaticality has to do with how a theory deals with the world, or how theoretical statements deal with their empirical predicates (what he later referred to as its *external* language of description). The stronger the grammaticality of a language, the more stably it is able to generate empirical correlates and the more unambiguous, because they are more restricted, are the field of referents. The weaker the grammaticality, the weaker is the capacity of a theory to stably identify empirical correlates and the more ambiguous, because it is much broader, becomes the field of referents. Thus knowledge structures with weak grammars are deprived of a principal means of generating progressive new knowledge, namely empirical disconfirmation. As Bernstein puts it, "Weak powers of empirical descriptions remove a crucial resource for either development or rejection of a particular language and so contribute to its stability as a frozen form" (2000, pp. 167–8). To summarize, whereas grammaticality determines the capacity of a theory to progress through worldly corroboration, verticality determines the capacity of a theory to progress integratively, through explanatory sophistication. Together, these two criteria determine the capacity a particular knowledge structure has to progress.

I have so far used the discursive arsenal of Bourdieu to describe the way in which fields historically evolve relations "to" (between scientists) through the achievement of conditions for autonomy; and the theoretical language of Bernstein to describe how those relations "to" are closely aligned to the properties of verticality and grammaticality, the internal logic of the knowledge, the two canonical forms of conceptual closure which are responsible for the relations "within". Like Bourdieu, Bernstein is, through this analysis, trying to pin down the possibilities and limits of his own field, sociology. Again like Bourdieu, Bernstein finds himself in the very act of firming up his analysis, confronted with the terms of its limits. Why does conceptuality in sociology have to be so weak? Why must sociologists be so fractious? Are they fractious because their thought is weak, or is their thought so weak because they are so fractious?

Bernstein suggests that one of the reasons schismatic knowledges like sociology are so weak is that they are *retrospective*, that is, they are oriented to describe an immediate past, rather than projecting a possible future. This is because the insulation of specialized languages in low-autonomy fields is so weak that "contributors to Horizontal Knowledge Structures have no means of insulating their constructions from their experience constructed by Horizontal discourse" (Bernstein 2000, p. 167). In terms quite reminiscent of Bourdieu's discussed above, Bernstein is suggesting that the weakness of field closure in these specialized languages induces speakers in these languages unwittingly to draw on their own everyday experiences and sensibilities as resources for their analyses; and since these sensibilities "are embedded in projections from the past" (Bernstein 2000) (rather than in generalizing projections into the future as adepts of strongly vertical theories are able to do), these languages have a built in "obsolescence", which fuels the survival-driven interlanguage competition to an ever higher pitch. These pressures together compound the tendency to "schismatism" (Moore 2007) and "fractionation" (Abbott 2001). Sociology is quite simply unable to insulate itself from the world – from worldly interests for Bourdieu; from situated commonsense for Bernstein – which means its truths can never entirely escape the context of their genesis.

High-autonomy fields tend thus to have fairly stable, if competitive, communities, with clear status levels, clear entry requirements, and clear progression requirements at the lower levels for neophytes. Although there is disagreement, the broader community is generally able to settle disputes internally about "bestness"; that is, they are able internally to broker the conditions and criteria for truth on an ongoing basis. This internal organization is achieved on the basis of organized collective work, synchronically realized in the autonomously organized institutions of the field (professional associations, strong journals), and diachronically embedded in the theoretical core of the knowledge structure – "on the shoulders of giants" (see Merton 1993; Muller 2006). In other words, autonomous scientific fields exhibit the social organization of Durkheim's organic solidarity, displaying a highly specialized division of labour and competence, held together by the closely coupled relations of "within" and "without". The cluster of specialized languages and their patronage-organized factions that characterize low-autonomy knowledge fields, on the other hand, resemble nothing so much as knowledge tribes in flight from statehood, with a de-specialized division of labour, with no principled means, because no notion of truth, for reconnecting the relations "within" (the internal logic of the discourse) to the relations "without" (the social organization of the field).

The essential tension

To recapitulate: with the first fault line (*Trivium* vs *Quadrivium*; the "two cultures") we saw a disciplinary argument between the sciences and the humanities, the disciplines of the "outer" and the disciplines of the "inner". With the second fault line, the debate is about the "hards" versus the "softs", the difference between the natural sciences and the social sciences. The humanities, although sometimes included as an afterthought, are *stricto senso* not part of this fault line.

There is a third fault line that in conclusion is worth examining, after hard/soft and inner/outer; this is the *past/future* (or near/far) tension. I have discussed above how Bernstein characterizes the schismatic languages of sociology as *retrospective*. This implies that sociologists are by and large mired in their past and in commonsense, both of which act as a brake on the "verticalizing" possibilities of each language. Sociologists are, it seems, unable to unshackle themselves from their pasts sufficiently to project a language that will serve not only present ends, but future, as yet unenvisaged, ones too. We may say that sociological theories by and large lack futurity; they lack the conceptual "carry forward" to account for life beyond their own particular horizons. This hastens the obsolescence of sociological theories, and hence promotes schismatism.

It is also possible to see how schismatism itself promotes theoretical restriction. In one of his more bizarre constructed examples (a "caricature"), Bernstein argues that schismatism "shrinks the moral imagination" (2000, p. 77); taking as his example short people (two-and-a-half inches under average height), he imagines that they collectively develop a voice from "valid scholarship and research" until a yet smaller person comes along with a narrower definition of shortness (three-and-a-half inches), which constructs new criteria for exclusion, hence shrinking both the social base and with it possibilities for imaginative projection. The very solution to premature obsolescence – schismatism – is the strategy that will exacerbate it.

What then is the alternative to schismatism, this endless "fictitious pursuit of difference" (Bourdieu 2004, p. 7)? Or have the "softs" always been schismatic, as Jacob Burkhard seemed to think already in the nineteenth century?[3] Both Bourdieu and Bernstein suggest an alternative. For Bourdieu, we will always have to deal with our own social identity as a ground for social theorizing. But instead of narcissistic reflexivity, we should try to practise a kind of "reformist reflexivity" (Bourdieu 2004, p. 91), which he then sets out to demonstrate by telling his own story ("self-socio-analysis"), hoping thereby to "objectivate the subject of objectivation" (Bourdieu 2004, p. 88). In the form of socio-analysis he has given us here, it is hard to distinguish this enterprise from that of narcissistic reflexivity.

Bernstein's route is different. If the problem of retrospective languages is that they are "forever facing yesterday rather than a distanced tomorrow" (Bernstein 2000, p. 171), if the intrinsic flaw in sociological theory is its lack of a future (its built-in "short-termism", so to speak), then the task of theory is to work against this short-termism by consciously aiming at greater "clarity", "control", "generality" and "delicacy" (p. 211): building "verticality", we might say. Greater grammaticality (more empirical studies) is emphatically a means towards this. But the theory itself must, in order to avoid schismatism, build links between the pasts of the theory and its futures. This is hard to do consciously, and in Bernstein's view of the progress of his own theory, is able to be discerned only retrospectively:

> Each paper from the earliest is really part of a future series, which at the time of writing was not known. In a way each paper stands alone incorporating and developing the previous paper and pointing to an unwritten and often unknown text ... the aim of a paper is productive imperfection. That is it generates a conceptual tension which provides the potential for development.
>
> (Bernstein 2000)

This models, through a compact summary of Bernstein's own history, the ideal trajectory for a vertical theory.

Not all theories have the potential for this kind of trans-temporal continuity and fecundity. Bernstein's has shown that his has. In perhaps his final reflection on his own theory, Bernstein comments that each conceptual language has a deep structural pivot, an initiating metaphor, that is productive only so long as it is able to continue producing "new more powerful sentences" (Bernstein 2000, p. xiii). In his own case, says Bernstein, his metaphor is "'*boundary*' (inside/outside, intimacy/distance, here/there, near/far, us/them)". Crucially, "boundary" signifies also "a tension between the past and possible futures" (Bernstein 2000), a tension that must remain so long as the theory remains productive. Built into his metaphor thus, is the condition for continuity that has ensured its productive longevity. Of course there is no future guarantee of its longevity, because sociologists of Bernstein's and Bourdieu's stature are few and far between. The obstacles are great, both in the conditions of the field (the relations "to") and in the internal features of sociology (the relations "within"). Bernstein shows us it can be done.

Notes

1 It would be misleading to convey the impression that Christianity was in principle inimical to science; in seventeenth-century England, Merton (1992) has shown that the then prevailing Puritan spirit with its values of reason and experience formed a powerful "spur" to the development of science.
2 The terms "hard" and "soft" were not Biglan's own. They had been used first by Bertrand Russell in 1929, and in the sociology of science by Storer (1967) and Price (1970) before Biglan.
3 Says Burkhardt of the humanists, "Of all men who ever formed a class they had the least sense of their common interests, and least respected what there was of this sense" (Burkhard 1878).

14 Reading Basil Bernstein, a socio-epistemological point of view

Nicole Ramognino

How can we read Basil Bernstein, think with him and beyond him? His last book, *Pedagogy, Symbolic Control and Identity*, offers a survey at once wide-ranging and concise of his experience as a researcher, of his objectives, of crucial moments in the development of his approach and of the sociological results stemming from it. His focus is on pedagogical relationships within schools and, more widely, on relationships, such as those between doctor and patient, through which "cultural production-reproduction is takes place" (Bernstein 2000, p. 7). Bernstein's sensitivity to the way his work has often been misunderstood and misinterpreted is also perceptible.

In the book, Bernstein explicitly defends a scientific normativity that all sociological approaches ought to adopt. *Pedagogy, Symbolic Control and Identity* thus constitutes an example of epistemology in action. My reading, and the discussion in this chapter about the relation between democracy and pedagogical relationships, will deal less with Bernstein's work and his results than with the normative exigency of his approach, both in order to fully apprehend its heuristic and sociological significance and to discuss, develop or reject it.

It is important, first, to stress a central point of Bernstein's sociology: the fact that he observes the inner activity of social practice and integrates it within his theory of cultural reproduction. This constitutes a radical revision of the theoretical frame of critical sociology. For Bernstein, in order to explain pedagogical practice one must observe the specific inner activity, the utmost social action that it entails. I argue that this perspective addresses both structure and agency and serves to bridge the macro- vs micro-sociological divide. However, I shall dispute the metalanguage that Bernstein develops to describe his approach, which at times has closing effects and limits its potential, particularly regarding the insight it lends to the issue of the dynamism of practice, a theme which constantly concerned Bernstein yet remains a somewhat unresolved enigma in his work.

Scientific normativity of the sociological approach

Bernstein does not propose to sociologists that his is the only valid method. However, when his research bears on the history of the field of sociology, his main reference remains Durkheim, promoter of the sociological specificity of the analysis of the "social". In this sense, Bernstein presents a precise view of what an analysis requires in order to reach this quality. His description of the disappearance of the concept of social class here captures his convictions well:

> Apple, among others, has remarked that class analysis has been disappearing in research in education as the focus has shifted to race, gender, region and indigenous groups.... To a very great extend the foregrounding of discourse as the crucial centre of gravity of social analysis by Foucault and other Parisians had made these authors the new definers of the social. Thus the concept of the "social" is being rewritten by non-sociologists and taken over by sociologists. It is not simply the evacuation from the use of social class but the evacuation from *sociological* analysis.
>
> (Bernstein 2000, p. xxvi)

I do not intend to discuss such positions holistically, but rather to reflect on what, specifically and sociologically, is entailed when the object of observation is the "social".

What, then, constitutes the scientific approach of sociology? I argue that it focuses on two crucial points: the social in action and the development and use of a specific descriptive language relevant to it. The combination of these will lead to a change in knowledge of the "social", which is no longer explained solely by socialization and the weight of past experiences, but which links this history to present action.

Observation of the normativity of action

Let us first discuss the issue of pedagogical practice as observable action. A heuristic description of it requires a standard allowing the researcher to measure and give meaning to pedagogical practice. Critical sociology of education has brought to light the macro-sociological effects of schooling, allowing it to identify and denounce educational and social inequalities. On the one hand, however, this exposure does not rest on the direct observation of schooling while, on the other hand, the analysis offered by the critical sociology of education remains insufficiently articulated with statistical evidence. There are several reasons for this. One of them (though not the only one) is that this "critical" analysis rests on implicit principles: neither the reader nor the researcher have at their disposal a standard allowing them to define, measure, and capture the school operations responsible for the production and reproduction of inequalities. Researchers have not sufficiently explicated the principles at the source of their criticism, principles that could explain the statistical evidence on inequality in education and society. Bernstein, meanwhile, clearly identifies the viewpoint from which he observes pedagogical action. This viewpoint is that of a democracy to be created, as he states: "I am going to start with some assumptions about the necessary and effective conditions for democracy" (Bernstein 2000, p. xix). His assumptions influence his observations: "I will derive from these assumptions of the conditions for a democracy a set of pedagogic rights for evaluating democracy in education which will provide principles for examining schools" (p. xix). He justifies this position by noting that:

> Biases in the form, content, access and opportunities of education have consequences not only for the economy; these biases reach down to drain the very springs of affirmation, motivation and imagination. In this way such biases can become, and often are, an economic and cultural threat to democracy.
>
> (p. xix)

Bernstein identifies three pedagogical rights – "the right to individual enhancement", "the right to be included" and "the right to participate" – and uses them to "set up a model against which [he] can compare what happens in various school systems".

It seems paradoxical to claim a scientific approach but to begin research by declaring such idealistic principles. My intention here is not to explicate a "model" allowing sociologists to expose, for example, educational and social inequalities. My aim is much more fundamental: it is to question whether, as soon as he or she observes social activities and actions, the sociologist can free him or herself from the normativity inherent in these specific activities and actions. One may then wonder whether the development of a model of the normativity of action extends beyond scientific work or whether, on the contrary, it achieves it. Should not the fact that social agents cannot act without norming their activities thus become an object of description? My hypothesis is as follows: a realist theory of action requires that its normativity be recognized and observed. Pierre Rosenvallon (2006), describing the political field, states that he is elaborating "a new type of realist theory of democracy", at a distance first from ideological theories and, second, from the "organized descriptions of history and of the sociologist" that polarize his field of research. He argues that a new theory ought to be developed, that of the forms of democracy, based on the thorough observation of the actions and normativities they give rise to (Rosenvallon 2006, p. 321). The aim is to "reconsider the role of scholarly work and to escape from the vacillation between disillusioned clear headedness and naïve enthusiasm" (Rosenvallon 2006, p. 322). More prosaically, my intention (as well as Bernstein's, no doubt) is to allow for the observation of actions which give form to, which norm, the social and, as a result, provide the means of observing this operative dimension of action.

Thus, Bernstein introduces a crucial change of theoretical perspective, stating:

I suggest that theories of cultural reproduction essentially see education, and in particular the school, as a site of pathology and that their concern is to diagnose education as essentially a pathological device. In these analyses, clearly, social class is necessarily – and crucially – fore-grounded. But in this analysis social class will not be foregrounded. What will be, I hope, will be an explication of the inner logic of peda-gogic discourse and its practices. If we want to understand how peda-gogic processes shape consciousness differentially, I do not see how this can be done without some means of analysing the forms of communica-tion which bring this about. I shall be more concerned to analyse how a pedagogic text has been put together, the rules of its construction, cir-culation, contextualization, acquisition and change.

(Bernstein 2000, p. 4)

The main difference, then, is the shift from a focus on relations "between" to relations "within". Or, to put it differently, we move from the statistical recording of the correlations between social and educational inequalities to the observation of the inner social action of schooling, the result of which is the preservation of external social inequalities. The objective, then, is to observe how the school's inner social action of differentiation operates and to apprehend the normativities of the "pedagogic discourse". Bernstein calls these "rules of its construction, of its circulation, etc." In fact, the word "rules" here is ambiguous: it does not correspond to empirical data but rather it is a concept developed to account for the normativities of the various actions that constitute the pedagogic discourse and the forms of communica-tion in pedagogic exchanges that inscribe, inform and produce the "social".

Another reason for the incompleteness of critical theories in the sociology of education arises from the way in which knowledge production is "diag-nosed". The diagnosis proceeds by stating the existence of a pathology without being able to account for its genesis. The shift from an external analysis of the school system to an inner analysis, that is to the description of "pedagogic" actions, makes it possible to avoid the culturalist use that might be made of the concept of "symbolic violence" and to better approach the realism of the operations through which the unequal "social" is constituted within and by the school. Thus, by focusing his observation on the forms of school exchanges as they are enacted by social agents, Bernstein brings to the sociology of education, and to sociology as a whole, a realist theory of peda-gogic action that displays its ontogenesis.

From scales of observation to the concepts of classification and framing

As a result of his contributions as detailed above, Bernstein allows for the incommensurability of the different scales of observation presently dominat-ing the sociology of education to be overcome. Antoine Prost, in 2001, highlighted the lack of cumulativity within educational research. The field of educational research actually surveys multiple dimensions of pedagogic action but fails to hierarchize them and to integrate them with one another. As an example, one could refer to research in critical sociology (situated at the macro-sociological level by statistical observations but ignoring what is accomplished within the school and the educational system), or to meso-sociological research examining the impact of "individual schools" and of "teachers", etc. These investigations go side by side with those of education-alists studying pedagogic relationships inside the classroom, at the local or micro-sociological level, or those of the didacticians relating apprenticeship in a subject matter to what Reuter and Lahanier-Reuter (2007) call the "subject matter awareness" of learners. The diversity of research and of the results stemming from it renders impossible any reflexive synthesis leading to practical lessons.

Bernstein's theory of pedagogic action serves, on this issue, as a unique contribution. His programme renders it possible to overcome the dilemma of "global vs. local" observation, since Bernstein, beginning with the various activities of the educational system (the selection and construction of what "counts" as school knowledge, the recontextualization of this knowledge according to various political and strategic objectives, its deliv-ery by diverse pacings and sequencings, its unequally distributed transmis-sion and acquisition, etc.), achieves a theoretical synthesis and develops two social operations he conceptualizes in terms of "classification" and "framing". He states:

> I will now proceed to define two concepts, one for the translation of power, of power relations, and the other for the translation of control relations, which I hope will provide the means of understanding the process of symbolic control regulated by different modalities of peda-gogic discourse. And, perhaps, one can add a note here. The models that are created must be capable of generating a range of modalities of peda-gogic discourse and practice. And the models must also be capable of generating pedagogic discourse and practices which at the moment do not exist.
>
> (Bernstein 2000, pp. 5–6)

How can we grasp these concepts and what gives them the capacity to inte-grate varying scales of analysis?

Regarding the concept of "classification", Bernstein warns the reader against a classical interpretation, stating that we must "use the concept of *classification* to examine relations between categories, whether these cat-egories are between agencies, between agents, between discourses, between practices" (Bernstein 2000, p. 6). If "normally classification is used to dis-tinguish a defining attribute which constitutes a category", classification here:

refers to a defining attribute not of a category but of the relations *between* categories. Thus, if I take a series of categories, concretely we could think about the categories of discourse in the secondary school: physics, geography, language, etc.... They could be the categories which constitute the division of labour in the field of production: unskilled, skilled, clerical, technological, managerial.

(Bernstein 2000, p. 6)

It is in this sense that, for Bernstein, the issue is that of the transfer of power relations. This transfer is achieved through a categorization that can either create directly, as in the above examples, the social division of labour, or that, indirectly, makes possible the hierarchy of school subject matter and disciplines (what Bernstein calls "singulars" as opposed to "regions of knowledge"). Fundamentally, the concept of classification, as applied here, makes it possible to understand the link, or "translation," between what happens outside the school and what happens inside it. Classification, it should be emphasized, is an operation which through categorization gives form and meaning to, and generates or allows for the relations between, the elements to which it is applied. It could be called an inscriptive (or perhaps semantic or informative?) operation of the social, an operation which serves both as a condition for the possibility of the social and as information of this very social. Bernstein states that we can clearly see that classification constructs the nature of the social space: its stratifications, distributions, locations and arises from the transformation of power relations into principles of classification and of the relations between those principles of classification and the metaphorical structuring of space. In his introduction to the revised edition of *Pedagogy, Symbolic Control and Identity*, Bernstein explains that Dr Joseph Solomon enlightened him about the "tacit metaphor" operating throughout his work, that of the "'boundary' (inside/outside, intimacy/distance, here/there, near/far, us/them)" (2000, pp. xii–xiii).

The second concept, "framing" points to a pragmatic dimension and refers to an operation of the organization of the social. As Bernstein states:

That is, I am going to look at the form of control which regulates and legitimizes communication in pedagogic relations: the nature of the talk and the kinds of spaces constructed. I shall use the concept of framing to analyze the different forms of legitimate communication realized in any pedagogic practice.

(Bernstein 2000, p. 12)

He adds: "As an approximate definition, framing refers to the controls on communication in local, interactional pedagogic relations: between parents/children, teacher/pupil, social worker/client, etc." (p. 12), For Bernstein "*two* systems of rules regulated by framing" can be distinguished. These rules "can vary independently of each other, that is, their framing values can change independently. These are rules of *social order* and rules of *discursive order*" (pp. 12–13).

It should be emphasized again that these "rules" are Bernstein's own constructions in his attempt to account for the normativity of observed social action. The difference between these two types of "rules" arises from the fact that pedagogic actions are mixed; they have both social and "cognitive" aims. Bernstein develops the notion of framing by stating that:

> Framing is about *who* controls *what*. What follows can be described as the internal logic of the pedagogic practice. Framing refers to the nature of the control over the selection of communication, its sequencing (what comes first, what comes second), its pacing (the rate of expected acquisition), the criteria and the control over the social base which makes this transmission possible.
>
> (Bernstein 2000, pp. 12–13)

Before proceeding, the relations between classification and framing should be further explicated. If classification inscribes the possible, framing is a concrete and specific shaping of this possible. The link between one and the other is termed "translation"; a "possible" may give birth to various realizations, though these are limited by its configuration. These two operations have been endowed with different functions. The first (classification) refers to an inscriptive (informative or semantic)[1] operation of the "social", whereas the second (framing) is one of its realizations among others and presents itself as a pragmatic (organizing) dimension. In following this reading of Bernstein, one may probe deeper into these two operations and demonstrate that the issue is that of the articulation between two main sociological paradigms: the paradigm, dear to Bourdieu, of classifying and classification, and the paradigm of regulation preferred by sociologists from Boudon to Reynaud. These two paradigms refer to two theories of located social action, one holistic, the other individualistic and situational. To establish this articulation, however, it was necessary to distinguish between two dimensions necessary to grasp the "social": a generic dimension and a pragmatic dimension. Both render possible the local and interactional level of pedagogic practice; the former dimension foreshadows the "social real" and gives it its orientation, while the latter dimension plays the crucial part of describing its constitution and materialization.

Social change and dynamism of the model

Bernstein insists on the potential of his model for analysing social change. According to Bernstein, social change is rooted, independently, in the unfolding of each of the two operations detailed above. He states that:

> Although framing carries the message to be reproduced, there is always pressure to weaken that framing. There is very rarely a pedagogic

practice where there is no pressure to weaken the framing because, in this formulation, pedagogic discourse and pedagogic practice construct always an arena, a struggle over the nature of symbolic control. And, at some point, the weakening of the framing is going to violate the classification. *So change can come at the level of framing.* Although classification translates power into the voice to be reproduced, we have seen that the contradictions, cleavages and dilemmas which inhere in the principles of classification are never entirely suppressed, either at the social or the individual level. ... I suggest the following: if a value changes from strong to weak, or vice versa, if framing changes from strong to weak or the classification changes from strong to weak, there are two basic questions we should always ask: which group is responsible for initiating the change? Is the change initiated by a dominant group or a dominated group? If values are weakening, what values remain strong?

(Bernstein 2000, p. 15)

Framing, as a pragmatic dimension of the "social real", is the very site of dynamism since it enforces the operativity of social action, here pedagogic action, which can be directly observed at the local and interactional level. It maintains or transforms, and in every case regulates, the already existing "social". The heuristic value of this theory of action, located in a concrete pedagogical context (the transmission and acquisition of knowledge), is evident here. Moreover, "pedagogic discourse" (the transformation, recontextualization and circulation of knowledge), is revealed as the result of many other situations preceding the pedagogic actions of transmission and acquisition, constructed by other social agents, situations and actions serving to shape the local pragmatic dimension. At these two related levels, struggles, conflicts, cooperations and compromises serve to give the school system its dynamism, transforming and regulating, through maintenance or innovation, the concrete modalities of "pedagogic discourse".

Next, I pose a question and offer a conjecture. Bernstein attributes to the concepts of classification and framing not only the internal/external property, which appears useful in distinguishing the levels or dimensions of the analysis, but also the property of strength/weakness. The introduction of this property somewhat confuses my understanding of Bernstein's writings and of their potential applicability to my own research. It is possible to interpret these properties nomothetically: the more these phenomena are characterized as "strong", the more reduced seem the possibilities of change, while the weaker they are, the stronger the possibilities of change. While this property may be necessary and useful in grasping social dynamism, Bernstein's terminological choice fails firstly to qualify the orientation and meaning of change (especially regarding the right to individual enhancement and the rights to be included and to participate). Moreover, it is linked, it seems, to a "structural" conception of the "social" that is not necessarily required by the theory of action: do classification and framing, either strong or weak, norm the action of social agents or, rather, do social agents translate and give material form to classification and framing? In assuming that the terms strong and weak refer to the notion of "strength", that is to the energy providing the social system its dynamism, I conject that this energy cannot but be a property of social agents and of the relations between them.

This point leads also to discussion of Bernstein's theory of cultural reproduction and the framing for which it allows. Bernstein insists that the objective of his language of description is to account for the "symbolic control of the production and reproduction of cultural change". If he demonstrates gaps and omissions in critical sociological theories and addresses them by widening the focus of the concepts of classification and framing, integrating them with the paradigm of regulation, the potential for change is reduced to the question of the "symbolic control" of cultural production and reproduction. In applying his theoretical model to historical contexts (the various modalities of the reproduction of educational and social inequalities), Bernstein takes into account, as Jean-Claude Passeron (1991) recommended, the historical nature of sociology as a "singular" discipline without pondering the consequences of this epistemological position. This entails two epistemic framing effects. On the one hand, modern historical consciousness is a particular form of the anthropological consciousness of time, a political form that is not the only one possible and imaginable (Molino 1986; Koselleck 1990). It has the drawback of dealing with social phenomena under the one dimension organizing political action. On the other hand, one could question the epistemic framing which consists of moving "from statistics to social dynamics". Molino's approach (1998) clarifies this:

> When, at the beginning of our century, historicism and evolutionism fell into disuse, sociology and human sciences as a whole turned to social statistics: they focused on functions, organizations, structures. The consequence was the shift to a problematic of change: change is the euphemistic name given to a future lessened to a subordinate statute. It is not a question of vocabulary only: it is the very balance of human sciences and their finalities that were modified.... It is, in fact, a fixist metaphysics which is hiding behind today's human sciences.

Bernstein's effort to propose a general model that would account for not yet achieved facts is thus limited in its potential by a political orientation towards history and by an epistemic framing that hierarchizes statistics over the future. Bernstein conceptualizes "pedagogic discourse" as being constituted by an "instructional discourse" embedded within a "regulative discourse". How, then, to develop observations of school phenomena referring to the "right to individual enhancement" if there does not exist a narrative, a taking into account of the virtual or certified effects of the "instructional discourse"? I argue that here we are reaching the limit of the "tacit metaphor", that of the "boundary", operating in Bernstein's work.

Once again, Bernstein's remarkable capacity for discussing his own work and for revising his own propositions is evident; he underlines its incompleteness, after an interview with Dr Solomon, by stating:

> The crucial metaphorising is what *the boundary signifies*. Condensing the past but not a relay for it, rather a tension between the past and possible futures. The boundary is not etched as in copperplate, nor as ephemeral as in quicksand, and is sometimes more enabling than disabling. I have been concerned with how distributions of power are realised in various, and often silent, punctuations of social space which construct boundaries. I have equally been concerned with how these boundaries are relayed by various pedagogic processes so as to distribute, shape, position and opposition forms of consciousness. However, engaging with such a metaphor as boundaries, whilst opening possibilities at the same time limits them. It is important to know when this limit is reached.
>
> (Bernstein 2000, p. xiii)

An unorthodox reading of Bernstein's "model"

In the second part of this chapter, I will discuss Bernstein's sociological and epistemological metalanguage. On the basis of the "tacit metaphor" and of the "boundary", I mean to demonstrate how sociology of education remains restricted in its capacity to analyse educational social phenomena by the epistemic framing of a theory of "cultural control", even when observations stemming from it offer the potential of other interpretations. This leads us back to the specificity of sociological analysis, as both an historical and anthropological science, in order to take more seriously into account the normative rights that serve as standards for measuring the efficiency (normativity) of pedagogic discourse and practice in action. Then I will examine the epistemological framework within which Bernstein narrates his work and I will suggest that his metalanguage does not do it the justice it deserves.

The "boundary" metaphor and its consequences

Let us start with the metaphor of the "boundary". It is a spatial and political metaphor which allows for or produces – it does not matter here – another one often employed in sociology, that of social space. It allows for social agents to be attributed places and positions within the social structure or situation and, of course, in doing so it entails stratifications, hierarchies and power relations. This lends Bernstein's model, and its integration into the theory of cultural reproduction, a strong coherence. Of course, this coherence means that the research also adjusts itself, as mentioned, to historical and cultural particularities which possess as a common feature the stamp of educational and social inequalities. The direct effect of the spatial metaphor is the translation (treason?) of social conflicts and divisions into a division of space, an "organization" of the world and of agents that appears almost natural. This aspect is particularly well perceived by Bernstein since his comments following the operation of this translation often emphasize that "spatial" social phenomena are but the trace of a stage in social change and of the conflicting dynamics behind it. But if Bernstein suggests this in his interpretation, if he provides us with the means of observing this conflicting interplay in his analyses concerning the construction of the "pedagogic text", its "contextualization" and its "inscriptive" or "generic" qualities, he does not provide us with the means for observing the pragmatic dimension of pedagogic action within the classroom. This is because he maintains, at the very moment of the observation of pedagogic practices and against his own recommendations concerning operations of categorization, the "normal" use of classification which "distinguishe[s] a defining attribute which constitutes a category" (Bernstein 2000, p. 6). In fact, in order to deal with the issues of the transmission and acquisition of knowledge, he returns to the "social space" of the classroom, where the transmitters (teachers) and the acquirers (students) are divided, separated, and thus remain locked into the semantic framing with which agents categorize the educational world and their pedagogic relationships.

This is understandable since, historically and culturally, the school situation has been observed only in those terms. But if the model is to be generalized, if historical and cultural relations are to be thought of in terms of an anthropological framing as well, then this vision of the school world should also be perceived as social exchange. This enables us, on the one hand, to better grasp the specific connections actually underlying these pedagogic relations (or the "working on other people" (Dubet 2002)) and, on the other hand, to qualify the properties of these relations compared with other possible types of relations (violent, hierarchical, egalitarian, democratic, etc.). This makes it possible to "measure" them or at the very least to compare them in terms of the "rights" that served as the starting point of the research: the "right to individual enhancement", the "right to be included" and the "right to participate". Bernstein's theoretical descriptions examine these issues from the vantage point of the operation of "transmission" or from the standpoint of an "identity model" that pedagogic discourse sets to work. But, if my reasoning is correct, pedagogic discourse sets to work "transmission" and "identity models" (*introjected or projected*, whether "competences" formative of the consciousness of the subject and/or "performances" required by the market are the aim) only virtually, since in order for "transmission" to occur or to succeed, reception ought to at least be achieved or actualized according to the "circulation of knowledge" model set into place. The spatial metaphor leads to a vision of "communication relations" that belongs to the paradigm of "circulation", not, as the operation of acquisition would demand, to that of an "appropriation" of knowledge that requires work, the production of knowledge. The "actual curriculum", the one acquired by the "students", is not dealt with. If it were, it would lead to a conceptualization of school social exchange no longer under the paradigm of communication "emission/reception" (transmission/acquisition), but rather under the paradigm of a co-production between social agents in determining how (and under what actual modalities, if "actual" corresponds to the school social exchange as a whole) the right to individual (and, I would add, collective) enhancement, the right to be included and the right to participate are realized. We would then have a different reading of the behaviour of "drop-out", "descholarized", "slow-achieving", etc. pupils, than is generally accounted for in terms of their deficits of various types. These agents would be considered as promoters of actions of "eviction" of the objectives of the educational institution. In the same way, violence and incivility at school could be characterized as pupils' actions (Ramognino *et al.* 1996, 1997) manifesting in return for and in answer to the absence of their rights "to be included" and "to participate", as capacities for putting to death or bringing down the pedagogic "social", and as "[translating] the locking of the negative sovereignty into its immediacy as a radically bare force, incapable of active criticism, [the] expression of a resigned violence" (Rosenvallon 2006, p. 268).

This reflection leads also to an exploration of the way Bernstein travelled towards other observations that might allow for the integration of the concepts of classification and classifying, the paradigm of regulation and the paradigm of the production of the "social". The latter, in interaction with the two former, makes it possible to account for the activity and social action of all the agents of social exchange (here, in schools) and possesses as a heuristic virtue two essential aspects. On the one hand, the analysis is freed from the enclosure of the spatial metaphor of the "boundary" while keeping its sense of the limits on the potential not only of the individual but also of the social and the collective. On the other hand, it invites the researchers to revise their descriptions of the behaviour of agents, particularly pupils, in order to narrate their actions less in terms of failure, incapacity, inertia or violence than in terms of actions showing competencies and potential, though unpolished, that schools are supposed to develop and improve. This is important, for if my reasoning is correct, then descriptions of pupils' behaviours could be revised and measured in terms of the rights to "individual (and, I would add, collective) enhancement", to "be included" and "to participate". The question of these "rights", then, would no longer be posed in an ethical and idealist way, but on a material and pragmatic level. Thus, the observation of the dynamism of practice in schools would not be reduced to an examination of how the "symbolic control of cultural production and reproduction" is transformed but rather would bear on issues of social change within an epistemic framing submitting the static to the dynamic.

The research narrative: an uncompleted reflection

Bernstein's (2000) last book is a remarkable synthesis of his approach, his work, his revisions and results. This synthesis follows the advancing stages of his work as a whole, offering both a distanced reflection on the development of his theory and a recognition of the new perspectives required as a result of the theory's interactions with and applicability to the field and to empirical data. The synthesis also presents itself as a narrative of his work over roughly 50 years, a narration which remains incomplete and which might ultimately have provided the opportunity for debate over the focus with which he started it. If my understanding of Bernstein's propositions is correct, they were born of a classical conception of a scientific approach which seems to represent, for the human and social sciences, the ideal model of the so-called "hard" sciences, the hypothetico-deductive model. Yet, this image[2] captures adequately neither the various approaches of researchers in the "hard" sciences, nor those adopted by researchers, including Bernstein himself, in the social sciences.

Scientific reasoning allows for several types of research approaches. It may proceed through models when the phenomenon analysed rises from a simple, homogeneous action. It is not impossible to imagine a complex model of action or its simulation, but this would require great inventiveness on the part of the researcher in order to articulate and give shape a priori to the coordination of the diverse activities, events, acts and processes which compose the complex social action of the "pedagogic discourse". This is a result of the multiplicity of activities of pedagogical action which are produced, articulated and translated at various levels (from inside to outside, from outside to inside), activities which have been redefined in this chapter as generic, inscriptive and semantic (such as the construction of the pedagogical text, the recontextualization of knowledge, and the circulation of knowledge) as well as pragmatic operations (such as the transmission and acquisition of knowledge). Bernstein's is not an inductive approach either, but an approach which may be defined on the one hand as iterative, since it consists of an organized and systematic see-saw motion between hypotheses and observation and, on the other hand, as a cumulative approach in the sense that the stages of his work advance as previous ones are revised and as he is constantly in search of new data in order to widen, deepen or revise concepts and temporarily accepted hypotheses. This is why Bernstein's work ultimately would have needed a different, better adjusted, metalanguage.

Moreover, the model implies causality. Even if Bernstein believes that it expresses causalities, his whole approach, as I have presented it to this point, does not rest on a scientific type of model but rather more pragmatically on "data analysis". As I have already demonstrated the relation between classification and framing is not really causal, neither is it generic in the sense that the inscriptive (semantic) orientations given by classification and the concrete modalities of framing are, according to Bernstein, relations of "translation". The relation of this last term to causality may be debated but, if we take seriously the present action and the ability of agents to invent other "possibles", it is supposed to account for the relations existing between two abstractly defined "possibles" and either their activation or their transformation.

Bernstein's narrative may contain major drawbacks regarding the relations of researchers with the so-called "model". The belief that it is a hypothetico-deductive and causal perspective may result in the adoption of a dogmatic and/or formalist use of the concepts proposed: thus, it might be concluded that adopting weak framing or classification at the level of school transmission might have beneficial effects on the reduction of inequalities, an interpretation Bernstein certainly does not make. But the temptation is great to give this meaning or orientation to the term "weak". The risk is all the greater as attempts at innovation in pedagogic matters have sometimes promoted such framing with the aim of reaching a more equitable social distribution of knowledge. The pioneering research of Viviane Isambert-Jamati (1995) concerning the profiles and pedagogies of secondary-level French teachers, for example, demonstrated that school achievement, and differences in achievement between pupils from different social backgrounds, did not indicate that a weak framing of the transmission of knowledge was beneficial to them. Similarly, a formalist use of the concepts may also neglect their operational quality and transform them into a metalanguage, cut off from reality, without contributing supplementary knowledge.

In this sense, my reading here of Bernstein's concepts is far from orthodox. I should probably explain why. When Bernstein provides examples of the operativity of his concepts, he usually does so by contextualizing them historically. These concepts lose their general meaning to specify a historical peculiarity. As a consequence, in the examples proposed, they become mixed concepts: they retain a general value but they also become sociohistorical, sociocultural, local concepts. He tends to proceed as if their operativity belonged to the order of an historical necessity and to forget that their necessity belongs to a different, more general and pragmatic order, linked to problematic social action in the sense that it is marked by uncertainty. As a result, the concepts shape responses to social phenomena and to general mechanisms that may be described as trans-historical, and in some way, anthropological.

Here, the vision of anthropology is not reduced to all that has ever been since the emergence of *homo sapiens*. It refers to a protracted process of hominization still in the making and it is constructed pragmatically by the interactions between social agents that cannot be summed up by what can be observed locally and punctually but that are generated by the already open "possibles", in and by the (particularly historical and cultural) process of hominization, but also by the opening of action towards different horizons.

Conclusion

This reading of Bernstein's last book is unorthodox, and undoubtedly a number of readers might have the feeling that I am cheerfully betraying him. Yet I believe that this reading renders more justice to the tenacious, perspicacious character of Basil Bernstein who, for more than 50 years, stubbornly kept questioning his own observations and interpretations without ever forgetting that sociology is an empirical scientific discipline and without ever allowing himself the right to write more metaphysical or ethical "essays". If his programme of research was always constructed around the issue of the "symbolic control of cultural production and reproduction", he never repeated himself, leaving aside concepts he deemed insufficiently operational and revising others to achieve an analysis of the school system that accounts for its complexity and for all its dimensions. It is for these rare qualities that I prefer this reading, clearly an unorthodox one when it comes to detailed sociohistorical and sociocultural descriptions, in order to better adjust myself to his project and the planning behind his different research programmes.

This reading refers to the order of a sociological epistemology and comprises two aspects. The first is sociological, through which I have tried to answer the following question: How does the synthesis Bernstein attempts, in his works as a whole, bring solutions to the explicit issues of the "singular" field of sociology, issues that can be defined in terms of divisions between paradigms, of the diversity of scales of observation, of a lack of cumulativity of the knowledge produced, or of unrecognized issues such as the necessity of accounting for the normativity of action? Concerning these issues, the progress made by Bernstein is crucial; the construction of a "model for democracy" serves as a standard and measure for historical and cultural observations, requiring from the researcher a description of the normativity of the actions and activities of social agents while the concepts of classification and framing, their internal/external properties defining operations of translation, going from "upstream" to "downstream" and back again, constitute an interesting heuristic solution to reconciling two sociological paradigms usually presented as opposites or as referring to different scales of observation, the paradigm of classifying and classification and that of regulation. At the epistemological level, I have tried to demonstrate that Bernstein's metalanguage for describing the history of his research and the knowledge and results produced by it remain underdeveloped to the openings his reflection and his thought development offer. I have examined his discovery of the "implicit boundary metaphor" governing his work, which could have helped him revise his work and his concepts once again in order to better approach the realities he was dealing with. He would likely have found a way to overcome the duality of these concepts which is evident in their mixture: elaboration of general concepts and their location, their sense linked to the contexts of historical and cultural description. These concepts are general and applicable to different modalities of the pedagogic relation; they govern various social phenomena, beyond the school institution and also beyond the historical and cultural realities already encountered; the concepts are, however, sociohistorical and sociocultural in nature, which should preclude their use in other contexts without renewed development.

Bernstein situated sociology among the historical sciences, even though it clearly relates also to anthropology: widening pedagogic relations towards the Maussian concept of social exchange, of which the "gift" is the archaeological expression. Far from the ethical transformation of the "right to individual enhancement", and to the "right to be included" and "to participate", gift "giving/receiving/repaying" is defined as a social obligation assuming, historically and culturally, various modalities of social benefits characterized by "*philia*" and the equality between agents and "*eros*", characteristic of hierarchy and competition, of power relations. These two relations, at their paroxysm, take the shape of either *agape* or of death, two different forms of sacrifice. The relation underlying the work of instructing the offspring of man – a specific activity creating a relationship between teacher and pupil, parent and child – is virtually akin to *agape* and may be concretized into relations of "symbolic violence" or of "school violence".

In order to demonstrate how this unorthodox reading might help further develop Bernstein's theoretical contributions, I conclude by touching on two of the themes dealt with in Bernstein's book. The first theme concerns precisely the issue of "democratic" exchange and of its locking by the modality of the pedagogic relations adopted. Bernstein examines exchange by adopting a "commonsense" viewpoint in terms of transmission and acquisition. In treating transmission not only as transmission through "instructional" discourse but also through "regulative" discourse (an observation rendered necessary by the paradigm of the "symbolic control of cultural production and reproduction"), Bernstein, through a close analysis of the model of competence emerging in the 1970s and of the performance model adopted around 1980, introduces the hypothesis that the various pedagogic processes distribute, shape, position, and oppose forms of consciousness. He develops two "identity models", terming them "*introjected*" and "*projected*". Here, his analysis converges with that of others, such as Virno (2002), who also demonstrates how the field of economic production demands a flexible workforce characterized less by its abilities than by its performances, such as those projected by the market. While such an interpretation is not erroneous, it is characterized mainly by its incompleteness. The interpretation moves too fast. Another observation of actual curricula, those really "delivered to" pupils, would have prevented this sort of overly fast reasoning and would have been better adapted to the economic market, itself plural and segmented.

The second theme is that of the transformation of subject matter discourse into the regionalization of knowledge, a consequence of which might be the disappearance of sociological analysis to the benefit of social analysis. It allows a reconsideration of the property of the strength or weakness of subject matter classifications. The regionalization of knowledge is achieved, in fact, along two lines. On the one hand, it is a spatial regionalization in which different research investigations depend on the creation of local (political or economic) markets. Clearly, the reform of higher education in recent years, particularly in France, seems oriented this way. On the other hand, the research and training demanded by these political and local economic markets, linked to territories largely overlying the cutting out of knowledge into "singulars", brings about a regionalization of knowledge of a different type. If the classification of subject matter discourse were strong, as it was in the nineteenth and twentieth centuries, this strong classification, while supporting diverse and fluctuating hierarchies between "singulars", would confer to the learned instructional discourse a strength allowing it, surely, to resist the power of political and economic markets. However, "singulars" abandoned the issue of the normativity of action, which can be regarded as impacting negatively the right to "individual and collective enhancement". A specific "field of knowledge", always more complete, its action and its pragmatic dimension require that the elements of knowledge contributed by other fields, whether from fundamental or applied subjects, be accumulated inside a given one. The emphasis Bernstein places on the observation of the pragmatic internal dimension (*within*) is crucial from this point of view: the analysis of curricula and of their appropriation in the classroom could show, at any given moment, the incompleteness and the potentialities of the configuration of a specific field of knowledge.

It should be evident that these two examples are an appeal to the pursuit of a research programme on Bernstein that would more particularly deal, on the one hand, with the second pole of the relation between transmission and acquisition and, on the other hand, with the upholding of the acquisition of specific subject matters ("singulars") during the process of the regionalization of scholarly knowledge.

Notes

1 I will leave open the issue of whether this dimension is informative or semantic, since the difference between these terms refers to different "scientific models" (informational model or semantic model), see Granger's propositions (1994).
2 Molino (1996) evokes Alistair Cameron Crombie's (1994) work, *Styles of Scientific Thinking in the European Traditions*, London: Duckworth, vol. 3, that lists six types of different scientific research approaches.

Bibliography

Abbott, A. (2001) *Chaos of Disciplines*, Chicago: Chicago University Press.

Al-Ramahi, N. and Davies, B. (2002) "Changing Primary Education in Palestine: Pulling in Several Directions at Once", *International Studies in Sociology of Education*, 12 (1), 59–76.

Alves, V., Calado, S., Ferreira, S., Morais, A.M. and Neves, I.P. (2006) *Instrumento de análise do currículo nacional de ciências naturais do 3º ciclo do ensino básico: Relações intradisciplinares – Conteúdos científicos/conteúdos científicos*, Lisbon: ESSA Group, Department of Education, School of Science, University of Lisbon.

Apple, M.W. (1995) "Education, Culture and Class Power: Basil Bernstein and the Neo-Marxist Sociology of Education", in A.R. Sadovnik (ed.), *Knowledge and Pedagogy. The Sociology of Bernstein*, Westport; London: Ablex Publishing, pp. 59–82.

Attali, J. *et al.* (1998) *Pour un modèle européen d'enseignement supérieur*, Paris: Rapport au ministre de l'Education nationale, de la Recherche et de la Technologie.

Aulagnier, P. (1986) *Un interprète en quête de sens*, Paris: Ramsay.

—— (1988) "Le champ des possibles", Conférence prononcée à l'AFPEP le 16 janvier, non publiée.

Bakhtin, M.M. (1981) *The Dialogic Imagination: Four Essays*, ed. Michael Holquist, (trans. Michael Holquist and Caryl Emerson), Austin: University of Texas Press.

Bakhurst, D. (1995) "Lessons from Ilyenkov", *The Communication Review* nos. 1–2, 155–78.

Ball, S. (1998) "Big Policies/Small World: An Introduction to International Perspectives in Educational Policy", *Comparative Education*, 34 (2), 119–30.

—— (2004) "Performativities and Fabrications in the Education Economy: Towards the Performative Society", in S. Ball (ed.) *The RoutledgeFalmer Reader in Sociology of Education*, London: RoutledgeFalmer.

—— (2007) *Education plc: Understanding Private Sector Participation in Public Sector Education*, London: Routledge.

Bautier, E. (2005) "Formes et activités scolaires, secondarisation, reconfiguration, différenciation sociale", in N. Ramognino, P. Vergès (eds), *Le Français d'hier et d'aujourd'hui. Politiques de la langue et apprentissages scolaires. Etudes offertes à V. Isambert-Jamati*, Aix-en-Provence: Publications de l'Université de Provence.

—— (ed.) (2006) *Apprendre l'école, apprendre à l'école. Des risques de construction des inégalités dès la maternelle*, Lyon: ed. Chronique sociale.

Becher, A. (1989) *Academic Tribes and Territories*, Milton Keynes: Open University Press.

—— (1994) "The Significance of Disciplinary Differences", *Studies in Higher Education*, 19 (2), 151–61.

Becher, A. and Parry, S. (2005) "The Endurance of the Disciplines", in I. Bleiklie and M. Henkel (eds) *Governing Knowledge*, Dordrecht: Springer.

Bennett, S. (2002) *Learning About Design in Context: An Investigation of Learners' Interpretations and Use of Real Life Cases Within a Constructivist Learning Environment Created to Support Authentic Design Activities*, unpublished PhD dissertation, University of Wollongong.

Berlin, I. (2000) *Three Critics of the Enlightenment: Vico, Hamann, Herder*, Princeton: Princeton University Press.

—— (2001) *The Roots of Romanticism*, Princeton: Princeton University Press.

Biglan, A. (1973a) "The Characteristics of Subject Matter in Different Academic Areas", *Journal of Applied Psychology*, 53 (3), 195–203.

—— (1973b) "Relationships between Subject Matter Characteristics and the Structure and Output of University Departments", *Journal of Applied Psychology*, 53 (3), 204–13.

Board of Studies NSW (BoS) (2006a) *English Stage 6. HSC 2006–2008. Prescriptions: Area of Study Electives and Texts*, Sydney: Board of Studies.

—— (2006b) *HSC Examination 2005, English, Paper 1 – Area of Study: Student Answers*, Sydney: Board of Studies.

Boltanski, L. (1964) *Prime education et morale de classe*, Paris: EHESS.

—— (1990), *L'Amour et la Justice comme compétences. Trois essais de sociologie de l'action*, Paris: Métailié.

—— (2009) *De la critique. Précis de sociologie de l'émancipation*, Paris: Gallimard.

Boltanski, L. and Chiapello, E. (1999) *Le nouvel esprit du capitalisme*, Paris: Gallimard.

Boltanski, L. and Thévenot, L., (1991) *De la justification. Les économies de la grandeur*, Paris: Gallimard.

Bolton, H. (2005) *Social Class, Pedagogy and Achievement in Art*, PhD thesis, University of Cape Town.

Bonal, X. and Rambla, X. (2003) "Captured by the Totally Pedagogized Society: Teachers and Teaching in the Knowledge Economy", *Globalization, Societies and Education*, 1 (2), 169–84.

Bonnéry, S. (2007) *Comprendre l'échec scolaire. Elèves en difficulté et dispositifs pédagogiques* (Preface, E. Bautier), Paris: ed. La Dispute.

Bourdieu, P. (1966) "Champ intellectuel et projet créateur", *Les temps modernes*, 246, pp. 865–906 (trans. "Intellectual Field and Creative Project", in M.F.D. Young (ed.) (1971) *Knowledge and Control: New Directions for the Sociology of Education*, London: Collier-Macmillan, pp. 161–8).

—— (1967) "Système d'enseignement et systèmes de pensée", *Revue internationale des sciences sociales*, 19 (3), 367–409 (trans. "System of Education and Systems of Thoughts", in M.F.D. Young (ed.) (1971) *Knowledge and Control: New Directions for the Sociology of Education*, London: Collier-Macmillan, pp. 89–207).

—— (1977) *Outline of a Theory of Practice*, Cambridge: Cambridge University Press.

—— (1980) "Une science qui derange", interview with Pierre Thuillier, *La Recherche*, 112, June (reprinted in *Questions de sociologie*, Paris: Minuit, pp. 19–36).

—— (1989) *La noblesse d'État*, Paris: ed. de Minuit (trans. *State Nobility: Elite Schools in the Field of Knowledge*, Cambridge: Polity Press).

—— (1991) *Language and Symbolic Power* (trans. G. Raymond and M. Adamson), Cambridge: Polity Press.

—— (2001) *Contre-Feux 2*, Paris: Raisons d'agir.

—— (2004) *Science of Science and Reflexivity* (trans. R. Nice), Cambridge: Polity Press.

Bourdieu, P. and Passeron, J.-C. (1977) *La reproduction. Éléments pour une théorie du système d'enseignement*, Paris: ed. de Minuit (1st edn 1970).

—— (1979) *The Inheritors, French Students and their Relation to Culture*, Chicago: University of Chicago Press.

Bourdieu, P. and Thompson, J. (2001) *Langage et pouvoir symbolique*, Paris: Seuil.

Bourne, J. (2004) "Framing Talk: Towards a 'Radical Visible Pedagogy'", in J. Muller, B. Davies and A. Morais (eds), *Reading Bernstein, Researching Bernstein*, London: RoutledgeFalmer, pp. 61–74.

Breier, M. (2004) "Horizontal Discourse in Law and Labour Law", in A. Morais, I. Neves, B. Davies and H. Daniels (eds) *Towards a Sociology of Pedagogy: The Contribution of Basil Bernstein to Research*, New York: Peter Lang.

British Journal of Sociology of Education (2002) "Special Issue: Basil Bernstein's Theory of Social Class, Educational Codes and Social Control", 23 (4).

Broadfoot, P. and Pollard, A. (2006) "The Changing Discourse of Assessment Policy: The Case Study of English Primary Education", in H. Lauder, P. Brown, J.-A. Dillabough and A.H. Hasley (eds) *Education, Globalization and Social Change*, Oxford: Oxford University Press, pp. 760–5.

Brown, P. (1995) "Cultural Capital and Social Exclusion: Some Observations on Recent Trends in Education, Employment, and the Labour Market", *Work, employment and Society*, 9, 29–51.

Burrows, L. and Wright, J. (2006) *Prescribing Practices Shaping Healthy Children in Schools*, unpublished paper, University of Otago and University of Wollongong.

Caille, J.-P. and O'Prey, S. (2005) "Accès en terminale sans redoublement en 2001 des élèves entrés en sixième en 1995", *Education et formation*, 72.

Canguilhem, G. (1977) *Idéologie et rationalité dans les sciences de la vie*, Paris: Vrin.

Carvalho, L. and Dong, A. (2007) "Knowledge and Identity in the Design Field", *Proceedings of ConnectED International Conference on Design Education*, Sydney: UNSW, July.

Carvalho, L., Dong, A. and Maton, K. (2009) "Legitimating Design: A Sociology of Knowledge Account of the Field", *Design Studies*, 30 (5), 483–502.

Certeau, M. (1980) *L'invention du quotidien*, vol. 1, *Arts de faire*, Paris: Union générale d'éditions.

Chambers, J.K. (2003) *Sociolinguistic Theory: Linguistic Variation and its Social Significance* (2nd edn), Oxford: Blackwell Publishers.

Charle, C. and Verger, J. (1994) *Histoire des universités*, Paris: PUF.

Charlier, J.-E. (2000) "La régulation de l'enseignement de la Communauté française: de la concurrence à la competition", *Recherches sociologiques*, xxxi (1), 29–40.

Charlot, B. (1999) *Du rapport au savoir. Eléments pour une théorie*, Paris: Economica.

Christie, F. and Derewianka, B. (2008) *School Discourse: Learning to Write Across the Years of Schooling*, London: Continuum.

Christie, F. and Humphrey, S. (2008) "Senior Secondary English: Responding to Literary Texts", in L. Unsworth (ed.) *New Literacies and the English Curriculum*, London: Continuum, pp. 215–37.

Christie, F. and Macken-Horarik, M. (2007) "Building Verticality in Subject English", in F. Christie and J. Martin (eds) *Language, Knowledge and Pedagogy*, London: Continuum, pp. 156–83.

Clerc, P. (1970) "La famille et l'orientation scolaire au niveau de la sixième", *Population et enseignement* (Introduction, Alain Girard), Paris: PUF, coll. Démographie et sciences humaines, pp. 142–88.

CNDP (2004) *Enseigner au collège, Français, programmes et accompagnement*, Paris: CNDP.

Cole, M. (1996) *Cultural Psychology: A Once and Future Discipline*, Cambridge, MA: Harvard University Press.

Cole, M. and Engeström, Y. (1993) "A Cultural-Historical Approach to Distributed Cognition", in G. Salomon (ed.) *Distributed Cognitions: Psychological and Educational Considerations*, New York: Cambridge University Press.

Crahay, M. (2006) *Un bilan des recherches processus-produit. L'enseignement peut-il contribuer à l'apprentissage des élèves et, si oui, comment*, Geneva: Carnet des sciences de l'éducation.

Daniels, H. (1989) "Visual Displays as Tacit Relays of the Structure of Pedagogic Practice", *British Journal of Sociology of Education*, 10 (2), 123–40.

—— (ed.) (1994) *Charting the Agenda: Educational Activity after Vygotsky*, London; New York: Routledge.

—— (1995) "Pedagogic Practice, Tacit Knowledge and Discursive Discrimination: Bernstein and Post-Vygotskian Research", *British Journal of the Sociology of Education*, 16 (4), 517–32.

—— (2001) *Vygotsky and Pedagogy*, London: Routledge.

Daniels, H., Edwards, A., Martin, D., Leadbetter, J., Warmington, P., Popova, A., Middleton, D. and Brown, S. (2005) *Learning in and for Interagency*, Working ESRC TLRP.

Daniels, H., Hey, V., Leonard, D. and Smith, M. (1999) "Issues of Equity in Special Needs Education as Seen from the Perspective of Gender", *British Journal of Special Education*, 26 (4), 189–95.

Daniels, H., Holst, J., Lunt, I. and Johansen, L. (1996) "An Intercultural Comparative Study of the Relation Between Different Models of Pedagogic Practice and Constructs of Deviance", *Oxford Review of Education*, "Special Issue on Vygotsky in Education", 22 (1), 63–77.

Daunay, B. and Denizot, N. (2007) "Le récit, objet disciplinaire en Français", revue *Pratiques*, 133–34.

Davies, B. (1994) "Durkheim and the Sociology of Education in Britain", *British Journal of Sociology of Education*, 15 (1), 3–25.

Davis, Z. (2005) *Pleasure and Pedagogic Discourse in School Mathematics: A Case Study of a Problem-Centred Pedagogic Modality*, PhD thesis, University of Cape Town.

DEPP (2007) *Information note*, 07-27, May.

Diaz, M. (2001) "Subject, Power and Pedagogic Discourse", in A. Morais, I. Neves, B. Davies and H. Daniels (eds), *Towards a Sociology of Pedagogy: The Contribution of Basil Bernstein to Research*, New York: Peter Lang, pp. 83–98.

Domingos, A.M. (now Morais) (1989) "Influence of the Social Context of the School on the Teacher's Pedagogic Practice", *British Journal of Sociology of Education*, 10 (3), 351–66.

Douay-Soublin, F. (2005) "Du discours à la dissertation: aspect du passage de la rhétorique à la litterature en France au XIXe siècle", in N. Ramognino and P. Vergès (eds), *Le français hier et aujourd'hui. Politiques de la langue et apprentissages scolaires. Etudes offertes à V. Isambert-Jamati*, Paris: PUF.

Douglas, M. (1967) *Purity and Danger: An Analysis of the Concepts of Pollution and Taboo*, London: Routledge.

—— (1970) *Natural Symbols: Explorations in Cosmology*, London: Barrie and Rockliff/ Cresset Press.

Dowling, P. (1993) *A Language for the Sociological Description of Pedagogic Texts with Particular Reference to the Secondary School Mathematics Scheme SMP 11–16*, PhD thesis, University of London, Institute of Education.

—— (1998) *The Sociology of Mathematics Education: Mathematical Myths/pedagogic Texts*, London: Falmer Press.

Draelants, H., Giraldo, S. and Maroy, C. (2004) "Les accompagnateurs pédagogiques et l'implantation de l'approche par compétences: rôle, identités et relations aux enseignants", in F. Frenay and C. Maroy (eds) *L'école, 6 ans après le décret "missions"*, Louvain-la-Neuve: Presses universitaires de Louvain, pp. 161–86.

Dubet, F. (2002) *Le déclin de l'institution*, Paris: Seuil, coll. L'épreuve des faits.

Durkheim, E. (1977) *The Evolution of Educational Thought: Lectures on the Formation and Development of Secondary Education in France* (trans. P. Collins), London: Routledge & Kegan Paul (1st edn 1938).

—— (1982) *The Rules of Sociological Method*, New York: Free Press.

—— (1995) *The Elementary Forms of Religious Life*, New York: Free Press (1st edn 1912).

—— (1997) *Suicide: A Study in Sociology*, New York: Free Press (1st edn 1897).

—— (1999) *L'évolution pédagogique en France*, Paris: PUF, Quadrige (1st edn Paris: Félix Alcan, 1938; 1969).

Engeström, Y. (1999) "Innovative Learning in Work Teams: Analysing Cycles of Knowledge Creation in Practice", in Y. Engeström, R. Miettinen, and R.-L. Punamaki (eds) *Perspectives on Activity Theory*, Cambridge: University Press.

Engeström, Y. and Miettinen, R. (1999) "Introduction", in Y. Engeström, R. Miettinen and R.-L. Punamaki (eds), *Perspectives on Activity Theory*, Cambridge: Cambridge University Pres, pp. 1–18.

Ensor, P. (2001) "Curriculum", in N. Cloete, R. Fehnel, P. Maassen, T. Moja, H. Perold and T. Gibbon (eds) *Transforming in Higher Education: Global Pressures and Local Realities*, Cape Town: CHAPS/Juta.

Eurydice (2000) *Two Decades of Reform in Higher Education in Europe: 1980 Onwards*, Eurydice Studies, Education and Culture, Brussels: European Commission.

Evans, J., Rich, E. and Davies, B. (2008) *Fat Fabrications: Education, Disordered Eating and Obesity Discourse*, London: Routledge.

Ferreira, S. (2007) *Currículos de ciências e as ideologias dos seus autores: Estudo centrado no currículo de Ciências Naturais do 3º ciclo do Ensino Básico*, Lisbon: master's thesis, School of Science, University of Lisbon.

Ferreira, S., Alves, V., Calado, S., Morais, A.M. and Neves, I.P. (2006) *Instrumento de análise do currículo nacional de ciências naturais do 3º ciclo do ensino básico: Relação Ministério da Educação-Professores – Critérios de avaliação quanto às dimensões da construção da ciência*, Lisbon: ESSA Group, Department of Education, School of Science University of Lisbon (adapt. from Castro and Morais, 2005).

Field, J. (2006) *Lifelong Learning and the New Educational Order*, Stoke on Trent: Trentham Books.

Fitz, J., Davies, B. and Evans, J. (2006) *Education Policy and Social Reproduction: Class Inscription and Symbolic Control*, London: RoutledgeFalmer.

Forquin, J.-C. (1987) *Le débat sur l'école et la culture chez les théoriciens et sociologues de l'éducation en Grande-Bretagne (1960–1985)*, Thèse de Doctorat d'État, Strasbourg: université des Sciences humaines.

—— (1989) *École et culture. Le point de vue des sociologues britanniques*, Bruxelles: De Bœck.

Francois, F. (2004) *Enfants et récits. Mises en mots et reste*, Paris: Presses universitaires du Septentrion.

Gamble, J. (2004) *Tacit Knowledge and Craft Pedagogy: A Sociological Analysis*, PhD thesis, University of Cape Town.

Gardin, J.-C. (1974) *Les analyses du discours*, Neuchâtel: Delachaux et Niestlé.

Gardin, J.-C., Lagrange, M.-S., Molino, J. and Natali, J. (1987) *La logique du plausible. Essai d'épistémologie pratique*, Paris: ed. Maison des sciences de l'Homme.

Gibbons, M., Limoges, C. and Nowotny, H. (1994) *The New Production of Knowledge*, London: Sage.

Girard, A. (1996) *Expériences touristiques et régime du patrimoine culturel-naturel: éléments pour une sociologie critique du tourisme*, Thèse de doctorat nouveau régime, Aix-en-Provence: Université de Provence.

Goffman, E. (1964) "The Neglected Situation", *American Anthropologist*, 66 (6).

Goody, J. (1977) *The Domestication of Savage Mind*, Cambridge: Cambridge University Press.

Granger, G.-G. (1994) "L'explication dans les sciences sociales", in G.-G. Granger, *Formes, operations, objets*, Paris: Librairie Vrin, coll. Mathesis.

Grignon, C. (1971) *L'ordre des choses, les fonctions sociales de l'enseignement technique*, Paris: Minuit.

—— (1988) "Ecriture littéraire et écriture sociologique", *Littérature*, 70 (May), 24–39.

Grignon, C. and Passeron, J.C. (1989) *Le savant et le populaire. Misérabilisme et populisme en sociologie et en littérature*, Paris: Gallimard, Le seuil.

Habermas, J. (1968) *Technik und Wissenschaft als "Ideologie"*, Frankfurt am Main (trans. (in part) by J.J. Shapiro (1970) *Toward a Rational Society: Student Protest, Science and Politics*, Boston: Beacon Press).

—— (1973) *La technique et la science comme "idéologie"*, Paris: ed. Gallimard (1st edn 1968).

—— (1973) "Connaissance et intérêt", in *La technique et la science comme "idéologie"*, Paris: Tel Gallimard (1st edn 1968), pp. 133–62.

Hakkarainen, K., Lonka, K. and Paavola, S. (2004) *Networked Intelligence: How Can Human Intelligence Be Augmented Through Artifacts, Communities, and Networks?* Online: www.lime.ki.se/uploads/images/517/Hakkarainen_Lonka_Paavola.pdf.

Halbwachs, M. (1997) *La mémoire collective* (édition critique établie par G. Namer), Paris: Albin Michel (1st edn 1950).

Halliday, M.A.K. (1973) "Relevant Models of Language", in *Explorations in the Functions of Language*, London: Arnold.

—— (1975) *Learning How to Mean: Explorations in the Development of Language*, London: Arnold.

—— (1978) *Language as Social Semiotic: The Social Interpretation of Language and Meaning*, London: Arnold.

Hamel, J. (1997) *Précis d'épistémologie de la sociologie*, Paris: L'Harmattan.

Hasan, R. (1992a) "Speech Genre, Semiotic Mediation and the Development of Higher Mental Functions", *Language Science*, 14 (4), 489–528.

—— (1992b) "Meaning in Sociolinguistic Theory", in K. Bolton and H. Kwok (eds) *Sociolinguistics Today: International Perspectives*, London: Routledge.

—— (1995) "On Social Conditions for Semiotic Mediation: The Genesis of Mind in

Society", in A.R. Sadovnik (ed) *Knowledge and Pedagogy: The Sociology of Bernstein*, Westport; London: Ablex Publishing, pp. 171–96.

—— (2001a) "The Ontogenesis of Decontextualized Language: Some Achievements of Classification and Framing", in A. Morais, I. Neves, B. Davies and H. Daniels (eds) *Towards a Sociology of Pedagogy: The Contribution of Basil Bernstein to Research*, New York: Peter Lang.

—— (2001b) "Understanding Talk: Directions from Bernstein's Sociology", *International Journal Of Social Research Methodology*, 4 (1), 5–9.

—— (2002a) "Semiotic Mediation and Mental Development in Pluralistic Societies: Some Implications for Tomorrow's Schooling", in *Learning for Life in the 21st Century: Sociocultural Perspectives on the Future of Education*, Malden, MA: Blackwell Publishers, pp. 112–26.

—— (2002b) "Ways of Meaning, Ways of Learning: Code as an Explanatory Concept", *British Journal of Sociology of Education*, 23 (4), 537–48.

—— (2004) "The Concept of Semiotic Mediation: Perspectives from Bernstein's Sociology", in J. Muller, B. Davies and A. Morais (eds) *Reading Bernstein, Researching Bernstein*, London, RoutledgeFalmer, pp. 30–43.

—— (2005) *Semiotic Mediation, Language and Society: Three Exotropic Theories – Vygotsky, Halliday and Bernstein* (manuscript).

—— (2006) "Literacy, Pedagogy and Social Change: Directions from Bernstein's Sociology", in R. Moore, M. Arnot, J. Beck and H. Daniels (eds) *Knowledge, Power and Educational Reform: Applying the Sociology of Basil Bernstein*, London: Routledge.

Hasan, R. and Cloran, C. (1990) "A Sociolinguistic Study of Everyday Talk between Mothers and Children", in M.A.K. Halliday, J. Gibbons, H. Nicholas (eds) *Learning Keeping and Using Language*, vol. 1, Amsterdam: John Benjamins.

Hedegaard, M. (2001) "Learning Through Acting within Societal Traditions: Learning in Classrooms", in M. Hedegaard (ed.) *Learning in Classrooms: A Cultural-Historical Approach*, Aarhus: Aarhus University Press.

Hoadley, U. (2005) *Social Class, Pedagogy and the Specialization of Voice in Four South African Primary Schools*, PhD thesis, University of Cape Town.

Holland, D., Lachiotte, L., Skinner, D. and Cain, C. (1998) *Identity and Agency in Cultural Worlds*, Cambridge, MA: Harvard University Press.

Honeger, M. (1996) "Temps musical", in M. Honeger (ed.) *Connaissance de la musique*, Paris: Bordas.

Hood, S. (2007) "Arguing in and across Disciplinary Boundaries: Legitimising Strategies in Applied Linguistics and Cultural Studies", in A. McCabe, M. O'Donnell and R. Whittaker (eds) *Advances in Language and Education*, London: Continuum.

IGAENR (2005) *La mise en place du LMD*, Paris: MENESR.

Isambert-Jamati, V. (1971) *Crises de la société, crises de l'enseignement, sociologie de l'enseignement secondaire français*, Paris: PUF, Bibliothèque de sociologie contemporaine.

—— (1995) *Les savoirs scolaires. Enjeux sociaux des contenus d'enseignement et de leurs réformes*, Paris: L'Harmattan, coll. Savoir et formation.

—— (2005) "Approches sociologiques des contenus d'enseignement", in N. Ramognino and P. Vergès (eds) *Le Français hier et aujourd'hui. Politiques de la langue et apprentissages scolaires. Études offertes à V. Isambert-Jamati*, Aix-en-Provence: Publications de l'université de Provence, pp. 18–36.

James, D. (2005) *Exogenous Change and Institutional Response: an Ethnographic Case Study of a School Inspection*, EdD thesis, Cardiff University.

Jephcote, M. and Davies, B. (2004) "Recontextualizing Discourse: An Exploration of the Workings of the Meso-Level", *Journal of Education Policy*, 19 (5), 547–64.

—— (2007) "School Subjects, Subject Communities and Curriculum Change: The Social Construction of Economics in the School Curriculum", *Cambridge Journal of Education*, 37 (2), 207–27.

Kimball, R. (1994) "The 'Two Cultures' Today", *The New Criterion*, 12 (6).

Knorr-Cetina, K. (1981) *The Manufacture of Knowledge: An Essay on the Constructivist and Contextual Nature of Science*, Oxford: Pergamon.

Kolb, D.A. (1981) "Learning Styles and Disciplinary Differences", in A. Chickering (ed.) *The Modern American College*, San Francisco: Jossey Bass.

Koselleck, R. (1990) *Le futur passé. Contribution à la sémantique des temps historiques*, Paris: ed. des Hautes études en sciences sociales.

Kuhn, T.S. (1970) *The Structure of Scientific Revolutions*, Chicago: University of Chicago Press.

Labov, W. (1964) "Phonological Correlates of Social Stratification", *American Anthropologist*, 66 (6).

—— (1978) *Le parler ordinaire*, Paris: ed. de Minuit.

Lahire, B. (1998a) *L'Homme pluriel*, Paris: Nathan.

—— (1998b) "La réussite scolaire en milieux populaires ou les conditions sociales d'une schizophrénie heureuse", *Ville-École-Intégration*, no. 114, "Les familles et l'école: une relation difficile", pp. 104–9.

Lamont, A. and Maton, K. (2008) "Choosing Music: Exploratory Studies into the Low Uptake of Music GCSE", *British Journal of Music Education*, 25(3), 267–82.

Latour, B. (1987) *Science in Action*, Cambridge, MA: Harvard University Press.

Leavis, F.R. (1972) "Two Cultures? The Significance of Lord Snow", in *Nor Shall my Sword: Discourse on Pluralism, Compassion and Social Hope*, New York: Barnes & Noble.

Leontiev, A.N. (1978) *Activity, Consciousness and Personality*, Englewood Cliffs: Prentice-Hall.

—— (1981) "The Concept of Activity in Psychology", in J.V. Wertsch (ed.) *The Concept of Activity in Soviet Psychology*, Armonk, NY: M.E. Sharpe.

Lessard, C. (2007) "Les usages politiques de la recherche en education", in V. Dupriez and G. Chappelle (eds) *Enseigner*, Paris: PUF, pp. 69–79.

Liénard, G. and Capron, M. (2000) "Justice sociale et reconnaissance de la dignité de l'autre: exigences et critères d'une mutation positive", in M. Capron and G. Liénard (eds) *Face à la mondialisation. Justice sociale, développement économique et contre-pouvoirs*, Brussels: Couleur Savoir, pp. 171–4.

Linehan, C. and McCarthy, J. (2000) "Positioning in Practice: Understanding Participation in the Social World", *Journal for the Theory of Social Behaviour*, 30, 435–53.

Lohdal, J.B. and Gordon, G. (1972) "The Structure of Scientific Fields and the Functioning of University Graduate Departments", *American Sociological Review*, 37, 57–72.

Luckett, K. (2009) "The Relationship between Knowledge Structure and Curriculum Structure: A Case Study in Sociology", *Studies in Higher Education*, 34 (4), 441–53.

Mangez, E. (2004) "La production des programmes de cours par les agents intermédiaires: transfert de savoirs et relations de pouvoir", *Revue Française de Pédagogie*, no. 146, pp. 65–77.

—— (2006) *Production, médiation et réception d'un nouveau référentiel pédagogique en Communauté française de Belgique. Une approche sociologique du champ pédagogique*, doctoral thesis, UCL Louvain, Belgium.

Maton, K. (2000) "Languages of Legitimation: The Structuring Significance for Intellectual Fields of Strategic Knowledge Claims", *British Journal of Sociology of Education*, 21 (2), 147–67.

—— (2005) "A Question of Autonomy: Bourdieu's Field Approach and Higher Education Policy", *Journal of Education Policy*, 20 (6), 687–704.

—— (2005) *The Field of Higher Education: A Sociology of Reproduction, Transformation, Change and the Conditions of Emergence for Cultural Studies*, unpublished PhD dissertation, University of Cambridge.

—— (2006) "Invisible Tribunals: Canons, Knower Structure and Democracy in the Arts and Humanities", *Proceedings of Fourth International Basil Bernstein Symposium*, July, Rutgers University.

—— (2007) "Knowledge-Knower Structures in Intellectual and Educational Fields", in F. Christie and J. Martin (eds) *Language, Knowledge and Pedagogy*, London: Continuum, pp. 87–108.

—— (2009) "Cumulative and Segmented Learning: Exploring the Role of Curriculum Structures in Knowledge-Building", *British Journal of Sociology of Education*, 30 (1), 43–57.

—— (2010) "Progress and Canons in the Arts and Humanities: Knowers and Gazes", in K. Maton and R. Moore (eds) *Social Realism, Knowledge and the Sociology of Education: Coalitions of the Mind*, London: Continuum, pp. 154–78.

Mead, G.H. (1934) *Mind, Self and Society*, ed. Charles, W. Morris, Chicago: University of Chicago Press.

Meirieu, P. (1998) *Quels savoirs enseigner dans les lycées?*, Paris: Rapport final pour le ministre de l'Education nationale.

Merton, R.K. (1992) *The Sociology of Science: Theoretical and Empirical Investigations*, Chicago: University of Chicago Press.

—— (1993) *On the Shoulders of Giants*, Chicago: University of Chicago Press.

Mignot-Gérard, S. and Musselin, C. (2002) "L'offre de formation universitaire: à la recherche de nouvelles regulations", *Education et Société*, 8 (2), 11–25.

Molino, J. (1986) "L'événement: de la logique à la sémiologie", *L'événement*, actes du colloque organisé par le Centre méridional d'histoire sociale, Marseille: Publications de l'université de Provence.

—— (1989) "Interpréter", in C. Reichler (ed.), *L'interprétation des textes*, Paris: ed. de Minuit.

—— (1996) "Le sociologue et la bataille de Poitiers", *Revue Européenne des sciences sociales*, xxxiv (103), 203–13.

—— (1998) "Du changement au devenir. Remarques sur la notion de changement dans les sciences humaines", *Revue Européenne des sciences sociales*, xxxvi (110), 185–97.

—— (2003) *Homo Fabulator. Théorie et analyse du récit*, Leméac: Actes Sud.

Mons, N. (ed.) (2008) "Évaluation des politiques éducatives et comparaisons internationals", *Revue française de Pédagogie*, 134, Dossier thématique, juillet-août-septembre, Lyon: INRP, pp. 5–98.

Moore, R. (2006) "Knowledge Structures and Intellectual Fields: Basil Bernstein and the Sociology of Knowledge" in R. Moore, M. Arnot, J. Beck and H. Daniels (eds) *Knowledge, Power and Educational Reform*, London: Routledge.

—— (2007) *Schismatism, the Pursuit of Difference and the Tradition of the New*, Homerton College, Cambridge University, mimeo.

—— (2009) *Towards the Sociology of Truth*, London: Continuum.

Moore, R. and Maton, K. (2001) "Founding the Sociology of Knowledge: Basil Bernstein, Intellectual Fields and the Epistemic Device", in A. Morais, I. Neves, B. Davies and H. Daniels (eds) *Towards a Sociology of Pedagogy: The Contribution of Basil Bernstein to Research*, New York: Peter Lang, pp. 153–82.

Morais, A. and Neves, I. (2001) "Pedagogic Social Contexts: Studies for a Sociology of Learning", in A. Morais, I. Neves, B. Davies and H. Daniels (eds) *Towards a Sociology of Pedagogy: The Contribution of Basil Bernstein to Research*, New York: Peter Lang, pp. 185–221.

—— (2006) "Teachers as Creators of Social Contexts for Scientific Learning: Discussing New Approaches for Teachers' Development", in R. Moore, M. Arnot, J. Beck and H. Daniels (eds) *Knowledge, Power and Educational Reform*, London: Routledge, pp. 146–62.

Morais, A.M. and Rocha, C. (2000) "Development of Social Competences in the Primary School: Study of Specific Pedagogic Practices", *British Educational Research Journal*, 26 (1), 93–120.

Morais, A.M., Fontinhas, F. and Neves, I.P. (1992) "Recognition and Realization Rules in Acquiring School Science: The Contribution of Pedagogy and Social Background of Student", *British Journal of Sociology of Education*, 13 (2), 247–70.

Morais, A.M., Neves, I.P. and Afonso, M. (2005) "Teacher Training Processes and Teachers' Competence – A Sociological Study in the Primary School", *Teaching and Teacher Education*, 21, 415–37.

Morais, A., Neves, I., Davies, B. and Daniels, H. (eds) (2001) *Towards A Sociology of Pedagogy. The Contribution of Basil Bernstein to Research*, New York: Peter Lang.

Morais, A.M., Neves, I.P., Medeiros, A., Peneda, D., Fontinhas, F. and Antunes, H. (1993) *Socialização primária e prática pedagógica*, vol. 2, *Análise de aprendizagens na família e na escola*, Lisbon: Gulbenkian Foundation.

Morais, A.M., Neves, I.P. and Pires, D. (2004) "The *What* and the *How* of Teaching and Learning: Going Deeper into Sociological Analysis and Intervention", in J. Muller, B. Davies and A. Morais (eds) *Reading Bernstein, Researching Bernstein*, London: RoutledgeFalmer, pp. 75–90.

Morais, A.M., Neves, I.P., Silva, P. and Deus, H. (2005) *What Do Teachers Make of Curriculum Guidelines and Syllabuses? Study of Differential Pedagogic Practices in the Primary Science Classroom*, paper given at the 11th Conference of the European Association for Research in Learning and Instruction, Nicosia: University of Cyprus, August.

Muller, J. (2004) "Introduction. The Possibilities of Basil Bernstein", in J. Muller, B. Davies and A. Morais (eds) *Reading Bernstein, Researching Bernstein*, London: RoutledgeFalmer, pp. 1–12.

—— (2006) "On the Shoulders of Giants", in R. Moore, M. Arnot, J. Beck and H. Daniels (eds) *Knowledge, Power and Educational Reform*, London: Routledge.

Muller, J., Davies, B. and Morais, A. (eds) (2004) *Reading Bernstein, Researching Bernstein*, London: RoutledgeFalmer.

Musselin, C. (2001) *La longue marche des universités françaises*, Paris: PUF.

Naidoo, R. and Jamieson, I. (2003) "Empowering Participants or Corroding Learning? Towards a Research Agenda on the Impact of Student Consumerism in Higher Education", *Journal of Education Policy*, 20 (3), pp. 276–81.

Nash, R. (2006) "Bernstein and the Explanation of Social Disparities in Education: Aa Realist Critique of the Socio-Linguistic Thesis", *British Journal of Sociology of Education*, 27 (5), 539–54.

Neumann, R. (2001) "Disciplinary Differences and University Teaching", *Studies in Higher Education*, 26 (2), 135–46.

Neumann, R., Parry, S. and Becher, A. (2002) "Teaching and Learning in their Disciplinary Contexts: A Conceptual Analysis", *Studies in Higher Education*, 27 (4), 406–17.

Neves, I.P. and Morais, A.M. (2001) "Texts and Contexts in Educational Systems: Studies of Recontextualizing Spaces", in A. Morais, I. Neves, B. Davies and H. Daniels (eds) *Towards a Sociology of Pedagogy: The Contribution of Basil Bernstein to Research*, New York: Peter Lang, pp. 223–49.

Neves, I.P. and Morais, A.M. (2005) "Pedagogic Practices in the Family Socializing Context and Children's School Achievement", *British Journal of Sociology of Education*, 26 (1), 121–37.

Neves, I.P., Morais, A.M. and Afonso, M. (2004) "Teacher Training Contexts: Study of Specific Sociological Characteristics", in J. Muller, B. Davies and A. Morais (eds) *Reading Bernstein, Researching Bernstein*, London: Routledge Falmer, pp. 168–86.

Opie, I. and Opie, P. (1959) *The Lore and Language of School Children*, New York: NYRB.

Passeron, J.-C. (1991) *Le raisonnement sociologique. L'espace non poppérien du raisonnement naturel*, Paris: Nathan, coll. Essais et recherches.

Petitat, A. (2006) "Fiction, pluralité des mondes et interpretation", *A contrario*, 4 (2).

Piaget, J. (1996) *L'épistémologie génétique*, Paris: PUF (1st edn 1970).

Pirkkalainen, J., Kaatrakoski, H. and Engeström, Y. (2005) *Hybrid Agency as Hybrid Practices*, mimeo in preparation.

Plaisance, E. (1986) *L'enfant, la maternelle, la société*, Paris: PUF.

Popper, K. (1973) *La logique de la découverte scientifique*, Paris: Payot (1st edn 1934).

Power, S. and Whitty, G. (2004) "Bernstein and the Middle Class", *British Journal of Sociology of Education*, 23 (4), 595–606.

Price, D. (1970) "Citation Measures of Hard Science, Soft Science, Technology and Nonscience" in C.E. Nelson and D.K. Pollock (eds) *Communication among Scientists and Engineers*, Lexington: DC Heath and Company, pp. 3–22.

Propp, V. (1968) *Morphology of the Folk Tale*, Austin: University of Texas Press.

Prost, A. (2001) *Rapport sur les recherches en education auprès du ministre*, Paris.

Ramognino, N. (2002) "Hétérogénéité ontologique du social et théorie de la description. L'analyse de la complexité en sociologie", *Revue européenne de sciences sociales*, xl (124), 147–64.

—— (2006) *Lectures actuelles de l'oeuvre de Balzac, Le procès littéraire ou l'extension du domaine du possible*, Paris: L'Harmattan, série Littérature et Société.

Ramognino, N., Frandji, D., Soldini, F. and Vergès, P. (1996) *De la violence en général et des violences en particulier. Les violences à l'école: l'étude de trois collèges à Marseille*, Rapport de recherche LAMES–MMSH.

—— (1997) "L'école comme dispositif symbolique et les violences scolaires", in

B. Charlot and J.-C. Emin (eds) *Violences à l'école/Etat des savoirs*, Paris: Armand Colin, pp. 117–44.

Reeves, C. (2005) *The Effect of "Opportunity to Learn" and Classroom Pedagogy on Mathematics Achievement in Schools Serving Low Socio-Economic Status Communities in the Cape Peninsula*, PhD thesis, University of Cape Town.

Reuter, Y. and Lahanier-Reuter, D. (2007) "L'analyse de la discipline: quelques problèmes pour la recherche en didactique", in E. Falardeau, C. Fisher, C. Simard and N. Sorin (eds) *La didactique du français. Les voies actuelles de la recherche*, Québec: Presses de l'Université de Laval.

Ricoeur, P. (1990) *Soi-même comme un autre*, Paris: ed. du Seuil.

Rochex, J.-Y. (1993) "Normes et normativité en sociologie de l'éducation", *Futur antérieur*, 19–20, "Sociologies", 195–206.

—— (1995) *Le sens de l'expérience scolaire. Entre activité et subjectivité*, Paris: PUF.

—— (1999) "Vygotski et Wallon: pour une pensée dialectique des rapports entre pensée et affect", in Y. Clot (eds) *Avec Vygotski*, Paris: ed. La Dispute, pp. 119–37.

—— (2000) *Expérience scolaire et procès de subjectivation. L'élève et ses milieux*, Note de synthèse pour l'Habilitation à diriger des recherches, université Paris VIII.

—— (2001) "Échec scolaire et démocratisation: enjeux, réalités, concepts, problématiques et résultats de recherché", *Revue suisse des sciences de l'éducation*, 2, 69–85.

Ropé, F. and Tanguy, L. (2000) "Le modèle des compétences: système éducatif et enterprise", *L'Année sociologique*, 50 (2), 493–520.

Rosenvallon, P. (2006) *La contre-démocratie. La politique à l'âge de la defiance*, Paris: ed. du Seuil.

Russell, B. (1929) *Our Knowledge of the External World*, New York: W.W. Norton.

Sadovnik, A.R. (ed.) (1995) *Knowledge and Pedagogy: The Sociology of Bernstein*, Westport; London: Ablex Publishing.

Santos, A. (2007) *Formação inicial de professores de ciências: Estudo de práticas pedagógicas e de aprendizagens*, master's thesis, School of Science, University of Lisbon (in progress).

Santos, A. and Morais, A.M. (2007) *Instrumento de caracterização da prática pedagógica do ensino superior: Contexto instrucional*, Lisbon: ESSA Group, Department of Education, School of Science, University of Lisbon.

Schneuwly, B. (1985) "La construction sociale du langage écrit chez l'enfant", in B. Schneuwly and J.-P. Bronckart (eds) *Vygotski aujourd'hui*, Neuchâtel: Delachaux et Niestlé, pp. 169–201.

—— (1986) "Les capacités humaines sont des constructions sociales. Essai sur la théorie de Vygotsky", *European Journal of Psychology of Education*, 1 (4), 5–16.

Scribner, S. (1985) "Vygotsky's Uses of History", in J.V. Wertsch (eds) *Culture, Communication and Cognition*, New York: Cambridge University Press, pp. 119–45.

Seibel, C. and Levasseur, J. (1983) "Les apprentissages instrumentaux et le passage du cours préparatoire au cours élémentaire", *Education et formations*, 2.

—— (1984) "CP-CE1, de la continuité des apprentissages", *Document de travail*, MEN.

Sennett, R. (1998) *The Corrosion of Character*, New York: Norton.

—— (2006) *The Culture of the New Capitalism*, London: Yale University Press.

Shay, S. (2008), "Beyond Social Constructivist Perspectives on Assessment: The Centring of Knowledge", *Teaching in Higher Education*, 13 (5), 595–605.

Silva, P., Morais, A. and Neves, I. (2003) *Instrumento de caracterização da prática pedagógica do primeiro ciclo do ensino básico: Contexto instrucional*, Lisbon: ESSA Group, Department of Education, School of Science, University of Lisbon.

—— (2005) *Characteristics of the Pedagogic Practice That Are Crucial for Children's Scientific Learning: Studying Their Interplay*, paper given at the International Conference of the European Science Education Research Association (ESERA), University of Barcelona, September.

Silverman, D. and Torode, B. (1980), *The Material Word: Some Theories of Language and Its Limits*, London: Routledge.

Skocpol, T. (1992) *Protecting Soldiers and Mothers: The Political Origins of Social Policy in the United States*, Cambridge, MA: Belknap Press.

Smeby, J.-C. (1996) "Disciplinary Differences in University Teaching", *Studies in Higher Education*, 21 (1), 67–79.

Snow, C.P. (1993) *The Two Cultures and the Scientific Revolution*, Cambridge: Cambridge University Press (1st edn 1959).

Stavrou, S. (2009) "Negotiating Curriculum Change in the French University: The Case of Regionalizing Social Scientific Knowledge", *International Studies in Sociology of Education*, 19 (1), 19–36.

Storer, N. (1967) "The Hard Sciences and the Soft: Some Sociological Observations", *Bulletin of the Medical Library Association*, 55, 75–84.

Terrail, J.-P. (1987) "Les vertus de la nécessité. Sujet/objet en sociologie", in M. Bertrand *et al.* (eds) *Je, sur l'individualité*, Paris: Messidor – ed. sociales, pp. 251–96.

Thomas, E. and Davies, B. (2006) "Nurse Teachers' Knowledge in Curriculum Planning and Implementation", *Nursing Education Today*, 26, 572–7.

Tyler, W. (2004) "Crosswired: Hypertext, Critical Theory and Pedagogic Discourse", in A. Morais, I. Neves. B. Davies and H. Daniels (eds) *Towards a Sociology of Pedagogy: The Contribution of Basil Bernstein to Research*, New York: Peter Lang.

Van Campenhoudt, L., Franssen, A., Hubert, G., Van Espen, A., Lejeune, A. and Huynen, P. (2004) *La consultation des enseignants du secondaire*, report drawn up for the Commission de Pilotage, Brussels: Facultés universitaires Saint-Louis.

Vincent, G. (1980) *L'école primaire française: étude sociologique*, Lyon. PUL.

Virno, P. (2002) *Grammaire de la multitude. Pour une analyse des formes de vie contemporaines*, Nîmes; Montreal: Conjonctures – L'éclat.

Vitale, P. (2006) *La sociologie et son enseignement. Curricula, théories et recherches*, Paris: L'Harmattan.

Vlasceanu, L. (1976) *Decision and Innovation in the Romanian Educational System: a Theoretical Exploration of Teachers' Orientation*, PhD thesis, University of London, Institute of Education.

Vygotsky, L.S. (1978) *Mind in Society: The Development of Higher Psychological Processes*, Cambridge, MA: Harvard University Press.

—— (1987) *The Collected Works of L.S. Vygotsky*, vol. 1: *Problems of General Psychology*, including the volume *Thinking and Speech*, ed. R.W. Rieber and A.S. Carton, trans. N. Minick, New York: Plenum Press.

—— (1994) "Problématique de l'arriération mentale", French translation in L.S. Vygotsky, *Défectologie et déficience mentale*, ed. K. Barisnikov and G. Petitpierre (1st edn 1935), Neuchâtel: Delachaux et Niestlé, pp. 195–236.

—— (1997) *Pensée et langage*, French translation (1st edn 1934), Paris: ed. La Dispute.

—— (2003) "La conscience comme problème de la psychologie du comportement",

French translation in L.S. Vygotsky, *Conscience, inconscience, émotions* (1st edn 1925), Paris: ed. La Dispute.

Wamain, S. (2004) *Le lycée professionnel aujourd'hui: une perspective scolaire ou profession-nelle*, doctoral thesis, University of Bordeaux 2.

Wertsch, J.V. (1985) *Vygotsky and the Social Formation of Mind*, Cambridge, MA: Harvard University Press.

—— (1991) *Voices of the Mind: A Socio-Cultural Approach to Mediated Action*, Cambridge, MA: Harvard University Press.

Willis, P. (1977) *Learning to Labour: How Working Class Lads Get Working Class Jobs*, Farnborough: England Saxon House.

Wright, R. (2006) *Music as Pedagogic Discourse: An Ethnographic Case Study of One Year 9 Class of Pupils and Their Music Teacher in a South Wales Secondary School*, PhD thesis, Cardiff: University of Wales Institute.

Young, M.F.D. (ed.) (1971) *Knowledge and Control: New Directions for the Sociology of Education*, London: Collier-Macmillan.

Bernstein

Bernstein, B. (1958) "Some Sociological Determinants of Perception: An Enquiry into Sub-Cultural Differences", *British Journal of Sociology*, 9, 159–74.

—— (1959) "A Public Language: Some Sociological Implications of a Linguistic Form", *British Journal of Sociology*, 10, 311–26.

—— (1959) "Sociokulturelle Determinanten des Lernens", *Koelner Zeitschrift für Soziologie und Sozial Psychologie*, 4, 52–79.

—— (1960) " 'The Lore and Language of Schoolchildren' by I. and P. Opie", book review, *British Journal of Sociology*, 11, 178–81.

—— (1960) "Language and Social Class: A Research Note", *British Journal of Sociology*, 11, 271–6.

—— (1961) "Social Structure, Language and Learning", *Educational Research*, 3, 163–76.

—— (1961) "Social Class and Linguistic Development: A Theory of Social Learning", in A.H. Halsey, J. Floud and C.A. Anderson (eds) *Education, Economy and Society: A Reader in the Sociology of Education*, New York: The Free Press of Glencoe.

—— (1961) "Aspects of Language and Learning in the Genesis of the Social Process", *Journal of Child Psychology and Psychiatry*, 1, 313–24.

—— (1962) "Social Class, Linguistic Codes and Grammatical Elements", *Language and Speech*, 5, 221–40.

—— (1962) "Linguistic Codes, Hesitation Phenomena and Intelligence", *Language and Speech*, 5, 31–46.

—— (1963) "Family Role Systems, Communication and Socialization", *Research for the Sixties*, Twentieth Century, 172, 92–5.

—— (1964) "Elaborated and Restricted Codes: Their Social Origins and Some Consequences", in J.J. Gumperz and D. Hymes (eds) *Ethnography of Communication, American Anthropologist*, 66, pp. 55–69.

—— (1964) "Social Class, Speech Systems and Psychotherapy", *British Journal of Sociology*, 15, 54–64.

—— (1965) "Speech and the Home", *NATE Bulletin*, 2, 18–21.

—— (1965) "A Sociolinguistic Approach to Social Learning", in J. Gould (ed.), *Penguin Survey of the Social Sciences*, Harmondsworth: Penguin, pp. 144–68.

—— (1966) "The Role of Speech in the Development and Transmission of Culture", *Public Lecture to the Bank Street Colleges Fiftieth Anniversary Symposium*, in G. Klopf and W. Hohman (eds) *Perspectives on Learning*, New York: Mental Health Materials Center, pp. 15–45.

—— (1966) "Sources of Consensus and Disaffection in Education", *Journal of the Association of Assistant Mistresses*, 17, 4–11.

—— (1966) "Elaborated and Restricted Codes: An Outline", *Sociological Inquiry*, 36, 254–61.

—— (1966) "The Formative Years: The Role of Language", *The Listener*, 75, 501–3.

—— (1967) "Play and the Infant School", *Where?*, Supplement 11: toys.

—— (1967) "Open Schools, Open Society?", *New Society*, 10, 351–3.

—— (1967) "Elaborated and Restricted Codes: An Outline", in S. Lieberson (ed.) *Explorations in Sociolinguistics*, *International Journal of American Linguists*, 33, 126–33.

—— (1969) "A Critique of the Concept of Compensatory Education", in D. Rubinstein, and C. Stoneman (eds) *Education for Democracy*, London: Penguin.

—— (1970) "Introduction", in W. Brandis (ed.) *Social Class, Language and Communication*, London: Routledge.

—— (1970) "Social Class, Language and Socialization", in A. Abranson (ed.) *Current Trends in Linguistics*, The Hague: Mouton.

—— (1970) "Education Cannot Compensate for Society", *New Society*, 387, 344–7.

—— (1971) "On the Classification and Framing of Educational Knowledge", in M.F.D. Young (ed.) *Knowledge and Control: New Directions for the Sociology of Education*, London: Collier-Macmillan.

—— (1971) *Class, Codes and Control*, vol. 1, *Theoretical Studies Towards a Sociology of Language*, London: Routledge & Kegan Paul.

—— (1971) "A Sociolinguistic Approach to Socialization with Some References to Educability", in D. Hymes and J. Gumperz (eds) *Directions in Sociolinguistics*, New York: Holt, Rhinehart & Winston, pp. 465–97.

—— (1971) "On the Classification and Framing of Educational Knowledge", *The Human Context*, 3, 339–86.

—— (1971) "Social Class, Language and Socialization", in S.A. Abramson (ed.) *Current Trends in Linguistics*, Amsterdam: Mouton.

—— (1972) "Sociology and the Sociology of Education: Some Aspects", *Eighteen plus*, The final selection, units 15–17, E282 School and Society, Unit 17, Milton Keynes: Open University Press, pp. 99–109.

—— (1973) *Class, Codes and Control*, vol. 1, *Theoretical Studies Towards a Sociology of Language*, revised paperback edn, St Albans: Paladin.

—— (1973) *Class, Codes and Control*, vol. 2, *Applied Studies Towards a Sociology of Language*, London: Routledge & Kegan Paul.

—— (1973) "Postscript: a Brief Account of the Theory of Codes", in V.J. Lee (ed.) *Social Relationships and Language: Some Aspects of the the Work of Basil Bernstein*, Block 3 of the Educational Studies second-level course Language and Learning, Milton Keynes: Open University

—— (1973) "Class and Pedagogies", *Educational Studies*, 1, 23–41.

—— (1973) *Class and Pedagogies: Visible and Invisible*, Paris: OECD, CERI.

—— (1974) *Class, Codes and Control*, vol. 1, *Theoretical Studies Towards a Sociology of Language* (2nd rev. edn), London: Routledge & Kegan Paul.

—— (1974) "Sociology and the Sociology of Education: A Brief Account", in J. Rex (ed.) *Approaches to Sociology: An Introduction to Major Trends in British Sociology*, London: Routledge & Kegan Paul.

—— (1975) *Class, Codes and Control*, vol. 3, *Towards a Theory of Educational Transmissions*, London: Routledge & Kegan Paul.

—— (1975) *Class, Codes and Control: Theoretical Studies Towards a Sociology of Language*, New York: Schocken Books.

—— (1977) "Foreword", in D. Adlam, G.H. Turner and L. Lineker (eds) *Code in Context*, London: Routledge & Kegan Paul.

—— (1977) "Class and Pedagogues: Visible and Invisible", in J. Karabel and A.H. Halsey (eds) *Power and Ideology in Education*, New York: Oxford University Press, pp. 511–34.

—— (1977) *Class, Codes and Control*, vol. 3, *Towards a Theory of Educational Transmissions* (2nd rev. edn), London: Routledge.

—— (1977) "Social Class, Language, and Socialization", in J. Karabel and A.H. Halsey (eds) *Power and Ideology in Education*, New York: Oxford University Press.

—— (1977) "Aspects of the Relation between Education and Production", in *Class, Codes and Control*, vol. 3, *Towards a Theory of Educational Transmissions* (2nd rev. edn), London: Routledge.

—— (1981) "Codes, Modalities and the Process of Cultural Reproduction: A Model", *Language and Society*, 10, 327–63.

—— (1982) "Codes, Modalities and the Process of Cultural Reproduction: A Model", in M.W. Apple (ed.) *Cultural and Economic Reproduction in Education: Essay on Class, Ideology and the State*, London: Routledge.

—— (1986) "Codes and their Different Sources and the Process of Cultural Reproduction", *Przeglad Socjologiczny*, 34, 7–40.

—— (1986) "On Pedagogic Discourse", in J.G. Richardson (ed.), *Handbook of Theory and Research for the Sociology of Education*, New York: Greenwood Press, pp. 205–90.

—— (1987) "On Pedagogic Discourse", *CORE*, 12.

—— (1987) "Elaborated and Restricted Codes: An Overview, 1958–1985", in U. Ammon, N. Dittmar and K.J. Mattheier (eds) *Sociolinguistics/Soziolinguistik: An International Handbook*, vol. 1, Berlin: Walter de Gruyter.

—— (1987) "Education and Democracy", paper presented at the Robert Finkelstein Memorial Lecture, New York: Adelphi University, Garden City.

—— (1987) "Class, Codes and Communication", in *Sociolinguistics: An International Handbook of the Science of Language and Society*, vol. 1, Berlin: Walter de Gruyter.

—— (1987) *Elaborated and Restricted Codes: An Overview, 1958–1986*, Occasional paper no. 2, Amsterdam: Amsterdam University, Centre for Race and Ethnic Studies.

—— (1988) "An Essay in Education, Symbolic Control and Social Practices", *Anglo-American Studies*, 8, 137–64.

—— (1990) *Class, Codes and Control*, vol. 4, *The Structuring of Pedagogic Discourse*, London: Routledge.

—— (1993) "Foreword", in H. Daniels (ed.) *Charting the Agenda: Educational Activity after Vygotsky*, London: Routledge.

—— (1995) "A Response", in A.R. Sadovnik (ed.) *Knowledge and Pedagogy: The Sociology of Bernstein*, Westport; London: Ablex Publishing, pp. 385–424.

—— (1995) "Code Theory and its Positioning: A Case Study in Misrecognition", *British Journal of Sociology of Education*, 16, 3–19.

—— (1995) "Codes Oppositional, Reproductive and Deficit: A Case of Red Herrings", *British Journal of Sociology*, 46, 133–42.

—— (1995) *Pedagogy, Symbolic Control and Identity: Theory, Research and Critique*, London: Taylor & Francis.

—— (1996) *Pedagogy, Symbolic Control and Identity: Theory, Research, Critique*, London: Taylor & Francis (rev. edn, 2000, Oxford: Rowman & Littlefield).

—— (1997) "Class and Pedagogies: Visible and Invisible", in A.H. Halsey, H. Lauder, P. Brown and A. Stuart Wells (eds) *Education. Culture, Economy and Society*, Oxford: Oxford University Press, pp. 59–79.

—— (1997) "Sociolinguistics: A Personal View", in P.C. Bratt and G.R. Tucker (eds),, *Summer Institute of Linguistics*, Dallas, pp. 43–52.

—— (1998) "Lo Strumento Pedagogico", *Studi di Sociologia*, 37, 107–20.

—— (1999) "Pedagogy, Identity and the Construction of a Theory of Symbolic Control: Basil Bernstein Questioned by Joseph Solomon", *British Journal of Sociology of Education*, 20, 265–79.

—— (1999) "Vertical and Horizontal Discourse: an Essay", *British Journal of Sociology of Education*, 20 (2), 157–73.

—— (1999) "Official Knowledge and Pedagogic Identities", in F. Christie (ed.) *Pedagogy and the Shaping of Consciousness: Linguistic and Social Processes*, London: Cassell.

—— (2000) *Pedagogy, Symbolic Control and Identity: Theory, Research, Critique* (rev. edn), Lanham, MD: Rowman & Littlefield Publishers (1st edn 1996, London: Taylor & Francis).

—— (2001) "From Pedagogies to Knowledges", in A. Morais, I. Neves, B. Davies and H. Daniels (eds) *Towards a Sociology of Pedagogy*, New York: Peter Lang, pp. 363–84.

Bernstein, B. and Brandis, W. (1974) *Selection and Control: Teachers Ratings of Infant School Children*, London: Routledge & Kegan Paul.

Bernstein, B. and Cook-Gumperz, J. (1973) "The Coding Grid: Theory and Operations", in J. Cook-Gumperz (ed.) *Social Control and Socialization: A Study of Class Differences in the Language of Maternal Control*, London: Routledge & Kegan Paul, pp. 48–72.

Bernstein, B. and Diaz, M. (1984) "Towards a Theory of Pedagogic Discourse", *Collected Original Resources in Education – CORE*, 8, 1–212.

Bernstein, B. and Henderson, D. (1969) "Social Class Differences in the Relevance of Language and Socialization", *Sociology*, 3, 1–20.

Bernstein, B. and Sadovnik, A.R. (1988) *Pedagogic Practice and Educational Reform: An Application of a Theory of Pedagogic Practice*, American Sociological Association.

Bernstein, B. and Young, D. (1967) "Social Class Differences in Conceptions of the Uses of Toys", *Sociology*, 1, 131–40.

Bernstein, B., Brannen, J. and Tizard, B. (eds) (1996) *Children, Research and Policy*, London; Bristol: Taylor & Francis.

Bernstein, B., Peters, R.S. and Elvin, L. (1966) "Ritual in Education", *Philosophical Transactions of the Royal Society of London*, Series B, 251, 429–36.

Publications traduites en français

Bernstein, B. (1975) *Langage et classes sociales, codes sociolinguistiques et contrôle social*, Paris: Minuit.

—— (1975) *Classes et pédagogies: visibles et invisibles*, CERI, OCDE (reproduit in

Jérôme Deauvieau et Jean-Pierre Terrail (dir.), 2007, *Les sociologues, l'école et la transmission des savoirs*, Paris: La Dispute, pp. 85–112).

—— (1992) "La construction du discours pédagogique", *Critiques sociales*, 3–4.

—— (1997) "Ecoles ouvertes, société ouverte", in J.-C. Forquin, *Les sociologues de l'éducation américains et britanniques*, Bruxelles: De Boeck.

—— (1997) "A propos du curriculum", in J.-C. Forquin, *Les sociologues de l'éducation américains et britanniques*, Bruxelles: De Boeck.

—— (2007) *Pédagogie, contrôle symbolique et identité. Théorie, recherche, critique*, Québec: Presses de l'université de Laval.

Index

Note: Page numbers in **bold** denote figures or illustrations, those in *italics* denote tables.

social handicap 11, 97
social inclusion 36, 67
social inequalities 5–7, 13, 21, 36, 87,
    104, 108–13, 116, 121–2, 155, 161,
    225–6, 227, 232, 233
socialization 9–10, 37, 54, 58, 83, 88,
    90, 108, 121, 124, 225; class 87;
    cognitive and linguistic 11, 99, 103,
    109, 114, 118, 123, 211
social and power relations 6, 12–13
social rupture 8
sociocultural 74, 237–8; handicap 50, 58
sociolinguistics 23, 34–5, 37, 58, 77,
    80, 87, 108, 175
sociological analysis 5, 80, 175, 225,
    233, 239
sociological interest 4, 14, 164
sociological research 1–2, 5, 10, 16, 34
sociology of education 5, 9, 17n8, 21–4,
    29, 33–6, 78, 108, 156, 160, 211,
    225, 227, 233; rehabilitation of 14,
    23, 88, 143, 217
Spanish-speaking world 34
special vocabulary 35, 57, 99, 103, 105,
    122, 179, 232
standards for certification 28–9
state-dominated systems 35, 39
state education 44n5, 45n7
statistical 5; analysis 8
Stavrou, S. 12
Storer, N. 223
strong classification 32, 85, 160, 166,
    192–4, 204, 240
strong framing 32, 151, 192–5
structuralist and post-structuralist 35,
    51
student assets or strenths 28
style 61, 181, 212, *214–15*; learning
    36, 42; prose 35, 182–3, 185
subjectification 52, 55, 59–61, 83, 89,
    92–3
subject position 63, 69
subsumption 128; of curriculum 7
symbolic 11–12, 24, 42, 80, 102, 104,
    106, 108, 127–8, 149, 156n14, 166,
    171, 173–4, 180, 215; control 1, 3,
    38, 50–1, 58–9, 79, 86–8, 154–5,
    162, 228, 231–2, 235, 238–9;
    development 91; domination 4, 16;

exchange 15; features 185; forms 56,
    184, 211; goods 12, 162; integration
    57; market 8, 53; power 217; violence
    5, 16n7, 227, 239
systemic follow-up of students 21

teacher 25, 28, 30–1, 33, 36–44, 71,
    74, 90, 111–15, 117–18, 120–1,
    123, 138, 160, 163–4, 166, 169–78,
    180–1, 184–9, 192–4, 196–8,
    203–5, 228–9, 234, 237, 239; effect
    32–3, 43; insecurity 13; practice 4;
    styles 31–2; vocational 23
teacher education 14, 24, 34, 191;
    de-intellectualized 35
teaching 32; of French 30, 179–81;
    methods 42, 111, 159, 197; practices
    109, 123; professionals 31
technical drawing 24–5
technical education 107
tensions 12, 15, 60, 67, 83, 86–7, 92,
    149, 181, 211, 221–3, 233; structural
    37; identity 4
Terrail, J.-P 77
Thatcher, M. 7, 44n2
The Discursive Field Today 37
The New Sociology of Education 29–30, 33
theory of activity and pedagogical
    practice 6
theory of education and pedagogy 3
theory of habitus 10
theory of pedagogical activity and
    practice 5
Thomas, E. and Davies, D. 39
Totally Pedagogized Society 37, 126–7
trade culture 24
trainability 7, 41, 45, 138
transformations 7, 10, 13
translation of power 177, 228
tribes 164, *213–15*, 221
Trivium and Quadrivium 29, 59–60,
    83, 212–13, 216, 221
Tyler, W. 37

undergraduate curriculum 21, 23, 25
underprivileged social classes 32, 85
university 12; autonomy 39, 146–7;
    courses 21; knowledge 147, 156n11;
    studies 28